D1470296

Impact Assessment for Development Agencies

Learning to Value Change

Chris Roche

Oxfam

Novib

First published by Oxfam GB with Novib in 1999   ISBN 0 85598 418 X (paperback)
© Oxfam GB 1999   ISBN 0 85598 424 4 (hardback)

A catalogue record for this publication is available from the British Library.

Available from the following agents:

for the USA: Stylus Publishing LLC, PO Box 605, Herndon, VA 20172-0605, USA;
tel. +1 (0)703 661 1581; fax +1 (0)703 661 1547; email styluspub@aol.com
for Canada: Fernwood Books Ltd., PO Box 9409, Stn. A, Halifax, Nova Scotia B3K 5S3, Canada;
tel. +1 (0)902 422 3302; fax +1 (0)902 422 3179; email fernwood@istar.ca
for Southern Africa: David Philip Publishers, PO Box 23408, Claremont 7735, South Africa;
tel. +27 (0)21 64 4136; fax +27 (0)21 64 3358; email dppsales@iafrica.com
for Tanzania: Mkuki na Nyota Publishers, PO Box 4246, Dar es Salaam, Tanzania;
tel./fax +255 (0)51 180 479; email mkuki@ud.co.tz
for India: Maya Publishers Pvt Ltd, 113-B, Shapur Jat, New Delhi-110049, India;
tel. +91 (0)11 649 4850; fax +91 (0)11 649 1039; email surit@del2.vsnl.net.in
for Australia: Bush Books, PO Box 1958, Gosford South, NSW 2250, Australia;
tel. +61 (0)2 043 233 274; fax +61 (0)2 092 122 468; email bushbook@ozemail.com.au

For the rest of the world, contact Oxfam Publishing, 274 Banbury Road, Oxford OX2 7DZ, UK.
tel. +44 (0)1865 311 311; fax +44 (0)1865 313 925; email publish@oxfam.org.uk

Published by Oxfam GB, 274 Banbury Road, Oxford OX2 7DZ, UK

Typeset in Garamond

Printed by Hobbs The Printers ,Totton, Hants SO40 3WX

Oxfam GB is a registered charity, no. 202 918, and is a member of Oxfam International.

Contents

Not everything that counts can be counted.
And not everything that can be counted, counts.

Albert Einstein

Acknowledgements

Writing this book has involved a large number of people and organisations. Although it fell upon me to write the book for publication, it would not have been possible without the case-study material upon which it is based, the comments and feedback I received on earlier drafts, and the ideas which arose from a workshop held in November 1998, which brought together many of the people who worked on the case studies.

I would particularly like to thank the following individuals, listed in alphabetical order of the organisations they are associated with: Professor AM Muazzam Hussain from the Bangladesh Rural Advancement Committee (BRAC) in Bangladesh; MC Jolly and Pran Gopal Das from the Centre for Youth and Social Development (CYSD) in Orissa, India; Enrique Reyes and Walter Gonzalez from the Fundación para la Cooperación y el Desarrollo Comunal de El Salvador (CORDES); Sthembile Mawoneke from Environment and Development Activities — Zimbabwe (ENDA) and Bowdin King, former staff member of ENDA; Mark Gale, former member of the Matson Neighbourhood Project (MNP) who is now with the Gloucester Neighbourhood Project Network, UK; Siapha Kamara and Robert Abaane, former staff of the Integrated Social Development Centre in Ghana (ISODEC); Andy Jarret from MNP, UK; Anamul Haque from Oxfam GB in Bangladesh; Yanci Urbina Gonzalez from Oxfam GB in El Salvador; Ben Pugansoa and Nafisatu Quarshie from Oxfam GB in Ghana; Yolette Etienne from Oxfam GB in Haiti; Mohammed Elmi from Oxfam GB in Kenya; Hidayat Narajo from Oxfam GB in Pakistan; and Abu Nasar from Proshika in Bangladesh.

A number of advisors, consultants and friends supported this study in various ways. They are Ojijo Odhiambo of the Resource Management and Policy Analysis Institute (REMPAI), Kenya; Sabina Alkire of Somerville College, Oxford, UK; Dr Anup Kumar Dash from Utkal University, Orissa, India; Stan Thekaekara ('Stan the Magic Man', as the kids of Matson call him) from ACCORD in India; Mick Howes and Kamal Kar, development consultants from the UK and India respectively; critical reader Ros David of Action Aid, UK; critical reader Rick Davies, research fellow at the Centre for Development Studies, University of Wales, UK; and critical reader Raul Hopkins from the Queen Mary and Westfield College, University of London, who prepared two important background papers for the study.

Several Oxfam GB staff based in Oxford also played crucial roles at various stages in developing this book. Thanks are due especially to Elsa Dawson who provided constant support, enthusiasm and ideas to the study, as well as writing some key background papers; to Margaret Newens and Fred Wessels for their detailed and thoughtful comments and ideas and, in Margaret's case, for doing part of my job while I was writing; to Suzanne Williams for doing the other part of my job with her usual panache; to Koos Neefjes for his innovative thinking and facilitation skills at the workshop as well as critical input and feedback; to Bridget Walker, Ivan Scott, Tahmina Rahman, Mohga Smith, Ines Smyth and Alan Reed for comments on specific chapters; and to Anke Lueddecke who did a fantastic job editing the original text.

I would also like to thank Yvonne Es, Adrie Papma, Allert van den Ham, and Peter van Tuijl from Novib, which co-funded this whole project; and Floris Blankenberg — Novib's 'Mr Impact' and now with SNV in the Netherlands — who was one of the main driving forces behind the study.

Also a special thanks to all those who made the impact assessment workshop such a great success: Kate Morrow who did a marvellous job recording the outcomes; Alison Farell and Lynne Perry who organised a vast amount of photocopying; Julie Allcock and Conchita Lloret, our patient and hardworking translators; Paresh Motla and Ann Burgess who provided administrative, logistical, and moral support with calm precision; Ken Garland who chauffeured participants at all hours of the day and night; Frances Lang and Peter of the Stanton Guildhouse who hosted the workshop; those residents of Stanton who put participants up in their homes; the staff and residents of the Matson Neighbourhood Project who hosted a visit from the workshop participants; and the Phoenix Club who gave us a delicious lunch.

It is customary at this stage to state that any mistakes or omissions that follow are the fault of the author. This is particularly relevant in this case as I have had to condense three years' work from more than ten case studies into a single volume. This inevitably means that I have skipped over some things and, possibly, have interpreted findings in ways that the original case-study participants might not recognise. I have tried to incorporate the feedback I have received on earlier drafts, but it is inevitable that the pressures of work and family life have meant that not everyone has had the time, or perhaps the energy, to go through the text as closely as they might have liked. My hope is that readers who are interested to learn more about the individual case studies will read the original material and make up their own minds. The case studies are available from Oxfam GB and from the organisations involved; a list of these is included in the Appendix.

Special thanks, as ever, go to Anna, Susie and Angus who at home put up with my nonsensical ramblings about impact assessment and many other things, with their usual good humour and healthy scepticism.

Chris Roche
8 June 1999

1

Introduction

This book is the result of an action-research exercise jointly undertaken by a number of international and local non-government organisations (NGOs) based in four continents. The research was initiated by Oxfam from Great Britain and Novib from the Netherlands (hereafter referred to as Oxfam and Novib). The book is an attempt to share with others the lessons learned from that experience, as well as some of the challenges that arise from thinking about and practising impact assessment.

It is aimed particularly at practitioners, and evaluation specialists may find that I skim over some of the more theoretical issues. This is not because these are unimportant, but because our research showed that there is a need to demystify the subject. The aim is to make impact assessment accessible without being simplistic about it. The book also explores those elements of impact assessment which look beyond the project level at organisational processes. I hope therefore that those involved in the development of monitoring and evaluation systems at an organisational level will find this book helpful. However, it is essentially about the insights gained from the case studies, rather than an attempt to cover the abundant literature on the subject.

Impact assessment – making the case for development aid

Despite the statistics in recent UNDP Human Development Reports and in the World Bank's annual reports, which record a marked improvement in a number of indicators of human well-being, the scale of world poverty remains a scandal which shames us all. In many parts of the world inequality, insecurity, and conflict are growing at alarming rates. Bilateral development aid has had its critics for many years, but during the past decade we have also seen a growing number of critiques of NGOs (Smillie 1995, de Waal 1996, Sogge 1996). These critiques together describe a vicious circle which the

NGO sector, particularly in the North, faces and which it has helped to create. This circle has five main elements (see Figure 1.1): there is increasing pressure on NGOs to demonstrate results and the impact of their work. Moreover, there is increased competition between NGOs, and a growing need for a high profile and press coverage in order to raise funds and to facilitate advocacy work. Poor institutional learning and weak accountability mechanisms are characteristic of many NGOs, which both leads to and is the result of the absence of professional norms and standards.

These elements combine to produce a growing gap between the rhetoric of agencies and the reality of what they achieve. They also fuel growing scepticism about the value of aid, and lessen trust between agencies — some argue that agreements and partnerships based on shared values have been replaced by bureaucratic trust based on plans, budgets, and accounts. Moreover, the elements of this vicious circle to perpetuate the tired old image of aid going from donor to 'victim', and a view of development as something that is done to other people, far away. This analysis, although based on little empirical evidence, holds a certain truth which NGOs ignore at their peril.

Figure 1.1: The vicious circle

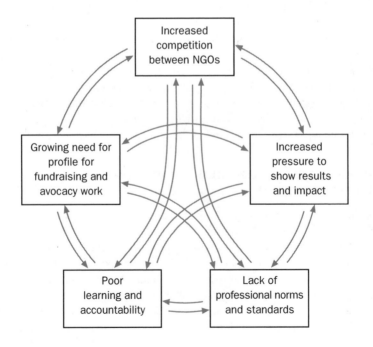

One recent study of NGO impact which had a stronger empirical base concluded that the true impact of NGO development work remained unclear and that there was little consensus on which tools and methods were the most appropriate to find out. This study, undertaken by Riddell et al. (1997) for the OECD/DAC Expert Group on Evaluation, reviewed 60 reports covering 240 projects in 26 countries, and undertook 13 country case studies.

Both the critique outlined above (mainly of Northern-based NGOs) and the findings of this OECD study point to the inadequacy of most current attempts to promote institutional learning, impact assessment, and greater accountability in the NGO sector — accountability to those who NGOs seek to support, as well as to those who fund this work. In a climate of increased competition, individual organisations and the sector as a whole tend to exaggerate the case for support just as their opponents tend to exaggerate the case against. This can have two consequences, the dangers of which have been pointed out for some time (Cassen 1986, Riddell 1987). First, support for development aid depends on the public's belief in its effectiveness. The moral case for providing support rests upon its achieving its objectives. However, a reluctance to admit that the effectiveness of much of that is done is unpredictable and difficult to assess, makes not just NGOs, but also international co-operation programmes, vulnerable to public criticism and the odd polemic attack.

Second, those making the case for co-operation must not create the belief that aid flows constitute the sole, or even principal, means available to donors and governments of improving the welfare of people living in poverty. Often, changes in policy and practice, for example improved terms of trade or greater debt relief, may be more beneficial.

In the long term, the case for aid can only be sustained by more effective assessment and demonstration of its impact, by laying open the mistakes and uncertainties that are inherent in development work, and by an honest assessment of the comparative effectiveness of aid vis-à-vis changes in policy and practice. The research project that forms the basis of this book was designed to make a contribution to this process, as well as to the institutional learning of the agencies involved. A broad range of intermediary and grassroots organisations in nine countries participated alongside the Northern NGOs Oxfam and Novib. More specifically, we had the following aims:

- to develop greater clarity about the key elements of impact assessment;
- to explore how unequal levels of power and participation of the various stakeholders can affect an impact assessment process;
- to test a range of approaches to undertaking impact assessment;
- to look at the organisational context in which impact assessments take place.

These issues are discussed in more depth in Chapters 2 and 3, and I will return to them in the final chapter.

The structure of this book

The second half of this Introduction describes the case studies and the organisations involved in preparing them. The case studies form the foundation of the book, and I have attempted to retain their richness and diversity. Chapter 2 discusses Oxfam and Novib's overall approach to impact assessment. It explores issues relating to ethics and participation, and emphasises the importance of ensuring that gender and other aspects of difference are embedded into all processes of impact assessment. Chapter 2 also sets out some of the assumptions and hypotheses which emerged from a literature review at the beginning of the research and which were subsequently tested in the case studies. For example, we confirmed the hypothesis that impact assessment must be seen as an integral part of development work throughout the project- or programme-cycle. Finally, this chapter summarises some of the key dilemmas regarding how to attribute any observed change to an intervention, and how to synthesise diverse and sometimes contradictory findings.

Although Oxfam and Novib feel that the distinction between emergency, development, and advocacy work is increasingly redundant, these terms do provide a convenient short-hand for different aspects of NGO work. So although Chapters 3 to 6 are structured along these lines, there is much overlap between them. Chapter 3 explores how the case studies were designed for assessments in single communities, across several communities, and across a range of projects. It also gives some guidance about basic operational matters which must be addressed in designing an impact assessment, such as how to go about sampling, what to do if there is no baseline data, and how to cross-check results. It also looks at how some of the most difficult issues such as setting indicators and measuring attribution were tackled in our case studies. In Chapter 4, I look at the wide range of different tools, methods, and approaches used as well as the problems encountered in the case studies. The reader will find summaries of the lessons learned about various kinds of tools and methods such as surveys, interviews and workshops, direct observation, participatory tools, and case studies. Chapters 3 and 4 make up the core of the book. Many of the chapters that follow refer back to some of the basic lessons described in these chapters.

Chapter 5 on impact assessment and emergencies refers mainly to one of the case studies as well as to some recent material. It explores some of the specific difficulties and challenges of undertaking impact assessment in crisis situations and compares them with the lessons described in previous chapters.

Because of the limited number of case studies directly dealing with emergency situations, this chapter should be seen as a preliminary exploration of the issue; it mainly focuses on relief interventions. The chapters on advocacy and organisations and impact assessment are also relevant to work in emergency situations. Recent events such as Hurricane Mitch and the Kosovo crisis may offer opportunities to work on more longitudinal and holistic approaches to emergency situations and their assessment.

In Chapter 6, which focuses on impact assessment and advocacy, I outline current approaches to this growing field of NGO activity. Drawing on the case studies and other experiences, I discuss both how to assess the impact of advocacy and how to use impact assessment in advocacy work.

Chapter 7 considers how we can assess the impact of projects and programmes on development organisations, and at how these organisations manage impact assessment processes. It also considers the impact that development organisations have on people's lives.

I draw some conclusions from this research in Chapter 8 and indicate areas which NGOs need to invest in if they are serious about impact assessment. I end by noting key policy implications that emerge from the case-study findings, and thinking about what these might mean for the future of NGOs. The appendices include a bibliography, further details of the organisations and individuals involved in the case studies as well as a list of acronyms.

The case studies

When Oxfam and Novib embarked on this study in 1994/5, we undertook an initial literature review as well as a rapid survey of what sort of work on impact assessment was happening in a number of countries where we supported projects and organisations. A number of reports resulted (Hopkins 1995 a and b, Dawson 1995 a, b and c) which gave a useful overview of existing concepts and tools as well as suggesting a number of principles and hypotheses for impact assessment, which are discussed in Chapter 2.

However, the literature review concluded that a more 'hands-on' approach was needed to test a range of approaches in diverse contexts with different types of organisations.

The most important challenge is to promote, through case studies, a systematic application of the methodologies on impact assessment. There has been in the past few years a significant production of tools of project evaluation ... but what is really lacking is both a vigorous and systematic application of techniques and methodologies and to learn from experience. (Hopkins 1995a)

Oxfam and Novib then approached a number of partner organisations and their own field staff to explore the potential for undertaking action-research on impact assessment and developing a number of case studies. As is common with this sort of exercise, willingness to participate became the most important criterion. So although we also wanted to ensure a good geographical balance, to include emergency and advocacy as well as long-term 'development' work, and to balance forward-looking with retrospective studies, these criteria were inevitably secondary.

In the end, case studies were carried out in Africa (Ghana, Kenya, Zimbabwe and Uganda), in South Asia (Pakistan, Bangladesh and India), in Latin America (El Salvador) and in Europe (the United Kingdom). They represent a balance of prospective work, mid-term assessments of ongoing work, and retrospective reviews — although it became clear during the exercise that these distinctions are in reality often blurred. Unfortunately, only two of the studies can be described as assessing an emergency programme. However, some of the others deal with work that emerged from responses to emergency or crisis situations. The case studies do not include rescue or acute emergency operations, but I refer to some material on assessments in these circumstances in Chapter 5.

Given the nature of the research and the diversity of programmes and partners involved, the case studies did not follow a set methodology. We adopted an open and flexible approach which was designed to encourage innovation, creativity, and 'learning by doing'. We hoped that this might lead to greater variation in the approaches, tools, and methods used and maximise the potential for learning across the case studies. A few of the original participants had to drop out due to unforeseen circumstances and were be replaced as other opportunities emerged: a fixed method would not have permitted such adaptation. On the other hand, this flexibility has made the job of synthesising the experiences all the more challenging!

Who was involved and why?

Table 1.1 gives an overview of the organisations involved in the case studies. These range from BRAC in Bangladesh, which has a budget of some $200 million, 20,000 full-time staff and works with nearly 2 million people, to the Matson Neighbourhood Project in Gloucester, UK, which has a budget of £300,000, 16 staff (eight of whom are part-time), and covers a single housing estate of 6,000 people. Information is provided for Oxfam GB and Novib as a whole as well as for specific country programmes. The difference in size and scope of the participating organisations is reflected in the size and scope of the impact assessment processes they have undertaken, as well as in the human and financial investments they have been able to make over and above the financial support of Oxfam or Novib. In all but one case (Matson), either Oxfam or Novib are — or have been — funding these organisations, in some cases for many years.

Given this relationship, it is of course possible that participants felt somewhat 'obliged' to take part in the research or hoped that it would have a favourable effect on their relationship with Oxfam and Novib. Some of the tensions and difficulties that emerged during the case studies can probably be attributed to this. Nevertheless the main reasons of agencies for participating can be summarised as follows:

- to learn more about impact assessment;
- to assess and improve performance, and plan for the future;
- to integrate learning from the research into management, monitoring and evaluation, and reporting systems;
- to share experiences of impact assessment with others;
- to improve the relationship with both communities and donors;
- to motivate staff and the communities supported;
- Three areas of consensus can therefore be defined as explicit reasons for involvement: learning, performance, and accountability.

Overview of the case studies

This publication cannot look in great depth at the background to the case studies or the context in which these projects and programmes developed. Below is a short summary of each of the projects, which is intended as a quick reference guide.

Institutional capacity-building in Northern Ghana (supported by Oxfam GB, Integrated Social Development Centre, Northern Ghana Development Network)

This programme was set up in 1995/6 to strengthen the capacity of more than 45 NGOs and community-based organisations (CBOs) which make up the Northern Ghana Development Network (NGDN). The project, undertaken by Oxfam in collaboration with the Integrated Social Development Centre (ISODEC) and the Northern Ghana Development Network, seeks to assess the impact of the institutional capacity-building programme on poverty in this region by establishing a baseline against which future changes in poverty levels and in organisational development can be measured. In doing so, past trends are also being identified. Changes will be tracked at regular intervals as the programme progresses, at the individual, community, and organisational level.

Table 1.1: Organisational profiles of case-study participants (1999 figures)

Country	Ghana	India	Kenya	Uganda	Pakistan
Organisation	Oxfam GB in Ghana, ISODEC and NGDN	CYSD	Oxfam GB in Wajir	Oxfam GB in Ikafe	Oxfam GB in Pakistan
Type of organisation	Local NGO and CBOs	Local NGO	International NGO and CBO	International NGO	International NGO
Established	1994	1982	1980	1994	1989
Number of staff	15 (Oxfam) 60 (ISODEC)	126	14 (local)	150	19
Number of volunteers	–	120	–	–	2
Income (£/US$)	£249,839	£620,000	£300,000	£2.5m	£350,000
Size of population they seek to benefit	50,000	43,646	40,000	55,000	50,000
Oxfam/ Novib funded	✓	✓	✓	✓	✓

Organisation	Oxfam	Novib
Type of organisation	International NGO	International NGO
Established	1942	1956
Number of staff	2,800	237 full-time equivalents
Number of volunteers	27,000	300
Income	£100m	£85m

UK	Bangladesh			El Salvador	Zimbabwe
Matson NP	Proshika	BRAC	NK GSS	CORDES	ENDA - ZW
Local NGO and CBO	Local NGO	Local NGO	Local NGOs	Local NGO	Local NGO
1988	1976	1972	NK 1974 GSS 1983	1988	1983
16 (8 part-time)	3,783	51,442 (31,009 part-time)	5,296 (GSS 1997)	112	45
36	–	–	–	–	–
£300,000	£53m	£125m	N.A.	£1.25m	N.A.
6,000	8,639,180	2m	NK: 112,208 GSS: 114,000	66,000	2m
✗	✓	✓	✓ GSS ✗ NK	✓	✓

This approach to impact assessment (often referred to as the longitudinal approach) helps us understand the relationship between these levels. It is hoped that the member organisations of NGDN will use the methods developed in this research for their own impact assessment needs.

The methods used in this study include a literature review, participatory rural appraisal (PRA) methods, repeated individual interviews, and organisational assessment exercises.

Integrated rural and tribal development programmes in Orissa, India (Centre for Youth and Social Development, Novib)

The Centre for Youth and Social Development (CYSD), supported by Novib, is exploring both retrospective and longitudinal approaches to assess the impact of their programmes.

The Integrated Rural Development Programme started in 1988 and works mainly with tribal people who migrated from neighbouring states to Orissa 30 to 40 years ago. It has focused on poverty reduction, stimulating alternative sources of income, building community-based organisations, watershed management, and promoting sustainable agriculture in 21 villages made up of some 869 households. CYSD is now looking back at results. This programme is referred to as CYSD 1 in the book.

The more recently established Integrated Tribal Development Programme, referred to as CYSD 2, also concentrates on several tribal communities who belong to the poorest groups in the State of Orissa. The project works with 1,787 households, constituting a total population of 8,935, and with the 24 CBOs that exist in the area. Areas of work include education, health, environment and livelihood issues, participation in local government institutions and cultural communication. CYSD is establishing a longitudinal study to assess the impact of this new programme as it progresses. The design of this study builds on the learning from CYSD 1.

Both studies have used a wide range of methods including reviews of secondary data, PRA tools, focus-group discussions, and case studies.

Pastoralist development programme in north-east Kenya (Wajir Pastoral Development Project, Oxfam GB)

Oxfam has provided relief services and other forms of assistance to nomadic communities in Kenya's Wajir District since 1984. Since 1993, Oxfam development assistance has been channelled through the Wajir Pastoral Development Project (WPDP), a nine-year programme consisting of three three-year phases. The first phase, which ran from July 1994 to July 1997, reached an estimated 40,000 beneficiaries in Wajir Town and Wajir Bor division. The aim of the WPDP is to reduce poverty and vulnerability of both pastoralists and settled communities by promoting sustainable livelihoods and creating opportunities and improving the conditions for self-reliance.

The work referred to in this book relates to an economic impact assessment exercise which has built upon continuous longitudinal monitoring and a more general mid-term review. It therefore involves a retrospective assessment of impact as well as a prognosis of likely future impact. The study used a questionnaire, focus-group discussions, case studies, and a range of participatory tools and methods.

A refugee settlement in Northern Uganda (Oxfam GB in Ikafe)

The Ikafe programme in Arua District of Uganda was developed in order to support about 55,000 Sudanese refugees who were relocated from nearby Koboko following security problems in 1994. Oxfam GB as the main implementing agency took on tasks ranging from infrastructure development, registration, health-care provision and management, land allocation, and food and water distribution, to aspects of community development, forestry, and income-generation. Oxfam's response attempted to incorporate a long-term, 'developmental' approach into an emergency response. For example, refugees are settled in small, dispersed groups, and agricultural land is allocated to enable them to develop a certain level of food self-sufficiency. Several other agencies work with the refugees and there is support from a number of donors.

This case study used a retrospective review (mainly based on participatory appraisal methods and reviews of project records) which was undertaken by a team made up of external facilitators, project staff, and representatives of the refugee and host populations. One objective of the study was to examine the various stakeholders' distinct perspectives of impact and progress, and to bring the groups together in meetings and 'assemblies' to discuss and negotiate their views.

Project impact assessment in Pakistan (Oxfam GB in Pakistan)

Oxfam in Pakistan supports a range of projects and organisations through funding and non-funding support. This impact assessment work reviewed a range of Oxfam-supported small-scale projects. It tested a systematic method of conducting group interviews with project participants to ask about non-economic impact. It also tested a checklist of indicators that look at broad dimensions of human development, as well as a method for cross-project comparison. In addition, the researchers used a specific process for assessing economic impact and making comparisons between economic and non-economic impact.

This method has been tested with different Oxfam staff as well as other NGOs in Pakistan. A particular effort was made to ensure that the process did not take up too much time for both staff and the local men and women involved.

Community-managed services in Gloucester, UK (Matson Neighbourhood Project)

The Matson Neighbourhood Project, set up in 1990, works on the largest housing estate in the town of Gloucester, UK. The project runs a range of community-managed services such as education and training, a community shop, an advice centre, a mental health drop-in club, and a drug-counselling service. This review of its ongoing work involved a relatively unstructured process of participant observation and key informant interviews, carried out by an Indian community development specialist over a period of eight-weeks. First and foremost, the study looked at change within Matson through the eyes of local people and project staff. The study then explored how important these changes were for local people as well as what they attributed those changes to.

Economic and social empowerment in Bangladesh (Proshika)

Proshika is one of the largest NGOs in Bangladesh and promotes economic and social empowerment of the poor through a wide variety of interventions in more than 11,500 villages. This case study covers two interrelated components: a large-scale survey comparing 18,00 households, half of them supported by Proshika and the other half not supported by Proshika; and a participatory impact study undertaken to explore discrepancies arising from the initial survey. Subsequently, the participatory study was also used to develop a new impact assessment methodology for future studies, to explore and document new indicators, and to improve staff skills in participatory planning, monitoring, and evaluation.

Rural development work in Bangladesh (Bangladesh Rural Advancement Committee)

BRAC started in 1972 as a small relief and rehabilitation organisation in the war-ravaged, post-liberation Bangladesh. Today it is the largest multi-dimensional rural development organisation in the country. Its main goals are to alleviate poverty and empower rural people living in poverty. This case study focuses on a follow-up impact assessment (IAS II) of its rural development programme which aims to reach some 2.5 million people. The original study (IAS I), BRAC's first comprehensive impact assessment, was undertaken in 1993/4. This follow-up involved a large household survey involving both households supported by BRAC and 'non-BRAC households', as well as qualitative and case-study research with 25 village organisations, and the development of village profiles.

Social mobilisation in Bangladesh (Nijera Kori, Gonoshahajjo Sangstha)

NGOs in Bangladesh mainly use group-based approaches to development. However, for many NGOs this is a means to individual empowerment rather than collective action. This study, funded by Oxfam, reviewed group formation undertaken by social mobilisation organisations, and the impact of their work. It involved in-depth work with 17 village groups, a study of over 70 individual case histories, and an analysis of two specific campaigns undertaken by a wider range of groups. The study developed specific tools for assessing institutional development and sustainablity, such as a leadership-type analysis and indices of group cohesion and NGO involvement.

Post-conflict reconstruction in El Salvador (Fundación para la Cooperación y el Desarrollo Comunal de El Salvador)

The Foundation for Co-operation and Community Development in El Salvador (CORDES) was created during the last years of the civil war of 1979-91 by the mandate of the communities which it works with. These include demobilised combatants and repatriated and marginal communities from the areas most affected by the armed conflict. Projects now concentrate on financing and marketing agricultural production, and institutional strengthening. Supported by Novib, CORDES is looking back to assess the impact of its work in three communities, and to develop an impact assessment method with those communities and within its own organisation.

The study involved the development of a systematic process of reconstructing project history and then relating this to the current situation (working with a small number of communities in a participatory way).

Livelihood support projects in Zimbabwe (Environmental and Development Activities Zimbabwe)

The primary goal of ENDA-Zimbabwe is to assist disadvantaged communities to generate income and wealth through their sustainable use of natural resources and increased capacity to raise their standard of living. This retrospective study assessed the impact of the Zimbabwe Seeds Action Network (ZSAN) Phase 1 and the Chivi/ Zvishavane Indigenous Woodland Management Demonstration Project. Both these projects ran from 1985-92, and the studies therefore had to go back to communities some years after the projects had ended. The studies used a literature review, key informant interviews, questionnaires, and focus-group discussions, but also attempted to explore changes in other institutions which may have been influenced by the projects.

13

Table 1.2: Overview of case studies

Country	Ghana	India	Kenya	Uganda	Pakistan
Organisation	ISODEC and NGDN	CYSD	Oxfam GB in Wajir	Oxfam GB in Ikafe	Oxfam GB
Scale of assessment	3 villages 3 organi- sations	2 integrated programmes	Programme- wide	1 refugee- affected area	Variety of micro- projects and organisations
Stage of assessment	Base-line analysis and review	Ongoing	Ongoing	Ongoing	Ongoing
Year project started	1995	1989	1992	1994	various
Beneficiaries	170 households	1. 869hh 2. 1787hh	40,000	55,000	5,000
Duration of assessment	2 years	1 year	2 weeks 2 weeks	6 weeks	1-3 days per micro-project
Cost	£35,000	£6,404	£18,000	£19,000	£5,000
Staff involved	2 half-time 2 part-time staff	7 full-time 8 part-time staff	3 consultants 7 part-time staff	2 leaders 7 full-time 50 part-time staff	Advisor: 12 weeks 4 staff part- time: 8 person weeks
Support	IDS, UK; World Neighbours; Oxfam GB	Novib workshop; external advisor	DfID; ITDG; REMPAI consultants	Oxfam GB	External advisor

How the case studies differ

Differences in scale

The most obvious difference between the studies is the scale of the projects or programmes being assessed. One aims to reach a single community of 300 people, another involves more than 68,000 village organisations. Although this mirrors the organisational differences outlined in Table 1.1, it is not as simple as this: a large-scale programme, such as Oxfam GB's in Pakistan, can be made up of a large number of micro-projects. In the case of the Matson Neighbourhood Project, the organisation *is* the project; in this sense,

UK	Zimbabwe	Bangladesh			El Salvador
Matson NP	ENDA – ZW	NK GSS	BRAC	Proshika	CORDES
1 community 1 organisation	2 projects 5 sites	17 groups	1 thematic programme	1 thematic programme	3 communities
Ongoing	Review (4 years after the project ended)	Base-line and review	Ongoing	Ongoing	Review (4 years after the project ended)
1990	1985	various	1986	1993	1990
6,000	120,000	9 villages	2.5m (1998)	11,530 villages	299
8 weeks	1 year	18 months	1 year	2 years	1 year
£5,000	£14,725	£41,437	£35,000	£60,000	£28,200
Peer reviewer: 8 weeks; existing part-time staff	4 part-time 2 full-time staff	2 consultants and existing staff	10 researchers and 60 enumerators	10 full-time 20 part-time staff	1 advisor and existing staff
Oxfam GB	Novib workshop	External advisor	IDS, UK	Novib workshop; external advisor	External advisor from local university

although the organisation is small in comparison to some of the others, the project it represents is relatively large.

Some of the other main distinctions between the case studies include the different stages at which the assessments were undertaken; differences in the degree to which the assessment was perceived as an opportunity to test tools and methods for the future rather than as a means of reviewing the past; differences in the availability of information on a project's history; and differences in the scope and duration of the assessment and therefore of the approaches adopted. Table 1.2 summarises the main characteristics of the various case studies.

Stages in the project-cycle

Figure 1.2 situates the case studies in the project-cycle (which can also be seen as a continuous spiral). The arrows illustrate the approximate position in a particular project's life-cycle at which the assessment was undertaken. The Ghana and the CYSD 1 studies stand out as attempts to establish baseline data and systems of impact monitoring (also called longitudinal data collection) at, or near, the beginning of programme implementation. Most of the other studies examine ongoing projects or programmes, looking both backwards and forwards. Some of these, for example the Wajir programme and BRAC's rural development programme, made use of longitudinal data collected during the course of the project or programme in question. The CORDES and ENDA studies represent retrospective assessments of programmes that had ended, in ENDA's case some four years previously.

Reliance on existing data

These case studies varied in the degree to which they were based on past processes of monitoring, evaluation, and impact assessment. For example, the Wajir and BRAC studies systematically tried to build on existing impact-data collection systems. BRAC's case study is actually builds on a previous impact assessment carried out in 1993/4. Other studies, although attempting to build on past documentation, have had to expend greater effort on retracing the past using a variety of recall methods, either because existing records were weak or because previous assessments did not capture those elements pertinent to the study in question.

Different approaches

A wide variety of approaches to impact assessment and to implementation timescales, some of which are summarised in Table 1.2 above, is represented in the case studies. They vary from an Indian consultant's eight-week intense involvement in the Matson Project in Gloucester, UK, using mainly participant observation and key informant interviews, to a year-long process with BRAC in Bangladesh, which involved ten researchers and 60 enumerators in a large-scale sample survey of 1,700 households, complemented by case study and focus-group discussions. This rich diversity indicates the range of approaches, organisations, and contexts through which and in which to conduct impact assessment.

Figure 1.2: Where the case studies fit in the project-cycle

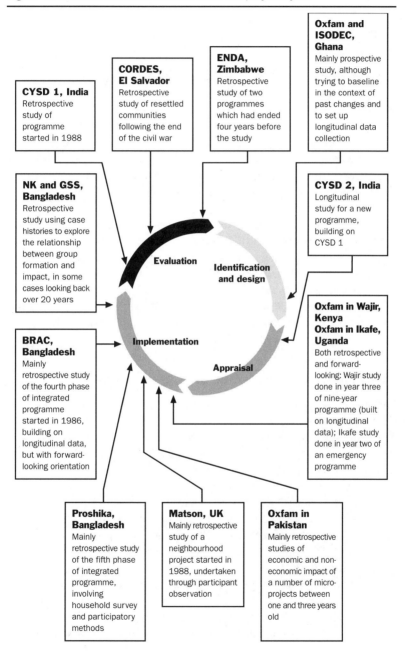

Oxfam and ISODEC, Ghana
Mainly prospective study, although trying to baseline in the context of past changes and to set up longitudinal data collection

ENDA, Zimbabwe
Retrospective study of two programmes which had ended four years before the study

CORDES, El Salvador
Retrospective study of resettled communities following the end of the civil war

CYSD 1, India
Retrospective study of programme started in 1988

NK and GSS, Bangladesh
Retrospective study using case histories to explore the relationship between group formation and impact, in some cases looking back over 20 years

CYSD 2, India
Longitudinal study for a new programme, building on CYSD 1

BRAC, Bangladesh
Mainly retrospective study of the fourth phase of integrated programme started in 1986, building on longitudinal data, but with forward-looking orientation

Oxfam in Wajir, Kenya
Oxfam in Ikafe, Uganda
Both retrospective and forward-looking: Wajir study done in year three of nine-year programme (built on longitudinal data); Ikafe study done in year two of an emergency programme

Evaluation

Identification and design

Implementation

Appraisal

Proshika, Bangladesh
Mainly retrospective study of the fifth phase of integrated programme, involving household survey and participatory methods

Matson, UK
Mainly retrospective study of a neighbourhood project started in 1988, undertaken through participant observation

Oxfam in Pakistan
Mainly retrospective studies of economic and non-economic impact of a number of micro-projects between one and three years old

17

2

Our overall approach to impact assessment

This chapter sets out the theoretical foundations which the case studies were based upon. These were informed both by a review of the relevant literature[1] and by a number of key questions which both Oxfam and Novib were keen to explore.

I outline our understanding of the nature and forms of change which underlies the case studies, and our principles regarding participation and the importance of paying attention to gender and other social relations. We are also convinced that impact assessment should be useful and relevant to local staff and partner organisations, and that it should be integrated into every stage of the project or programme. In terms of methodology, I give some thought to the central issues of attribution and aggregation, and conclude with some views on the ethics of impact assessment.

Historical overview of impact assessment

Initial approaches to impact assessment date from the 1950s; development agencies began to use these approaches — which were about predicting, before the start of a project, its likely environmental, social, and economic consequences — in order to approve, adjust, or reject it. Environmental impact assessment (EIA), social impact assessment (SIA), cost-benefit analysis (CBA) and social cost-benefit analysis (SCBA) are some of the most common approaches (see Howes 1992). In recent years, there have been several efforts to integrate social and environmental impact assessments into more coherent forms (see Barrow 1997); impact analysis, on the other hand, was essentially confined to an assessment of impact several years after a project had ended.

The next generation of planning in international development agencies saw the introduction of logical framework analysis (LFA), which attempts to set out a clear hierarchy of inputs, activities, and objectives and to relate these to assumptions made about the external environment. Today the logical framework and its variants are the most common planning framework used by bilateral and multilateral agencies. LFA was used in several of the case studies: for instance, Chapter 4 looks at how the Wajir programme in Kenya explored cause-and-effect relationships between what the project did and what it sought to achieve.

From the early 1980s, new methods of enquiry emerged which sought to make people and communities subjects and active participants, rather than objects of impact assessment. New methods such as rapid rural appraisal (RRA), participatory action research (PAR), participatory rural appraisal (PRA) — now often termed participatory learning and action (PLA) — and other methods all blossomed during this period (Chambers 1997). This in turn led to a number of efforts to achieve a greater synthesis of these strands. The development of objectives-oriented project planning (ZOPP) in Germany attempted to introduce notions of participation into the logical framework approach (GTZ 1988a). In contrast, approaches to the evaluation of social development (Marsden and Oakley 1991) and 'fourth-generation' evaluation ideas (Guba and Lincoln 1989) have built on historical and anthropological ideas and see evaluation more as a negotiation of diverse opinions and perspectives. This latter approach, in combination with participatory methods, thus seeks to understand the opinions of various interest groups, especially those whose views are not normally heard. In recent years, national-level planning and development strategies have also begun to include participatory poverty assessments (PPAs), seeking to incorporate local perspectives and opinions by including participatory research methods within national frameworks (Norton et al. 1995).

Figure 2.1 (originally developed by Mick Howes) indicates the evolution of these different approaches. He also illustrates the origins of these approaches in relation to various development paradigms such as modernisation, limited participation, and extended participation. Modernisation here refers to an approach largely premised on promoting economic and infrastructural development as a means for 'third-world' nations to catch up with the 'first' world. By contrast, the extended participation approach begins with the belief that poverty is primarily caused by injustice and inequality and that overcoming poverty is impossible without people's full participation. This paradigm demands that outsiders relinquish control and act as catalysts for locally owned processes of empowerment and development. The limited participation approach, in Howes's view, represents a compromise between these two poles and was most apparent in the multilateral agencies' shift to embrace participatory approaches, while retaining a strong planning tradition and an emphasis on economic development.

Figure 2.1: Approaches to appraisal and evaluation 1950s-90s

(adapted from Howes 1992)

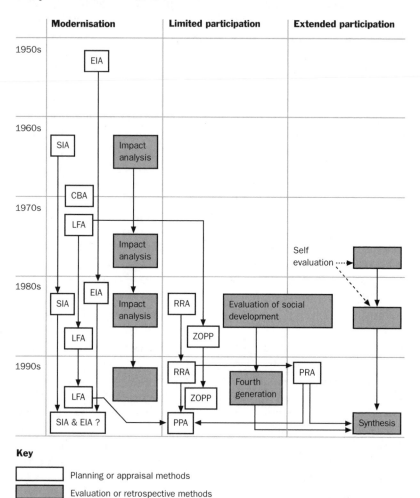

Key

Planning or appraisal methods

Evaluation or retrospective methods

What do we mean by impact assessment?

At the outset of the research, Oxfam GB and Novib used the working definition of impact as *'sustained changes in people's lives brought about by a particular intervention'*. Impact thus referred not to any immediate outputs or effects of a project or programme but to any lasting and sustained changes brought about.

We therefore defined impact assessment as an evaluation of how, and to what extent, change had occurred. This required an understanding of the perspectives of various stakeholders in a development intervention, as well as of the social, economic, and political context in which it takes place.

Following the first stage of our research it became clear that — particularly in areas experiencing rapid and unpredictable change such as conflict zones or emergency situations — the emphasis on sustained or lasting change was a problem. It was obvious that in such situations the provision of clean water, for example, could literally save someone's life, which could only be described as a significant impact, if not a lasting one. The definition of impact therefore changed to *'significant or lasting changes in people's lives, brought about by a given action or series of action'*. In other words, programmes can make an important difference to people's lives even if that change is not sustained over time.

The consultant who was recruited to review the existing literature and to undertake some initial discussions with Oxfam and Novib partners also proposed that, given the complexity of the task, there should be two different levels of impact assessment. First,he recommended a focused appraisal with regards to the original objectives of the project, and second, a wider assessment of overall changes — positive or negative, intended or not — caused by a project. All the case studies, while recognising the importance of assessing performance against objectives, opted for the latter, wider definition.

A common definition therefore emerges from the studies: *Impact assessment is the systematic analysis of the lasting or significant changes — positive or negative, intended or not — in people's lives brought about by a given action or series of actions.*

The consultant who carried out the initial research had recognised that

[i]n a certain sense, most of us have been doing impact assessment for a long time. What is new in the discussion is the emphasis on the outcomes and consequences of a project; and the attention given to the systematic *nature of such an effort.* (Hopkins 1995, p.5)

Figure 2.2 illustrates this focus on outcomes and impact, using the example of a legal rights programme. In this case, impact assessment would need to measure the degree to which an improved awareness of rights has led to people actually using the legal system and whether this has improved the participants' quality of life. It also reminds us that although the emphasis may be on significant change and not the inputs, activities, or outputs, all these will need to be examined in order to see if there is a logical link between them and the impact achieved.

Figure 2.2: The orthodox view of the focus of impact assessment

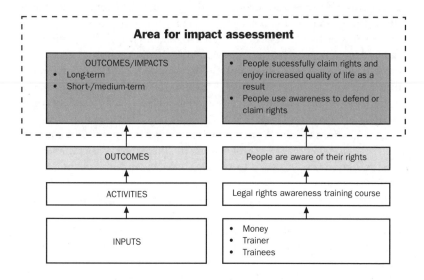

In much of the literature, and in some of the case studies which follow, a further distinction is made between outcomes or effects and impact. In the above example, the actual use of the legal system to claim a right would be considered an outcome or effect, whereas the actual change in quality of life that this brings about would be considered as impact.

These definitions[2] are often used in distinguishing between different kinds of assessment which examine the efficiency, effectiveness, consistency, and impact of an intervention (see Figure 2.3). The first of these analyses the relationship between the resources put into a given project or programme and the outputs and outcomes achieved. Thus, an efficiency assessment helps to decide whether the same results could have been achieved at less cost, or whether significantly better results could have been achieved with only a small amount of additional resources. An effectiveness assessment looks at the degree to which a project has achieved what it set out to do. Third, one can evaluate the degree to which the process or methods adopted were consistent or in harmony with the outcomes achieved: for example, a non-participatory project design and implementation would not be consistent with intended outcomes that sought to strengthen people's capacities to solve their own problems. Impact is then assessed by analysing the degree to which an intervention's outcomes led to change in the lives of those who it is intended to benefit.

Figure 2.3: Distinguishing between efficiency, effectiveness, consistency, and impact

(adapted from Paul Willot, 1985)

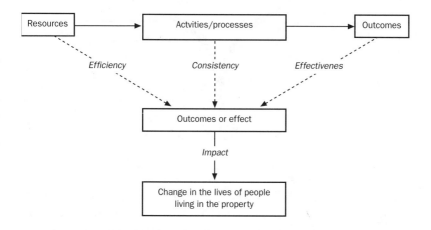

Judgements made in assessment

In practice, the distinction between outcomes or effects and impact, although useful, can be very blurred. Taking up the example of a legal rights programme, this distinction between outcomes and impact can ignore the fact that a person who is now sufficiently aware and confident to use the legal system may consider this a significant change in his or her life, even if it does not immediately lead to a positive legal result or a demonstrable change in their quality of life. This reveals that although impact assessment is about systematic analysis, it is also centrally about judgements of what change is considered 'significant' for whom, and by whom; views which will often differ according to class, gender, age, and other factors.

These judgements are also dependent on the context within which they are made. In some of our case studies, income or assets are considered key indicators of change, and these would have to *increase* over time to be assessed as an impact. In other cases, the *preservation* of current levels of food security over a number of years for the poorest households is considered a significant impact. Clearly, these judgements can only be made for each specific situation, which leads to the important conclusion that change is brought about by a combination of the activities of a given project or programme and the ongoing dynamics of the context in which these activities occur (see Figure 2.4).

Figure 2.4: Actions and context combine to produce change

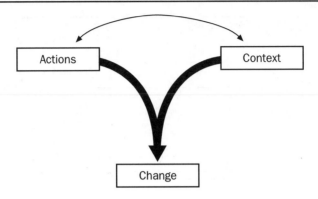

The nature of change

Impact assessment is therefore essentially about the measurement and/or valuation of change. For many years, development planning models have been associated with a linear notion of change, which assumes that an input A leads to an output B and an outcome or impact C.

$$A \longrightarrow B \longrightarrow C$$

However, in recent years there has been a growing interest in non-linear models of change, which recognise not only that may A and B may influence each other,

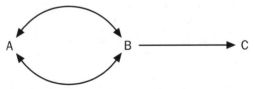

but also that this interaction may result in the same input producing divergent, and possibly unexpected, outputs over time or in different places.

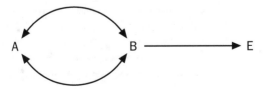

This means that the change which occurs is contingent on the specific events, people, and conditions present in a given situation as well as on the action or activity undertaken. In other words, the resulting change may be due to a myriad of factors combining in a particular way. This means that using the same inputs will not necessarily produce the same results in the future. Given the nature of development projects, and of the organisations that run and support them — which are not machines but involve people who have their own ideas, dreams, and interests — it is particularly important to recognise the contingent nature of the change they produce.

The second characteristic of non-linear change is that it may be sudden, discontinuous, and unpredictable rather than drawn-out, stable, and forecastable (Uphoff 1993, Roche 1994, Fowler 1995). When a coup-d'état occurs, when currency speculation takes hold, or when an earthquake happens, a whole chain of unexpected events can disrupt the status quo. This might provoke considerable changes in social, economic, or political systems which hitherto would have seemed unlikely or impossible. Given the interdependence of environments, and the growing links between economies, communication systems, and in some cases political systems, the possibilities for systemic shocks, whose ripple effects reverberate around the world, are increasing. Such sudden changes can also occur at a local level, for example when the charismatic leader of a local organisation suddenly resigns, or when a new feeder road is built.

These issues are important for the purposes of impact assessment as they remind us that development and change are never solely the product of a managed process undertaken by development agencies and NGOs. Rather, they are the result of wider processes that are the product of many social, economic, political, historical, and environmental factors — including power struggles between different interest groups. Understanding these processes is important if the changes brought about by a given project or programme is to be properly situated in its broader context.

The impact chain

The degree to which the context of a project influences change will increase the further up the 'impact chain' we move (see Figure 2.5). Going back to our legal rights example, the likelihood of the training course being held is largely dependent on the organisers doing their job and the funds being available. However, whether this course results in trainees' increased awareness of legal rights depends not only on the trainers' skills and abilities, but also on whether the trainees pay attention, are able or willing to read any course texts, or whether women trainees have their husbands' permission to attend.

At the level of outcomes and impact, people's ability to use the legal system and benefit from it in turn depends on how the legal system functions in that context — whether particular groups are discriminated against, whether support and funding for plaintiffs is available, and so on.

Figure 2.5: The impact chain and the importance of context

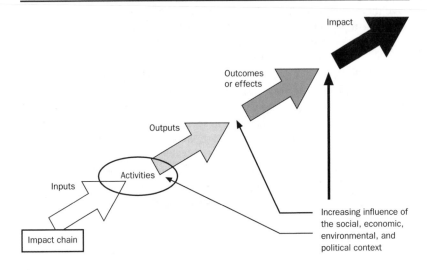

However, although the impact chain provides us with a useful way of distinguishing between different levels of change, these differences may not be evident in practice, may be meaningless to people in communities — who assess change in their lives without distinguishing between 'outcomes' and 'impacts' — and need to be clearly situated within, and analysed in relation to, the context.

Although I may refer to examples which relate to different parts of the impact chain in the following chapters, most impact assessments will need to explore the entire chain if reliable conclusions are to be drawn about the degree to which any observed change in people's lives can be attributed, at least in part, to a given project or programme.

Impact assessment in relation to monitoring and evaluation

Some of the case studies suggest the following distinctions between impact assessment, monitoring and evaluation.

Timing: Monitoring occurs frequently and evaluation periodically. Impact assessment, however, occurs infrequently, usually towards or after the end of an intervention.

Analytical level: Monitoring is mainly descriptive, recording inputs, outputs, and activities. Evaluation is more analytical and examines processes, while impact assessment is mainly analytical and concerned with longer-term outcomes.

Specificity: Monitoring is very specific and compares a particular plan and its results. Evaluation does the same but also looks at processes, whereas impact assessment is less specific and in addition considers external influences and events.

Figure 2.6 represents what one might call the 'classical' view of the distinctions between monitoring, evaluation, and impact assessment. From this perspective impact assessment has been seen either as part of the appraisal stage (in order to anticipate potential environmental, social, or economic consequences and to redesign a project if necessary) or as a specific type of evaluation which occurs near or after the end of a project (in order to review past impact and to inform future plans or revised policies). In addition, in this view impact assessment is understood to examine only the outcome or impact level of an intervention (illustrated in Figures 2.2, 2.3 and 2.5). Recently, the importance of mid-term reviews or evaluations has been increasingly recognised; these are intimately linked to monitoring, and are increasingly addressing issues of impact. However, in the classical model monitoring, i.e. the ongoing collection and analysis of information during the course of the project, is generally seen as referring to input, activity, and output data, not to impact.

Figure 2.6: The 'classical' view of the difference between monitoring, evaluation, and impact assessment

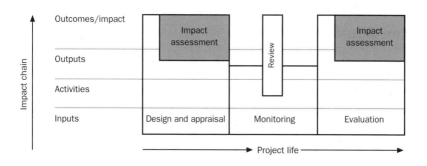

Although the clasical model can be useful in distinguishing between different elements of recording and reviewing progress, there can be major limitations in adopting this framework too rigidly. Indeed some of the studies conclude that 'impact monitoring' is an essential part of impact assessment and that too rigid a distinction between monitoring, evaluation and impact is unhelpful. What is clear is that monitoring, evaluation, and impact assessment are all intimately connected and draw on each other.

In view of the complexities of definition, we have been guided in this research by the following considerations. Although various stakeholders will have their own perspectives in judging the impact of a given project, far greater attention must be paid to the views of those who are intended to benefit. Second, it is important to assess all changes (whether these are positive or negative), including unintended and unexpected ones, rather than simply looking at the intended impact of an intervention. These changes may also affect people other than those who the project intends to benefit. Moreover, among the groups intended to benefit, as well as among those outside an intervention's reach, people will have different experiences and perceptions of what change has been achieved. Views will diverge particularly between men and women, but also between other social groups.

While the intended impact of a development intervention is often defined in terms of long-term, sustainable changes that it wishes to bring about, there may be short-term results which are attributable to the intervention and which people judge to be significant too. For example, a dam-building project which displaces people from their land has a significant impact on them from day one, whether this is intended or not, and whether they eventually regain some land! One of the most important questions to answer is whether the project or programme in question has brought about results that would not have occurred otherwise. This involves not only an assessment of the input-output-impact 'chain', but also of the context in which the project evolved and how this context interacted with the project activities to produce change.

Power and participation

At the outset of the research Oxfam and Novib stated that they saw the development of participatory monitoring and review processes as the basic building block for impact assessment. This was based on the view that significant and lasting change in people's lives must take account of *their* values, priorities, and judgements; projects cannot be deemed to have been a 'success' or 'failure' if the perceptions of those who the intervention aims to benefit diverge seriously from those of the project staff or an external evaluator.

In addition, the literature review concluded that monitoring and evaluation systems have tended to be 'top-down and bureaucratic' and that a 'frequent way to impose authority has been to introduce sophisticated jargon' which now needs demystifying (Hopkins 1995a). Valuing the wisdom and judgement of ordinary people is therefore a critical element of any impact assessment process. 'The main challenge facing organisations such as Oxfam and Novib is how to incorporate these opinions, especially those of women, into our monitoring and evaluation systems.' (Dawson 1995)

However, we also recognise that there are other stakeholders who require information and that it is often extremely difficult to satisfy everybody's needs. Thus while insights and lessons can be drawn from participatory processes of assessment, a large organisation can only use these in a selective way. It is therefore suggested that organisations should not seek 'to aggregate and summarise the richness of this type of information, or to seek standard indicators across diverse projects and programmes' (Hopkins 1995a). Rather than simply adding up results, project-level findings can be incorporated into wider processes of review and learning. This approach explicitly acknowledges a number of interest groups, who have different and possibly conflicting objectives, are involved in any process of intervention. As these interest groups will judge impact in different ways, the search for an 'objective truth' or reality that all can agree on is, at best, fraught with difficulty and, at worst, impossible. In this scenario, impact assessment becomes far more of a negotiation of different interpretations of what has happened or will happen.

It was not made explicit in the literature review that these various interest groups bring different status, resources, and ultimately power to the negotiation process, and that some group's views on what has occurred can therefore become dominant. The question, as Robert Chambers put it, becomes 'whose reality counts?' or, as Estrella and Gaventa ask in relation to impact assessment, 'who counts reality?' (Estrella and Gaventa 1997). The meaning of the now widely used term 'participation' therefore needs greater clarity. Among the questions that need to be addressed are:

- What do we mean by participation?
- Who participates and on what terms?
- How can we trust processes which claim to be participatory?

I will return to these questions in the final chapter.

The importance of gender and other social relations

Oxfam and Novib both believe that social relations are a critical determinant of well-being or poverty, a view shared by most of the case-study participants.

Confronting gender-related inequalities is seen not only as a pre-requisite to 'achieving sustainable development and alleviating poverty' (Oxfam Gender Policy, 1993) but as a objective for social justice in its own right. It is well known that within communities, factors such as gender, class, ethnicity, religion, ability/disability, and age are important elements and that communities do not share a single identity, goal, or ambition.

We also know that in recent years, the understanding of the household[3] has changed enormously from an approach which stressed sharing and co-operation to models which include the possibility of negotiation, bargaining, and conflict. The old approach viewed the household as a single unit, rather than one made up of individuals who are connected to wider structures and networks, such as kin or age groups, mutual support groups, or more formal organisations. Moreover, the household was described as if it were the same everywhere, rather than recognising the large differences between households within and between societies as well as over time.

Given these insights about power and participation, those planning an impact assessment must reflect carefully not only on what needs to be assessed and how this is done, but who is involved, and what level and unit of analysis is most appropriate.

In the past few years increasing attention has been paid to gender issues in the design, implementation, and evaluation of development projects. Several frameworks have been developed in order to assist better gender analysis, including Practical and Strategic Needs, the Harvard Framework, the Capacities and Vulnerabilities Framework, and Social Relations Framework (see March et al. 1999 for detailed discussion of the advantages and disadvantages of these).

The case studies made different assumptions about gender and other factors that shape social relations; they therefore explored the issues in different ways and emphasised different aspects. I will explore these and present some of the tools and methods used.

Impact assessment and the project- or programme-cycle

The literature review stressed that 'it is not possible to carry out impact assessment activities successfully if the more basic task of evaluating activities and their immediate effects is not done properly' (Hopkins 1995a). A better assessment can be made if a baseline study has been carried out, indicators have been monitored efficiently, and clear objectives have been defined, with corresponding activities and indicators. This means that impact assessment is an activity that must be done *throughout* the project cycle; what changes is the nature of the exercise. In the preparatory stages, it is anticipatory or prospective. In the process of implementation, it checks what consequences a project is currently having. After completion, the emphasis is on examining what effects the project has had.

Moreover, because most interventions aim to improve the quality of life of a target group of people, their input needs to be captured at all stages of the project-cycle. Figure 2.7 details the typical form of various elements of the impact assessment process at specific stages of the project-cycle.

Figure 2.7: Key elements of impact assessment at specific stages of the project-cycle

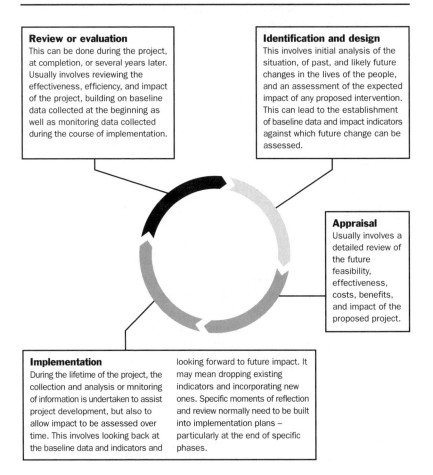

Review or evaluation
This can be done during the project, at completion, or several years later. Usually involves reviewing the effectiveness, efficiency, and impact of the project, building on baseline data collected at the beginning as well as monitoring data collected during the course of implementation.

Identification and design
This involves initial analysis of the situation, of past, and likely future changes in the lives of the people, and an assessment of the expected impact of any proposed intervention. This can lead to the establishment of baseline data and impact indicators against which future change can be assessed.

Appraisal
Usually involves a detailed review of the future feasibility, effectiveness, costs, benefits, and impact of the proposed project.

Implementation
During the lifetime of the project, the collection and analysis or mnitoring of information is undertaken to assist project development, but also to allow impact to be assessed over time. This involves looking back at the baseline data and indicators and looking forward to future impact. It may mean dropping existing indicators and incorporating new ones. Specific moments of reflection and review normally need to be built into implementation plans – particularly at the end of specific phases.

The image of the project-cycle has a number of well-known weaknesses: projects do not endlessly repeat the same 'cycle' as they evolve; rather, the process can be described as a 'spiral' with continual adaptation and modification. Another weakness is that a project approach tends to be rigid, inflexible, and to ignore the context. Third, while the project tends to dominate the lives of those who manage and support it, it may make up a very small part of the lives of those it seeks to benefit.

With this in mind, I will explore what the case studies tell us about the utility of a project-cycle conceptualisation of impact-assessment, and what the findings suggest in relation to more programme- or process-oriented approaches.

Impact assessment and organisations: The problems of attribution and aggregation

All organisations, be they a community-based group, a local NGO, or an international agency, need to make sense of what they are doing. They also generally want to know what difference they are making. This raises two central problems: how organisations can synthesise or summarise what they are doing (aggregation), and how they can find out to what extent any changes they observe were brought about by their actions (attribution). These issues are further complicated if the organisation has to communicate their achievements to many other people, both inside and outside the organisation.

Attribution

'Success has many parents ... failure is an orphan.'

In the current climate, despite the vogue for development organisations to proclaim partnership and the need for 'synergy', raising money and gaining in reputation largely depend on demonstrating what a single organisation has achieved, what difference it has made, and what value it has added, usually to the exclusion of other actors or agencies. As Neil Thin points out, NGOs, like other organisations, tend to blame others and/or the external environment when things go wrong (Thin 1992). Similarly, they tend to neglect to mention the role played by other organisations or concomitant events when things go right.

Yet one of the most problematic parts of impact assessment is determining causality, because in real life, a combination of several factors is likely to have caused any observed change. In the laboratory, different possible sources of change are isolated so as to observe, and precisely measure, their different effects. Outside the laboratory, and particularly in the area of social development or emergency work, it is not usually possible, or appropriate, to rely solely on this form of scientific observation, for the following methodological and ethical reasons:

- It is usually impossible to find a control group similar to the group of people benefiting from an intervention, who are subject to exactly the same influences, except for the specific agency input, and whose situation mirrors that of the beneficiary group over the life of a given project.

- Withholding support from a control group in order for it to remain 'uncontaminated' is not only difficult (you might have to persuade other agencies not to support them!), it is in most cases unethical and may contravene their human rights.

- A particular intervention does not occur in isolation from those of other organisations, from the local context, wider economic and political policies and, more importantly, from the actions and reactions of those who it aims to support. It will interact with these in different ways in different places. Unpicking what caused an impact in this situation in any scientific way is likely to be very difficult and usually very expensive (Hulme 1997).

Often the most that can be done is to demonstrate through reasoned argument that a given input leads logically towards a given change, even if this cannot be proved statistically. This in turn can be cross-checked against the views of other actors to see if important areas of agreement or disagreement emerge. In some cases, quasi-experiments with control groups or non-beneficiaries used in combination with other methods may be appropriate.

But it should always be remembered that a common principle of development is that agencies such as Oxfam or Novib should be trying to 'work themselves out of a job'. In doing so we usually aim to enable people to take ownership of achievements: this directly affects how one might look at attribution. If a group says 'we did it ourselves', this is an indicator of their empowerment. While they may recognise the role that others have played in supporting them, if others start claiming the success as their own, then this might undermine the group's sense of self-worth and self-confidence[4].

In the case studies, various approaches are used to deal with the problem of attribution such as the use of control groups, statistical analysis, and cross-checking. I explore the advantage and disadvantages of these different approaches and their appropriateness for different context and types of organisation in Chapters 3 and 4.

Aggregation and synthesis

All organisations need to organise, categorise, synthesise, and aggregate information. The larger the organisation, the bigger the problem. The problem can be posed in terms of practical issues — how does an organisation cope with the large amounts of information generated from participatory processes? It can also be defined in terms of utility or rigour: does the aggregated data actually mean anything? And is it of any use?

Organisations cope with this by demanding that certain categories of information (such as budgets) are included in, for example, project proposals, reports, and evaluations. In addition to formal reporting structures, staff also communicate to others in their organisation in ways which 'filter' information: how they share information depends on what use they assume will be made of it. For instance, when an Oxfam staff member from Africa was asked how he knew that a tomato-growing project was successful, he replied 'because the men in the village are marrying second wives'. He was then asked why he did not report this fact in his annual report, and commented: 'Because that's not what you want — you want "10 tonnes to the hectare" or "income up 50 per cent"'. It is beside the point that this quantitative data had not been demanded — he *assumed* that it was required. This underlines the importance of recognising the informal signals that an organisation may send out to its staff or partners, in addition to its formal procedures and guidelines.

The case studies aggregated and synthesised findings in different ways. I shall explore these as well as the strategies which some of the organisations involved have adopted in order to meet the needs of various stakeholders.

Avoiding bias

The case studies take different starting points regarding the assumed objectivity or subjectivity of particular approaches to impact assessment. This is not surprising, given the intensity of the debate that sometimes surrounds these notions.

The BRAC team decided not to rely solely on participatory methods.

[A]lthough the criteria used in the participatory approach tell us more about local people's multidimensional conception of poverty than conventional consumption and expenditure measures, these are, by their very nature, subjective and only definable within the norms and customs of a given society. (BRAC case study)

In contrast, the Matson study deliberately started with the 'subjective' opinions and perceptions of local people, precisely because the researcher believed that understanding their views counted most.

No one can be entirely objective, of course, and the measures that researchers develop, even quantitive ones, always contain a degree of subjectivity. For example, who decides that $1 a day is an accurate poverty line? In addition, the choice of approach is often the result of rather pragmatic concerns: BRAC was attempting to assess the impact of a programme that covered over 60,000 village organisations, and therefore felt that they needed to be able to compare results across communities, whereas the Matson study covered a single housing estate.

We will return to this issue at several points in the next chapters, because it goes to the heart of several issues related to the design and implementation of impact assessments, the choice of assessment methods and teams, and the importance of cross-checking or triangulation.

The ethics of impact assessment

The case studies highlighted several ethical questions associated with evaluation processes which need to be borne in mind, some of which become particularly acute in emergency or conflict situations.

At the community level, the dangers of raising expectations and of taking up too much of people's time are commonly raised in the studies. This suggests that a critical ethical issue is the degree to which an impact assessment is meaningful and intrinsically worthwhile to those involved. If impact assessment work is purely interested in extracting information and does not allow *all* participants to gain insights, to reflect on their observations, and to look to the future, then the cost to some of those involved will far outweigh the benefits. In this case, it may be appropriate to recompense them in some way. This issue is explored further in relation to different approaches to impact assessment.

A further ethical issue relates to the danger of impact assessment processes exacerbating existing conflicts of interest within communities. For instance, in a programme which is having negative effects for women, or another group within a given community, it may be difficult for them to express their feelings about this, because a more powerful group is benefiting. Anybody assessing impact therefore must make efforts to understand who the winners and the possible losers might be, and seek the opinions of both. Promoting the continuation of activities that negatively affect certain groups clearly has an ethical dimension.

There are some specific issues realted to work in conflict zones or with traumatised populations such as refugees. In these cases, simply talking to evaluators may be dangerous (particularly if the evaluation subsequently leads to unpopular decisions being taken) or disturbing (if it leads to people having to recall traumatic events). In very tense situations the evaluation process may well lead to the emergence of conflicting views, which precipitates more conflict and generates risks for local populations, agency staff, and others. Agencies or individuals commissioning assessments need to be aware of these dangers and seek to minimise them. They should also recognise that evaluators may be particularly at risk in conflict zones, especially given that they may uncover facts that some would like to remain unknown.

However, these ethical concerns must be balanced against the moral question of accountability to others such as donors or supporters, who have often given money on the assumption that a particular impact or outcome will be achieved. There are further ethical considerations in relation to future performance, in terms of the degree to which an assessment can contribute to future positive impact for other people. Trying to balance these various concerns involves complicated trade-offs, which I shall look at particularly in Chapters 4 and 5.

3

Designing an impact assessment process

This chapter explores how to design an impact assessment process drawing upon the experience of the case studies. It attempts to cover some of the critical issues that must be considered when planning an assessment process, be it before a project starts, during its course, or after it has finished. I discuss what preparatory steps need to be taken, the questions of baseline data and indicators, as well as the difficulty of how to attribute change to a given intervention. The chapter concludes by analysing how the studies approached the need to cross-check findings and synthesise them in such a way that the results could be used and communicated. Some of the major lessons highlighted in this chapter relate to the importance of all stakeholders being clear about the purpose and focus of an impact assessment exercise; and to the necessity of deliberately exploring negative and unexpected impacts, of proactively involving those whose voices may not normally be heard, and of preventing bias by cross-checking findings.

Preparatory steps

When designing an impact assessment, whether it is at the beginning of the project, in the middle, or at the end, time spent in preparation is rarely wasted. Being clear about the purpose of the assessment, who it is for, who should be involved, and what resources are available, are just some of the questions that need to be addressed. The case studies answered them in different ways.

Defining the purpose of the impact assessment

This may seem an obvious point, but it is often overlooked. The purpose of most impact assessments is to demonstrate past impact and to improve future practice, and there may be tensions between the two. These tensions will be more difficult to handle if there is a large number of diverse stakeholders with an interest in the exercise, but who have different expectations of it.

Clarifying expectations and what different interest groups mean by impact can help to create a shared understanding of the process.

In most of the case studies, introductory workshops or meetings were held to discuss understandings about impact assessment and to define the purpose of each study. In some cases this involved Oxfam and Novib, who in most cases not only funded the impact assessment work but also the organisations involved. In the case of the Wajir study, representatives of the British Department for International Development (DFID), the funder of the Oxfam programme, were also present. In only one case (Ikafe) were representatives of intended beneficiaries directly involved at this stage. In many cases, the introductory workshop was held before it was decided where and with whom the impact assessment was to be undertaken. However, in some cases (such as the CORDES study) once communities had expressed interest in getting involved, similar workshop were held with them.

In Zimbabwe, an introductory workshop was held over five days and was attended by two members of staff from NOVIB and ten ENDA staff members.

The workshop provided a forum for debate and understanding of the [impact assessment] project [and] played a very important role in educating the participants on the expectations of the project. It is unlikely that a total understanding of the concepts of the impact assessment study could have been taken up easily without such a workshop. Of particular concern among staff were issues of whether future funding was related to the outcome of the impact assessment. Again the suspicion of the study being an evaluation may have been lingering in some minds. This was settled by having the participants choose which projects they would like to assess. (Bowdin King, ENDA case study report)

The issue of funding relations was touched upon explicitly and implicitly at several of the workshops and indicated the slight suspicion which many felt about this research, despite Oxfam and Novib's insistence that this was a mutual learning process, designed to find out about ways of assessing impact. These workshops did allay some of these fears, but at least in some cases, the question remained, because relationships between agency and partner organisation and decisions about future funding were being negotiated during the same period. It was inevitable that in some cases it was impossible to 'insulate' the impact research from these other processes — we shall return to this issue in Chapter 7.

Another important element of the workshops was to define the boundaries and focus of the case studies. This meant taking into account the financial and human resources available, the time scale envisaged, the scale and stage of the project being assessed, the types of activities undertaken and how long they had been running and the supposed impact of the project in question. As a result of these considerations, some components of projects were dropped from the assessment. For instance, BRAC deceided to exclude the issue of institution-building from their study, because staff felt that not enough time had elapsed since they had adopted a new strategy for this.

Workshops of this type can be a useful step to determine and agree the nature, scope, and purpose of impact assessment studies. In several of the case studies they also proved important in overcoming suspicions and mistrust between the stakeholders. The workshops also encouraged a sense of ownership of the assessment work within the organisations involved, particularly when more staff than those who would implement the project were involved, as was the case with ENDA, CYSD, and CORDES.

Perhaps most importantly, the workshops gave participants the opportunity to define what models of change they were using and what kinds of impact they envisaged.

Defining models of change: What has changed and why?

All impact assessment processes make assumptions about how change happens and why it has occurred, or that it will occur in the future. Sometimes these assumptions are made explicit but often, as David Hulme states, 'in many smaller scale exercises the framework is implicit and may be seen as 'common sense' (Hulme 1997). In those case studies where these assumptions were made explicit they were found to be based on certain theoretical frameworks relating to poverty or well-being.

In their study, which covers some 68,000 village organisations which are a part of its rural development programme, BRAC took a conventional approach to poverty measurement (looking at consumption and expenditure) because, although they recognise that poverty is multidimensional, they believe that 'its characteristics are sufficiently well correlated with consumption and expenditure to allow us to focus on these two variables'. This approach was then complemented by a range of qualitative techniques which aim to explore people's own perceptions of poverty. In their study of Nijera Kori (NK) and Gonoshahajjo Sangstha (GSS) — local Bangladeshi NGOs whose work emphasises social mobilisation — Rao and Hashemi explicitly rejected the assumption 'that poverty stems from a lack of access to scarce resources and that once a channel to such resources has been established it can continually be harnessed. In contrast, we begin with the assumption that poverty is created and reproduced through structural inequalities'. This led Rao and Hashemi to put less emphasis on assessing individual income and consumption and more on understanding the extent to which village organisations and their federations 'pit their interests first against the local power structure and then against the state'.

The Wajir study team, building on the programme documents, concluded that the reduction of poverty and vulnerability in a remote pastoral zone in north-eastern Kenya is dependent on strengthening and diversifying pastoral livelihood strategies. They agreed that this could best be achieved through improved access to market and state services (particularly concerning human and animal health, and provision of water, credit, and education servies); through a legal and policy framework which endorses common grazing and enforces existing property rights; and through stronger pastoral associations which can take collective action in order to claim and defend their rights. As a result, the Wajir study looks at change in pastoral livelihoods, at possible differences in pastoral livelihoods (and therefore in welfare) between project and non-project sites, and at the performance of service-delivery by local state and non-state institutions.

The Pakistan study on the other hand, which explored the impact of a number of micro-projects, started from an assumption that human development or well-being is multi-dimensional. The approach they adopted was explicit about what these dimensions are, in order not to miss important elements, and in order to ensure that the study focused on the ends of development, not just the means. The study uses a number of dimensions of human development from the field of ethics which are considered universal, irreducible, and non-hierarchical. These are life (which encompasses health, nutrition, security and so on), knowledge, excellence in work and play, relationships, beauty/ environment, inner voice/ peace, religion, and empowerment. The Pakistan study thus focused on the degree to which the projects in question produced change in these dimensions, and which ones the beneficiaries considered the most important. This was done without any prior judgement about the relationship between the dimensions, nor about the relationship between the project and its stated objectives.

This range of assumptions led to important differences in emphasis between the studies, particularly in terms of the main units of assessment chosen (individual, household, community, organisations, institutions), the areas or dimensions of change which were investigated, and the tools and methods chosen. Given how important these assumptions are in shaping the study, it makes sense to spend time clarifying and agreeing them. Summary 3.1 outlines some of the lessons learned in the course of this process, as well as other important issues that need to be clear at this stage.

Summary 3.1: Key lessons about preparing for an impact assessment process

- It is important that all stakeholders are clear about the purpose and focus of the assessment as well as the resources available — initial workshops or meetings can help in creating this shared understanding.

- Difficult issues that may need to be raised at this stage include how the results may or may not influence future funding.

- It may be necessary to clarify what is meant by impact assessment as opposed to any other evaluation or review exercise.

- At this stage, one should make explicit different stakeholders' assumptions about how change happens, what area of work they consider important to explore, and how they view the context within which an impact assessment exercise will be undertaken.

What areas of change and indicators are to be assessed?

Once the purpose of the assessments was clear and the assumptions about change made explicit, most of the case studies then defined the areas or kinds of impact to be assessed. The choice of indicators is often seen as one of the most crucial steps in the process of impact assessment, but there is no agreed method of doing so. Three different approaches were used in the case studies.

The first approach, used in restrospective studies, is largely project-led and involves an initial review of the current state of both the project in question and its external environment, in order to determine which indicators are most important to explore. In some case, new indicators were identified in this review, or previously established ones modified. This sometimes involved a process of consultation with communities and focus groups in order to determine the indicators.

For BRAC, whose team had already undertaken an impact assessment study (IAS 1) in 1993/4, this meant reviewing the indicators they had used to see if they remained relevant for IAS 2. Given that they wanted to compare the two studies, this posed certain problems.

Comparing with IAS 1 required the retaining of as many indicators of IAS 1 as possible. This raised a dilemma. We finally decided to exclude redundant or poorly specified variables included in IAS 1 ... [o]nly those indicators were retained which were of substantial value and relatively easy to repeat. (BRAC case study)

However, in other cases the projects being studied had either not previously established any indicators, or those that they had established proved difficult to assess or were simply not relevant. In cases where indicators were not available, for example in the CYSD retrospective study of an integrated project supporting tribal people in Orissa, India, researchers decided to engage with local communities to establish a set of indicators — related to the sectors which the project had worked on such as agriculture, literacy and so on — which could then be used to assess the project.

The project personnel have not given much effort in identifying/ visualising long term tangible/ intangible indicators and standards in participation with target population during different stages of the project. In this context there were no proper yardsticks (indicators) for the researcher to assess the level of achievement. Hence a set of indicators were framed by the research team from the villagers perspective through focus-group interview (with representatives from all social strata). Here they were asked to express their indicators (according to sector) by which they expect the project can withdraw from the area. These intangible indicators were then considered as best criteria for assessing the level of achievement. (CYSD 1 case study)

The second approach is more open and first and foremost explores changes brought about by the project as stated by various stakeholders, using generic checklists which are broader than the original scope of the project. The checklist in the Pakistan study, for example, included health and security, knowledge, excellence in work and play, relationships with others including gender relations, inner voice and empowerment, and beauty and religion. Men and women in the communities involved were then asked if change had occurred in these areas and to specify what the change was. As such these 'indicators' represent people's own examples of specific changes that has happened in their lives, rather than functioning as general, verifiable indicators.

The third approach is similar to the second, but attempts to 'turn the telescope round'. Rather than looking at impact solely from the perspective of an organisation or the project it supports, it starts by looking at what change is considered most significant in people's lives, irrespective of any project. It then goes on to explore with those concerned what are the processes bringing about such change, among which NGO-initiated projects and programmes may be one, and possibly minor, element. This approach was used in the Matson and Ghana studies.

In the first approach, indicators are established and the exercise of assessment is then essentially about verifying the degree to which these indicators can be confirmed. In the latter two, however, indicators exemplify broader areas of change in people's lives.

The importance of looking beyond predetermined indicators was deemed important in some studies due to what some have called the indicator dilemma (Goyder et al. 1998). This dilemma, as illustrated in Figure 3.1, notes that indicators which are used to verify impact can, by definition, only capture expected change and will only reflect those areas of change which can be made explicit or are agreed upon by key stakeholders. This leaves out situations where unexpected change occurs, or areas of change that have not been agreed or are left hidden by one or more stakeholders.

Figure 3.1: The indicator dilemma: What kind of change is captured?

Source: Action Aid Participatory Impact Study, Goyder et al. (1998)

	Expected	Unexpected
Agreed	✓✓✓	???
Not agreed	???	???

For instance, a review of a goat-rearing project (carried out as part of the Pakistan case study) revealed that the project had an important impact on women's' religious life because it enabled them to sacrifice animals for the Muslim festival of Eid. This had not been made an explicit area of change at the beginning of the project, and although the women may always have viewed it as an indicator of success, it was not seen as such by Oxfam. If Oxfam had only assessed change in line with the project indicators, it might well have not discovered this. Clearly this sort of surprise can be prevented by better pre-project discussions between communities and those supporting their projects. However, it may often be the case that these sorts of impact are unexpected, and there will be areas which some groups may feel uncomfortable or unwilling to declare as future indicators of success, for a variety of reasons. An evaluation of an Oxfam-supported credit and income-generation programme in Chad some years ago revealed that one of the women's own success criteria was that as a result of the project, they were now able to purchase bigger cooking pots. This in turn had allowed them to participate more fully in community celebrations, a critical element in feeling part of a social network. As Bridget Walker, formerly of Oxfam, observes, 'I wonder whether Oxfam would have initially supported a project to purchase bigger cooking pots for weddings and circumcision ceremonies!'

The indicator dilemma also illustrates the problem of assessing negative impacts. Although indicators may provide information about poor levels of attainment of agreed and expected changes, these are nearly always phrased in a positive way: increasing income, reducing animal mortality, and so on. Unexpected negative impacts will not necessarily be exposed. As similar studies have found (Goyder et al. 1998), the unequal relationship between an NGO and those who it seeks to support, may make the expression of negative impacts less likely. The method used in the Pakistan case study underlines this.

There will be positive impact and negative impacts. There are negative impacts even of very good activities. It is nothing to be embarrassed of. For example, if a women gets married, she spends less time with her parents; if I have a good job, I have less time to drink tea with friends. (Pakistan case study)

In the Pakistan study, the methodology developed put great emphasis on raising the issue of negative impacts at the beginning of any meeting with communities, and repeating questions about negative impacts at the end. However, this study also stresses to the researchers (local Oxfam staff) that their attitude and willingness to hear about negative impacts is also critical.

You yourself must really want to know what has gone wrong, or is going wrong — if you don't, how can you diffuse it? And you must welcome criticism. (ibid.)

The importance of developing trust and openness is brought out in the CORDES study. It seems that due to the very close relationship between CORDES and the community, the negative effects of a failed collective credit programme were clearly expressed. This in turn allowed important lessons to be learned not only about the technical aspects of credit management, but also about the knock-on effects in terms of the community's increased tendency to act as individuals.

Other research teams deliberately sought out those who might have been negatively affected by a project or who might have more critical opinions. For example, BRAC included individual case studies which were selected from those households that had dropped out of the programme. The Ghana study purposely chose women and men who were not benefiting from NGO projects in its sample of interviewees in order to assess possible negative effects upon them. Several studies specifically explored changing gender relations, and the effects on women, given the well-known history of negative impact that development projects have had on women's workload and status.

Types of indicator

Obviously the choice of indicator reflects the different projects undertaken. However, there are also differences between the case studies in the degree to which attempts were made to trace all stages of the projects' development, which means covering a wide range of indicators related to outputs and process as well as impact. Doing this of course depends in part on the extent to which a project has been well documented. Those projects which had to do more to reconstruct project activities and indicators (CYSD, ENDA) tended to have greater difficulty in defining and prioritising key indicators, whereas those projects with a greater emphasis on monitoring and recording progress (Wajir, BRAC, Proshika) were clearer about which impact indicators were critical to assess.

Table 3.1 lists examples of the key areas of change, within which more specific indicators were chosen, examined in the BRAC, Proshika, and Wajir case studies. This indicates that while there are important differences between the contexts of the case studies from Bangladesh and the study from Kenya, they have certain basic categories or dimensions of change in common. There are three main categories.

Material wealth: This encompasses assets (land, cattle, housing), income, credit and savings, occupational status, wages, expenditure, food security and quality of diet, dependency on money lenders or on food aid.

Social well-being or human capital measures: These terms refer to health status and more specifically infant and child mortality, water and sanitation, and education — especially literacy and school-attendance rates.

Empowerment or political capital measures: These include ownership and control over assets, perceptions of well-being and quality of life, participation in decision-making and public institutions, access to public resources, dependency and mobility, and family-planning rates as a proxy for women's empowerment. It is important to apply this category specifically to women, whose measure of empowerment will in most cases differ significantly from that of men.

Whilst these broad areas of change are similar, the means by which they are assessed may differ. For example, in the pastoralist community in Wajir, Kenya, which has been severely hit by drought and insecurity, animal mortality, dependence on food aid and the law and order situation were deemed critical indicators of the security of livelihoods. In rural Bangladesh access to land and credit were assumed to be critical determinants of general well-being, and of women's well-being in particular, in addition to their control and ownership of assets.

Table 3.1: Key areas of change within which specific indicators were selected

BRAC	Proshika	Wajir
Economic well-being	**Economic empowerment**	**Change in welfare/ livelihood**
• land holding	• indebtedness	• animal mortality
• occupation	• assets	• occurrence of peri-urban destitution
• assets	• income	
• housing status	• savings	• need for food aid
• household expenditure and consumption	• investment	• quality of diet
• food security	• market mobility and power	• rate of return to investments provided through credit
• credit and savings		
• ability to cope with crisis		• law and order
Social aspects of well-being	**Social empowerment**	**Social empowerment**
• literacy and educational level	• literacy	• school-attendance rates
		• parental satisfaction with education quality
• health, sanitation, and family planning	• health education and awareness	• reliability of water supply
	• family planning	• child mortality
• demographic and other household characteristics	• environmental awareness and practice	
	• infant mortality	
Women's empowerment	**Women's empowerment**	**Women's empowerment**
• involvement in income-generating activities	• access to public resources	
• ownership and control over assets	• participation in local institutions	
• perceptions of own well-being		• perceptions of changes in quality of life
• economic dependence on husbands		
• mobility		

By contrast, in the ENDA study each part of the project process was analysed at three levels: output, effect, and impact. The research team at first selected more than 20 indicators, which were subsequently found to be inappropriate and difficult to use as a basis for assessing impact. They therefore decided to begin indicator selection all over again in order to 'assess impact with a smaller number of relevant and manageable indicators. This gave some prospect of understanding the change that had taken place, rather than an unmanageable and ambitious list' (ENDA case study). ENDA's initial approach was to look for impacts and influences at every stage of the project-cycle. One of the assumptions they made was that each activity has an output that may lead to an impact.

The model therefore pointed to getting as much detail about the implementation process as possible. In retrospect, we feel that ... a lot of time could be spent in the reconstruction and understanding of the project. Although an understanding of the situation and conditions that prevailed during the project is required, we found that despite the masses of data that were generated these data were difficult to relate to tangible project impacts. (ENDA case study)

The Pakistan study, mentioned above, uses a generic checklist of possible impacts (see Table 3.2) and then systematically examines changes in each area to determine if there have been positive or negative changes in each category, to record specific examples of those changes, and to assess the relative importance of each category.

Table 3.2: Checklist for dimensions of impact used in Pakistan case study

Dimensions of impact	Description
Life — health — security	• changes related to physical survival
Knowledge	• technical , practical, about others, about themselves
Excellence in work and play	• impact on skills used at work, and at home during relaxation
Relationships, especially gender relations	• within community, family, with outsiders, within group • between men and women
Inner voice	• at peace with themselves, with their conscience, sense of harmony
Empowerment	• ability to make meaningful choices and decisions and to influence others
Beauty/environment	• impact on environment, sense of harmony with nature: has the intervention created or destroyed things of beauty or culture?
Religion	• impact on deeper values, sources of meaning

This technique of offering groups a broad framework of dimensions, which they then define and explore from their own experience, seems to offer several benefits. First, it solves the problem of people being more likely to report those impacts that they think will be of interest to the NGO or researcher — in a purely open-ended process this can be a real danger. Moreover, this technique can also be a starting point for the development of participatory indicators to be monitored in the future, or for planning how the community can deepen certain positive impacts and address negative impacts. Finally, if the facilitator is accompanied by a discreet note-taker, this method can help the NGO to capture the impacts in the words of the beneficiaries.

Properties of indicators

The desired properties of indicators will depend very much on the approach adopted and the nature of the project. For the purpose of verification and planning, establishing appropriate indicators is a critical part of the process. The acronym SMART (specific, measurable, attainable, relevant, timebound) is a commonly used shorthand to describe the necessary properties of these indicators. Table 3.3 defines each of the characteristics in detail.

Table 3.3: SMART properties of indicators

Properties	Definition
Specific	Indicators should reflect those things the project intends to change, avoiding measures that are largely subject to external influences
Measurable and unambiguous	Indicators must be precisely defined so that their measurement and interpretation is unambiguous
	Indicators should give objective data, independent of who is collecting the data
	Indicators should be comparable across groups, projects thus allowing changes to be compared and aggregated
Attainable and sensitive	Indicators should be achievable by the project and therefore sensitive to changes the project wishes to make
Relevant and easy to collect	It must be feasible to collect data on the chosen indicators within a reasonable time and at a reasonable cost
	Indicators should be relevant to the project in question
Timebound	Indicators should describe by when a certain change is expected

Several of the case studies underline the difficulties that arise if some of these criteria are not met. For instance, in the CYSD study a household survey undertaken in 1992 stated that literacy levels of 60 per cent had been achieved in the village Berena by the end of 1992. But a repeat survey in 1997 has observed this to be only 38 per cent. On further examination, the researcher learned from the former survey team that a person who can sign their name was considered literate. However the 1997 survey defined literacy as the ability to read, write, and do minimum accounting. This lack of precision in the indicator — literacy — led to problems in assessing levels of change over time.

However, when indicators are used more as specific examples of change, different characteristics become important. These relate to the process of defining indicators as well as how they are measured. Table 3.4 outlines another set of characteristics, called SPICED (subjective, participatory, interpreted, cross-checked, empowering, diverse) in shorthand.

Table 3.4: SPICED properties of indicator development and assessment

Properties	Definition
Subjective	Informants have a special position or experience that gives them unique insights which may yield a very high return on the investigators time. In this sense, what may be seen by others as 'anecdotal' becomes critical data because of the source's value.
Participatory	Indicators should be developed together with those best placed to assess them. This means involving a project's ultimate beneficiaries, but it can also mean involving local staff and other stakeholders.
Interpreted and communicable	Locally defined indicators may not mean much to other stakeholders, so they often need to be explained.
Cross-checked and compared	The validity of assessment needs to be cross-checked, by comparing different indicators and progress, and by using different informants, methods, and researchers.
Empowering	The process of setting and assessing indicators should be empowering in itself and allow groups and individuals to reflect critically on their changing situation.
Diverse and disaggregated	There should be a deliberate effort to seek out different indicators from a range of groups, especially men and women. This information needs to be recorded in such a way that these differences can be assessed over time.

Clearly this does not mean that SMART and SPICED objectives and indicators cannot be combined. Indeed, most of the case studies attempted exactly that. In Wajir, quite specific indicators (such as the number of meals eaten in a day) were defined by the researchers on the basis of previous participatory planning exercises, and then verified by the population. These were combined with much broader, open questions such as asking people to score changes in their quality of life over time. This raises the question whether emphasis should be placed on developing indicators at the outset of a given intervention and on monitoring them or whether one should assess significant change regardless of pre-determined indicators.

In recent years there has been a growing interest in 'indicatorless' reporting, for example in the work of the Christian Commission for Development in Bangladesh supported by Rick Davies (Davies 1998). In this approach, staff are requested to report the most significant changes (positive or negative, planned or unplanned) over the last period and explain why they have chosen these. This exercise is then repeated at each level in the organisation.

Indicators and the project-cycle

The experience from the case studies suggests that the assumptions about indicator development and the project cycle-outlined in Chapter 2 are perhaps too neat and tidy. At the outset of a project it is important to understand both past *and* current change, as well as its indicators, and what has brought it about. This helps to understand people's changing circumstances and perceptions about the past before future desired change is explored (people's lives don't begin when projects start). Moreover, it is vital to understand existing trends so that any significant changes to those trends can be traced (which can make attribution easier — see p.79).

Equally, during the course of a project, monitoring current performance must be complemented by reviewing what has changed and looking to the future in order to modify existing indicators. In the same way, even an impact assessment undertaken many years after a project has finished (for example, ENDA in Zimbabwe) needs to consider future policies and practice rather than concentrating on past events — although this it may be of less benefit to communities no longer engaged with a given institution, than to the institution itself and the groups it might work with in the future.

It is not always possible or desirable to define impact indicators at the outset of a process and track these same indicators over time. In fact, the way in which people's own indicators of poverty change over time is an important element in understanding how their needs, attitudes, and values evolve. For example, when exploring changes in women's situation, CYSD in India found that women stressed that the main difficulty they had faced before the project was male dominance and the subordinate role of females. But these women had not considered this as a problem when the project first started. Their involvement with CYSD and their changing self-analysis had led them to this understanding. The fact that women's indicators of change had evolved was an important indicator in itself that the project's efforts to change awareness and perceptions had borne fruit.

A recent impact study by Action Aid[1] also emphasises the importance of capturing *emerging* indicators. Interestingly, one reason why they came to this conclusion was the fact that women originally had not included changes in their own status as indicators, but subsequently did. The study proposed that changes in the type and nature of indicators was in itself an important indicator or 'meta-indicator'. For women, these might include change in the number of indicators they propose; change in the scale of desired change; change in the degree to which indicators are also desired by men or not.

The Wajir study came to a similar conclusion.

[T]he impact on project beneficiaries livelihoods and welfare often calls for the continuous integration of (new) impact indicators during the project implementation period. Only in this way can we know whether the project is having any impact on the beneficiaries. The constant integration of impact indicators ... is also necessary because of the uncertain and unpredictable nature of the project environment. (Wajir Economic Impact Assessment)

Summary 3.2 outlines some of the key lessons learned about indicators and their measurement.

Summary 3.2 : Key lessons about indicators

- At the outset of projects, determine key areas of change, as well as some specific impact indicators, with ultimate beneficiaries and local staff. This is necessary in order to assess progress, and can be empowering in itself, but it is also useful in meeting the demands of other stakeholders, particularly funders.

- Ensure that these indicators are sought from different groups — men/ women, well-off/ less well-off, etc. — and differences noted.

- When circumstances change, update and reformulate existing indicators, as well as introducing new indicators and dropping others. This requires monitoring the project's context and environment.

- Reduce the number of impact indicators to a manageable proportion based on key areas of change. Anecdotal indicators can be used to exemplify past changes in key areas of people's lives, even if they have not been pre-defined. These may need to be interpreted so that others can understand their significance.

- Explore significant changes which occurred as a result of the project/ programme, but which lay outside these initial indicators. Use this information to develop indicators for the future.

- Deliberately set out to capture negative change and to seek out those who might report it, particularly groups who are often disadvantaged such as women, minority groups, or people who have dropped out of the project.

What are the units of assessment?

Any impact assessment exercise needs to determine what its key units or levels of assessment are. Will the study focus on change at the level of individuals, communities, organisations, or all of these? What are the advantages and disadvantages of concentrating on one level as opposed to another? Clearly this decision depends on the objectives of the programme in question and the types of impact to be assessed. However, being clear about what needs to be assessed at different levels can help to focus studies and concentrate resources, as well as helping to understand important linkages between these levels.

Although all studies looked at more than one unit of analysis, they varied in emphasis. For example, BRAC, in order to assess the impact of its programme on material well-being, used the household as the main unit of analysis as 'it is the household as a whole, not the programme participant alone, which experiences the impact of the programme intervention' (BRAC). In the NK and GGS study in Bangladesh, Rao and Hashemi emphasised village organisations and their evolving relationships with intermediary NGOs, concentrating on transformation in the community. Several of the studies explore the relationship between the individual and groups/organisations as well as on wider institutions (Ghana, Wajir, CYSD).

The following lists the levels explored in the case studies, with the main focus in italics.

Ghana: *individuals*, households, communities, *support NGOs*

CYSD: *individuals, households*, CBOs, *community*

Wajir: individuals, *households*, *CBOs*, support NGOs, institutions

Ikafe: *individuals*, household, *communities*, institutions

Pakistan: *individuals*, organisations

Matson: *individuals* and organisational

Proshika: *individuals, households, groups*, villages

BRAC: *individuals, households, groups*, villages

NK and GSS: individuals, *groups*, federated structures, *support NGOs*

CORDES: *individuals*, household, *communities*, institutions

ENDA: *individuals*, household, *communities*, institutions

It is clear that nearly all the studies focused particularly at individual and household levels. Some looked at organisational change within community based organisations and local NGOs, and fewer still attempted to look at changes in community or societal norms. Within this some, but not all, of the studies looked at women's position, status and empowerment in particular, at both an individual and household level.

While this primary focus on individuals and households is understandable, focusing on only one level provides a very partial picture of impact. Given the complexity of including all these levels in an assessment, and given the definition of impact as significant change in people's lives, there are advantages and disadvantages in focusing on a range of units or levels of assessment. As we see from Table 3.5, focusing on more than one level not only allows for a wider range of impacts to be explored, but also allows the linkages between levels to be examined. However this can also make the study more complex and time-consuming. Prioritising the most important levels and linkages and focusing on these, is necessary if the study is to remain manageable.

Table 3.5: Advantages and disadvantages of various units of assessment

Unit of assessment	Advantages	Disadvantages
Individual	• Easily defined and identified • Allows social relations and gender issues to be explored • Allows inter-household relations to be explored • Can allow personal and intimate issues to emerge	• Most interventions have impact beyond the individual • It may be difficult to speak to the most marginalised people • Difficulty of attribution through long impact chain • Difficult to aggregate findings

Table 3.5: Advantages and disadvantages of various units of assessment (continued)

Unit of assessment	Advantages	Disadvantages
Household	• Permits appreciation of income, asset, consumption and labour pooling • Permits appreciation of link between individual, household and group/community • Permits understanding of links between household life-cycle and well-being	• Exact membership is sometimes difficult to assess • Inter-household relations are often ignored
Group/ CBO	• Permits understanding of collective action and social capital • Permits understanding of potential sustainability of impacts • Permits understanding of potential transformation community in the community Exact membership is sometimes difficult to assess	• Group dynamics are often difficult to understand • Difficult to compare using quantitative data
Community/ village	• Permits understanding of differences within the community • Can act as sampling frame for household/individual assessments • Permits understanding of collective action and social capital • Permits understanding of faction and clan relations • Permits understanding of potential transformation community in the community and beyond	• Exact boundary is sometimes difficult to assess • Community dynamics are often difficult to understand • Difficult to compare

Table 3.5: Advantages and disadvantages of various units of assessment (continued)

Unit of assessment	Advantages	Disadvantages
Local NGO	• Permits understanding of potential sustainability of impacts • Permits understanding of changes brought about by capacity-building • Allows assement of performance (especially in terms of effectiveness and efficiency) • Allows exploration of links between change at the community, group, and the individual level	• NGO dynamics are difficult to understand • Difficult to compare various local NGOs
Institutions	• Permits wider change and influence to be assessed • Permits assessment of how favourable future context is likely to be in helping sustained change to continue	• Greater problems of attribution • Internal processes and dynamics are difficult to explore or understand

Adapted from Hulme (1997) and related to case studies

What information already exists?

Once it is clearer what information is required and what levels of assessment are appropriate, it is important to find out if the information that is required already exists, or there are systems in place for its collection. The collection of secondary data is important, not least in order to ensure that individual's and communities' time is not wasted collecting information that already exists. In addition this data can also reveal gaps in official records, existing trends, and contradictions between official statistics and the study's findings.

In the case studies secondary data were collected from the following sources:

Literature reviews: Researchers searched academic and aid agency sources to discover more about specific issues, such as the relationship between local institutions and poverty in Northern Ghana (Wolmer 1996), or on the issue of impact assessment itself (BRAC). In the case of Ghana, although it took some time for this material to be absorbed by those undertaking the impact assessment, it did allow village-level findings on changing gender relations to be verified by comparing them to longer-term anthropological work. Literature reviews also provide important information on changing trends in the area as a backdrop to exploring changes brought about by NGO projects,

Official records and surveys: Undertaken by government agencies, multi-lateral institutions, research institutes, or other aid agencies, these are valuable sources of data that can inform impact assessment exercises. Some of the major sources of information which may be of use are listed in Summary 3.3. As I mention later in the section on reconstructing baselines, using data from external sources, particularly government agencies, on education, agriculture, and health was important in several of the studies.

Project document and record reviews: The first phase of the Wajir mid-term review consisted of project staff gathering information for their 'mid-term review status report'. This report summarised information that had already been collected by the project as part of the monitoring process, and included issues which had been raised by project staff as important and considered necessary for the review to look at. Although this preparatory work at the time seemed over-long to staff, they recognised its value at a later stage. For example, the impact assessment team in the ENDA case study prepared a 'baseline analytic report', which was then presented to all ENDA staff at an internal workshop.

Box 3 indicates some key sources of secondary information identified by Renata Lok of the United Nations. Certain ministries, such as Health, Education, Social Welfare, Agriculture, Employment, and Public Works can all provide useful information in addition to National Statistical Offices which may have a role in synthesising information and therefore may already have done some of the analysis of data that may be important for impact assessment purposes. In addition, a number of relevant specific surveys, often undertaken by International Agencies in co-operation with local ministries, may also exist. The kind of survey pertinent to impact assessment exercises includes the household survey; specialised surveys which analyse income, consumption, agricultural production, prices, employment rates, and so on; and hybrid methods which combine household or individual data-collection with other survey methods.

Of particular relevance among the hybrid surveys are sentinel studies (for example, those undertaken by UNICEF which track changes in the health of a given group of people over time); knowledge, attitudes and practices (KAP) studies, which try to look at changes in areas that are often more difficult to assess; and participatory poverty assessments (PPAs), which have been used mainly by the World Bank, and attempt to combine participatory approaches of assessing poverty and its causes with data gathered and analysed in more formal ways.

Summary 3.3: Key external sources of information

Government sources

Ministry of health: May have data on health services provided through hospitals, clinics, and health campaigns (such as vaccination drives), including information on child nutrition status, disease incidence, inpatient and outpatient visits, and so on.

Ministry of education: Source of data from schools on numbers and profiles of students and teachers, educational attainment, literacy levels etc.

Ministry responsible for social welfare: May have synthesised local records on the poverty status of households which some countries maintain.

Ministry of agriculture: May hold records of poverty-related services.

Ministry of labour or employment: Source of unemployment and wage statistics.

Ministry of finance: Will have financial data, consumer price trends, and so on.

Ministry of public works: Has data on water provision, sanitation, and distribution of electricity.

National statistical office: In some countries, this institution may collate a lot of the above data.

Surveys carried out by international agencies and government ministries

Multi-topic household surveys

- Living standard measurement surveys (LSMS)
- Surveys associated with social dimensions of adjustment (SDA) undertaken by the World Bank: the integrated survey (IS) and the priority survey (PS)
- 'Core welfare indicators' questionnaire

Specialised surveys

- Household income and expenditure surveys (HIES)
- Demographic and health surveys (DHS)
- Labourforce and employment surveys
- Food-consumption and nutrition surveys
- Consumer price surveys
- Agricultural surveys, agricultural sample surveys, agro-economic surveys
- Other specialised household surveys

Hybrid survey methodologies

- Sentinel site surveillance (SSS)
- Knowledge, attitudes, and practices (KAP) studies
- Poverty assessments and participatory poverty assessments (PPA)

Source: Renata Lok (1996)

Who should be involved?

Chapter 4 gives a detailed account of the tools and methods which were used to involve a wide range of stakeholders, particularly beneficiaries, in the case studies, and discusses some of the associated problems. Here I will simply describe the main groups involved in the studies and look at issues relating to the composition of the assessment team. I return to the question of how to assess the quality of participation in the final chapter of the book.

Men and women, rich and poor

As stated in Chapter 2, issues of power and participation are central not only to impact assessment but also to understanding impoverishment and injustice. Some of the case studies were more concerned with distinguishing between project and non-project groups (see below). Others made more effort to ensure the involvement of both men and women or worse-off groups; other aspects such as age and ethnicity were also relevant in several studies. In some cases, specific research was undertaken in order to identify who to involve, such as wealth-ranking exercises which determined the least well-off households (see next chapter). In others, targets were set for the proportion of women to be interviewed in a given community, and reserachers ensured that various members of a household were interviewed. Those studies which considered gender-related issues particularly important made greater efforts to ensure not only that these issues were explored (which was done in most studies), but also that the choice of assessment team members, the methods used, and the timing of the exercise were all designed to making women's involvement easier.

Beneficiaries

All the case studies involved the ultimate beneficiaries in some way. However, both the proportions of beneficiaries involved and their levels of participation varied enormously. In the CORDES study, almost the entire population of the three communities that are part of the project participated throughout the study and were involved in its design. In the studies involving much larger programmes, such as BRAC or Proshika, only a small sample of the many thousands of village organisations they support were involved. Table 3.6 indicates the level of participation at different stages of the impact assessment process in the case studies. It indicates that despite the willingness to involve beneficiaries, few of the studies managed to do this at *all* stages of the process. Although beneficiary groups were involved in most or all of the case studies during the reconstruction of project histories and in determining and verifying indicators, they participated much less in defining what was meant by impact assessment, in the design stage, and in the analysis and feedback stages towards the end of the process. This suggests that despite the professed desire of all the organisations to involve communities in the impact assessment process, there were still significant differences in the depth and quality of participation.

Non-project respondents

Non-project respondents are individuals who have deliberately not been involved in the projects assessed, but who have similar characteristics to those which these projects seeks to support. They were interviewed in a number of case studies which used them as 'control groups'. The lessons from comparing changes in the lives of project and non-project respondents are described in detail in this chapter's section on attribution.

Excluded and drop-out groups

It is well known that some members of the community which an invention is intended to benefit may well be excluded from or even disadvantaged by it. Some of the case study teams sought to identify these groups and individuals in order to understand why this had happened and what negative effects it might have had. In both the Ghana and the UK case studies, efforts were made to contrast the views of these 'excluded' groups with those of project participants. In other cases, project participants who had left the project or dropped out of groups the project was supporting, were identified and interviewed.

Table 3.6: Participation of beneficiaries at different stages of the impact assessment process in the case studies

Stage of impact assessment process	Occurrence in case studies
At the outset, defining what is meant by impact and designing the impact assessment study	Beneficiaries were fully involved in this stage in only one of the case studies, although partially in one other.
Reconstructing project history and changes in the context	Benficiaries participated in most case studies, although in some, assessment of changes was limited to changes directly associated with the project in question.
Determining the areas of change, objectives, or indicators necessary to assess past or future impact	Beneficiaries were involved in most case studies. In some cases, people did not participate in prioritising the updated indicators, although they might have been involved at an earlier date.
Verifying if project objectives had been achieved, or indicators met	Beneficiaries took part in this in nearly all the case studies, although in a few cases, objectives and indicators were unavailable or not sufficiently specific to do this.
Analysis and interpretation of results	In some of the studies, benficiaries participated as a matter of course; in others in some aspects; and in some hardly at all or on a very limited basis.
Feedback of results	This occurred in a few of the studies, both informally and as a result of a systematic attempt to feed back to beneficiaries.
Presentation and communication of findings	This really happened only in one case study, where it was part of the study design.

Project staff

The involvement of project staff varied particularly according to the size of the project, its stage in the project-cycle, and the degree to which the exercise was also perceived as a capacity-building process for staff themselves.

However, as the ENDA study revealed, the involvement of project staff —
although it has many advantages in terms of building 'ownership' of the
process, in providing the exercise with unique knowledge and insights, and
contributing to feasible future plans and policies — also has a down side. Staff
may fear that the evaluation will affect their jobs, reputations, or future
resource allocation, in which case they may feel defensive, become
obstructive, or seek to manipulate results so as to promote themselves.

Donors

Although donors were only explicitly involved in a few case studies (for
example, agreeing the terms of reference and scope of the impact assessment
or attending introductory workshops), their unseen presence was very much
evident in considerations of study design and implementation. This particularly
affected the selection of the impact assessment team, which projects were
selected, and the degree to which independence and 'objectivity' were sought.

Others

Local government, other NGOs, and international agencies also were
important stakeholders in some of the case studies. This was particularly true of
the refugee programme in Ikafe in Northern Uganda. Chapter 5 explores the
issue of how this impact assessment exercise attempted to cope with the
diverse perspectives involved.

The impact assessment team

Depending on the purpose of the study, the information required, and its likely
sources, decisions must be made about whether an impact assessment team
needs to be established and who it should include. The case studies vary in their
approaches, in their use of local project staff or external specialists, and in the
degree to which external staff were perceived as evaluators, people offering
support, facilitators, or peers. Table 3.7 summarises the degree of involvement
of outsiders, ranging from purely external teams in two cases, mixed teams in
two cases, to internal teams supported by external specialists or internal
research units in six cases. The Matson project team in the UK invited an
external reviewer as a peer and facilitator rather than as an evaluator.

Clearly the use of external specialists will also depend on the level of
experience available 'in-house', the degree of independence or 'objectivity'
certain stakeholders may demand, and the extent to which the exercise is seen
as a training or capacity-building process in its own right. The Ikafe and the
CORDES studies were the only ones where representatives of beneficiaries were
included in the assessment team.

Table 3.7: Degree of involvement of outsiders in the case studies

Degree of involvement of outsiders	Case study
External evaluation team	Wajir, Kenya; NK and GSS, Bangladesh
Internal evaluation or research team:	
• supported by external specialists	Pakistan; Ghana
• run by, or supported by, internal research/ evaluation unit or impact assessment co-ordinator	ENDA, Zimbabwe; BRAC and Proshika, Bangladesh; CYSD, India (sometimes with external support or with specific tasks contracted out)
Mixed evaluation team involving outsiders, staff, and beneficiaries	Ikafe, Uganda; CORDES, El Salvador
Peer review by outsider	Matson, UK

There are well-known advantages and disadvantages to various combinations of 'insiders' and 'outsiders' in a team (Rubin 1995). However, the case studies reveal that the individual's attitude and skill, as well as their ability to build rapport, are more important than their affiliation. For example, Stan Thekaekara from India, who undertook the Matson study in the UK, was able to gain important insights from informants due to good interpersonal skills (not least with children thanks to his magic tricks!), many years' experience in grassroots work, and an inquisitive yet humble approach. Over an eight-week period, Stan mainly used participant observation techniques, which allowed him sufficient time to get to know the community and vice versa. The message that Stan was a colleague involved in similar work elsewhere and that he also wanted to learn from Matson meant that he was not seen as an expert coming to judge the project. He offered the project staff some very useful insights into their work, but he was essentially a peer who had come to listen, learn, and share what he had learned with project staff, community members, and other stakeholders.

The definition of who is an 'outsider' varies enormously. For example, in the ENDA and Ghana studies the impact researchers were 'outsiders' to the communities where the assessments took place, although they were local staff of the agencies involved in the assessment (ENDA, Oxfam, and ISODEC). They too faced difficulties, in having to overcome the attitudes of both staff and community members who saw them as a threat to the continuation of the project, in sometimes having to work through translators, and in having to overcome their lack of specific knowledge of the projects or communities in question. However, there also were advantages: in Ghana, people felt able to talk about certain aspects of their lives with outsiders, precisely because they were not members of the community or project staff. Yet because this sort of information is confidential, great care must be taken to ensure that it remains so not only in the final report, but also in any feedback sessions held with the community.

In most case studies care was taken to ensure a gender balance on the research teams, or to include at least one woman. The benefits of this are well known. A review workshop on the impact assessment work in Ghana revealed that the female researcher managed to elicit sensitive information in individual interviews related to child-spacing, household relations, and female income which would have been difficult, if not impossible, for a man to find out. But workshop participants also pointed out that the researcher's attitude and approach were equally critical (being a woman may be a necessary but not sufficient condition!). Some of the information was revealed not simply because the researcher was female, but also because she was an outsider.

Most of the impact assessment teams were made up of two to three people, with the exceptions of BRAC, Proshika, Ikafe, CORDES, and Matson. In Matson, the main reason for this was the approach adopted: participant observation by a peer over an extended period. In Ikafe, the complexity and insecurity of the situation (involving refugees and host populations) and the number of stakeholders involved (central and local government, several relief agencies, United Nations specialised agencies, refugees and host populations, and private contractors) prompted the researchers to establish a large team with representatives from all the major actors. At the end of the study the managers acknowledged the risk inherent in this choice.

The large number of team members / facilitators produced very much information and analysis, especially through working in sub-teams. The team functioned well and was able to discuss, cross-check and reach consensus on many issues, but such a large team and process if not successfully managed can also result in unmanageable, unfocused amount of information from which no consensus analysis arises. On reflection a smaller team would be recommended for future work of this kind. (Neefjes et al. 1996, p.48)

In creating a team, the challenge is to combine individuals whose skills complement each other. There are therefore several considerations for establishing an impact assessment team.

Questions of training and support

External support at the outset

Two of the case studies (Ghana and Pakistan) used external trainers or facilitators at the outset of the studies in order to develop team skills for impact assessment work. In both cases this involved field-based exercises using a variety of participatory research tools (see Chapter 4). This approach has the advantage of providing hands-on experience and a practical understanding of the advantages and disadvantages of different tools and methods. However, care must be taken to ensure that staff do not feel they have to use the same number of tools and methods in each community, but that they are familiar with a range of ways in which questions about impact can be asked and answered.

Support from internal staff

In five of the case studies (BRAC, CYSD, ENDA, Proshika, CORDES), most of the training, support, and advice was provided by internal research or monitoring and evaluation units, sometimes supported by sympathetic local academics. Clearly internal support offers major advantages such as continuity and an understanding of the context, programme, and organisation. If these units have links with wider networks of expertise, they can also communicate critical external experience, in a way that is appropriate to the local situation and the organisation.

However, there can also be problems with internal support: satff may be busy with other tasks, which means that the necessary advice is not available when needed; they may lack the expertise relevant for the research in question, and feel reluctant to admit it; they may have personal interests in the organisation which are threatened by building the capacity of others or by the discovery of certain findings; they may represent certain interests according to their gender, class, ethnicity, race, faith, and so on; they may be seen as the representatives of senior management and project staff may therefore be less likely to divulge problems, errors, or mistakes in the fear that this may threaten their jobs or affect future resource allocation. Of course external trainers also have their own personal interests and biases, but internal units may have institutionalised dominant personal interests which can influence the support and advice that is given, particularly to contentious impact assessments.

External team which includes capacity-building in their work

Three of the case studies (Ikafe, Wajir, Proshika) involved external evaluators whose role it was, either implicitly or explicitly, to undertake the assessment in such a way as to enhance local staff and partners' impact assessment skills. This is difficult, and there is a risk of doing neither the capacity-building nor the impact assessment properly. In Wajir, however, the evaluation team gave staff some helpful advice on how to improve their 'impact tracking' which also validated a more flexible approach that recognises the importance of capturing emerging impact indicators as well as monitoring existing ones. The way in which the assessment was conducted also provided useful experience in determining how the project could monitor impact, rather than just inputs and outputs.

Equally, the Proshika experience highlights the important role that credible external support can play in institutionalising new (in their case participatory) approaches to impact assessment, especially if there is some scepticism about how these compare with existing approaches.

Peer review/ mutual learning

The Matson review was set up in a different way to all the other studies. Oxfam acted as a go-between by putting a neighbourhood project team, who wanted to learn more about impact assessment, in touch with an Indian community development worker who wanted to explore cross-cultural community exchanges. Therefore the relationship was one of peers seeking to learn from each other and gain experience. This involved no training as such, but a lot of observation, debate, and exchange of ideas — some of it relating to the impact assessment, but a lot of it developing in wholly unpredictable directions, such as the possibility of Matson residents bagging tea sent from Southern India for sale in the UK. This review is now seen by both parties as a first step in developing longer-term relations between the two communities, which may include training Matson staff and volunteers in community animation techniques developed in India.

Summary 3.4 lists the main lessons learned about establishing an impact assessment team.

Summary 3.4: Questions to consider when establishing an impact assessment team

- What balance of insiders and outsiders is appropriate? Is the best way to ensure that the views of some stakeholders are voiced to havie them represented on the team? Are there alternative, better ways of doing so?

- What is required to achieve an adequate gender balance on the team?

- What are the attitudes and behaviour required of all team members? How can these be verified?

- What technical/ sectoral knowledge is required?

- What conceptual and methodological skills are required in order to solve problems specific to impact assessment, such as attribution?

- What balance of quantitative and qualitative methods will be used and what skills will these demand?

- What co-ordination, facilitation, and diplomatic skills are required, particularly in managing the assessment?

- How will the findings be communicated? What writing and communication skills are needed for this?

- What is the best way of ensuring that the findings actually make a difference to people's lives, to the projects being assessed, or to the organisations involved? Who might need to be involved in order for this to happen?

- What kind of training and support will team members require? What resources are available for this? What degree of capacity-building of project staff, partner organisationsm and beneficiary groups is possible or appropriate?

Sampling

There is very rarely the time or the money to talk to, or contact, everybody in a given community, organisation, network, or region. This means choosing or sampling from a larger 'population'. In the following, I describe some of the types of sampling that exist. Most observers distinguish between sampling that is done in order to generalise findings about a given group of people or organisations (which usually involves random sampling), and sampling undertaken in order to identify specific groups of people or organisations about which more information is needed (which usually involves non-random sampling). Again, it is crucial to be clear about the purpose of the study, because this will determine the sampling frame or the 'population' under study.

The sample population may involve different units of assessment such as individual women, men or children, households, communities, organisations, or institutions. For example, the Ghana study team wanted to explore the relationship between organisational development and poverty reduction; they therefore chose a sampling frame of the 30 organisations which are part of the Northern Ghana Development Network and the communities they supported. By contrast, the Matson study's sampling frame included the entire population of Matson neighbourhood.

Once the type of sampling and the units of assessment have been identified, the next step is to decide on sample size. Cost, staffing levels, and availability of researchers, and logistics often are the key factors in determining sample size, as is the willingness of organisations or communities to get involved. However, one must also consider how valid particular sample sizes will make the study. If the study primarily aims to confirm that existing small-scale findings apply to the entire population, and to do so in a way that is statistically significant, then there are agreed statistical procedures for estimating how confidently this can be done for different sample sizes (Paul Nichols, pp.53-56). If, however, the aim is to understand in depth how a given impact was achieved or to explore possible impacts, a much smaller sample size will probably be appropriate. But again, sample sizes must be set without losing sight of practical concerns.

[A] small sample, properly managed and carefully analysed is always better than a poorly supervised, large sample which is never fully analysed for lack of time. Will the sample size you can afford answer your research questions? If not, then consider how you might either get more resources, or scale down your research questions to something more realistic. (Nichols, p.53)

There are numerous methods for selecting the sample once the sample size is clear. Summary 3.5 describes some of the best known types of random and non-random sampling as well as repeat sampling methods.

The case studies mainly used non-random sampling methods, although larger studies (Wajir, Proshika and BRAC) did use stratified sampling methods such as random sampling within particular sub-groups. In addition, most studies went through staged sampling processes, although not usually on a random basis. The Ghana study team first selected three organisations from the 30 members of the Northern Ghana Development Network, according to criteria determined by the researchers and the Network. They then selected three communities from among those the organisations worked with. Within each village, ten men and ten women were selected following wealth-ranking exercises, in order to include each wealth grouping in repeat interviews over a longer period. This process was chosen in order to develop tools and methods for impact assessment which could capture the opinions of those whose voices were seldom heard, as well as to understand the relationship between organisational support and poverty reduction.

Summary 3.5: Types of sampling

Random sampling

Simple random sampling: A group of people are selected at random from a complete list of a given population.

Stratified or systematic random sampling: This ensures that sub-groups within a population are included in the sample, by randomly sampling within each of these sub-groups.

Cluster sampling: By selecting geographic clusters of villages or households within a given population, time and money is saved; this technique thus allows more people or groups to be contacted in the time available.

Staged sampling: For large populations, one may need to sample within samples. For example, BRAC's Rural Development Programme works with 63,846 village organisations through 372 area offices. Each of these villages contains a number of households. Therefore BRAC selected a sample of areas, within which a random sample of households was interviewed.

Random walk: Instructions are given to the interviewer to follow a random route and interview individuals ('take first road right, interview at second house on your left, continue down the road, interview tenth household on your right', and so on).

Non-random sampling

Quota sample: Based on information about a population, quotas of certain types of people or organisations are selected for interview; common criteria for quotas are age, gender, occupation, and whether people live in project or non-project areas.

Genealogy-based sample: Select entire families and their relatives rather than households.

Chain sampling or snowballing: Select a first contact and then ask them who you should talk to next. This method is useful for identifying minority groups or occupations within communities.

Matched samples: Similar pairs of villages, projects, or groups of people are selected in order to compare them (project groups and non-project groups are an example).

Repeat sampling methods

Panel or cohort surveys: A set of people or organisations is contacted several times over a relatively long period.

Repeat survey: The entire survey process is repeated, including sampling.

Rotating survey: This is a combination of the panel and repeat survey methods: one fraction of the sample is changed each time the survey is repeated, another fraction remains the same.

For more details see Nichols, P (1991) *Social Survey Methods: A field guide for development workers*, Oxfam Development Guideline No.6

The Proshika study used a two-stage cluster-sampling technique. As the organisations works in over 4,000 villages, obtaining a complete list of all households in these villages was considered unnecessary and too costly. Instead, they first 'clustered' the villages into units of about eight villages each. As a result, they reached a number of 500 clusters in areas where Proshika worked and 380 clusters where they did not. The researchers selected nine of these clusters from areas they worked in and ten from those areas where they were not involved. The second stage was to compile a complete list of households for these 19 clusters, from which 190 households were selected at random — 100 from Proshika areas and 90 from other areas.

Although the larger studies used quite sophisticated sampling procedures to generate representative findings, they also included non-random samples for more in-depth, qualitative assessments and for case-study material. Thus BRAC, in addition to the 1250 BRAC sample households and 250 non-BRAC households which were randomly selected, also surveyed 200 households who had demonstrated very high economic performance as well as 25 village organisations. The Wajir study for example added women who were beneficiaries of a loan scheme, and families who had been involved in an animal restocking project, to its original sample as well as selecting a number of Pastoral Associations and Women's Groups for workshop and focus-group discussions.

Given that impact assessment usually attempts to combine both quantitative and qualitative questions, sampling is likely to include a number of important 'purposive' criteria — criteria that are deemed critical because of the research team's knowledge of the area, the organisations involved, and the project objectives and history. Some of the key 'purposive' criteria used for sampling in the case studies are included in Table 3.8. There are three main groupings:

context-related criteria, which are about ensuring that social, economic, and environmental differences are taken into account; organisation-related criteria, which range from the pragmatic — looking at capacity and willingness to get involved — to questions of stakeholder participation; and project-related criteria, which aim to ensure that both beneficiaries and non-beneficiaries are included, and that those involved in different ways and for different lengths of time are adequately represented.

Table 3.8: Key 'purposive' criteria used for sampling in the case studies

Context-related	Organisation-related	Project-related
• Gender and age • Wealth and well-being • Geography and agro-ecology • Proximity to markets and roads • Cultural/ethnic composition	• Willingness and capacity to get involved • Balance of types of organisations, for example community-based organisations and intermediaries • Stakeholder balance • Mix of targets for advocacy/influencing	• Project and non-project sites • Participants and non-participants of the project within the same community • Good and poor performers, including disbanded groups and drop-outs • Length of involvement in projects/programme (asking whether an intervention has been running for long enough to have made an impact, or selecting from a scale of length or intensity of involvement in order to compare) • Involvement at particular moments of the intervention (a community was the project entry point, or the last area to be included in a programme) • Involvement in particular interventions • Availability of information • No, or not too many, previous studies

Sampling represents a critical stage in most impact assessment work and can affect the results as well as the perception of the study by others. Key questions that might be asked at this stage are included in Summary 3.6.

Summary 3.6: Some key questions related to sampling

If the sample claims to be representative of a larger population:

- What might have occurred to make the sample atypical of the wider group?

- Could certain types of participant be less likely to be selected than others?

- Could pragmatic criteria such as cost or time constraints introduce bias into the sample selection?

If the sample's main purpose is to identify particular groups or people and to find out more about qualitative aspects or impacts, other questions may be more relevant:

- Does the sample cover those whose views and opinions are particularly important or normally overlooked, in particular women and the poorest groups?

- Whose views and opinions will not be covered by a given sample, and does their exclusion matter?

- Does the sample cover all groups likely to have differing opinions or views? Does the sample help us understand the linkages between different units of analysis (such as individuals and organisations)?

Timing of assessment

The timing of the assessment is another important issue and relates to the project-cycle, to seasonal conditions, and to people's daily rhythms and work schedule.

Timing and the project-cycle

When is it appropriate to carry out an impact assessment? As we have seen, in an impact assessment exercise, certain activities have to be undertaken throughout the project-cycle in order to determine objectives and indicators, monitor progress to date, and to monitor and adapt to changes in the external environment. However, there are probably moments when intense reflection on and analysis of impact are more appropriate then others.

The first such moment is the initial situation analysis and appraisal, when likely future impact is assessed and baseline data collected. The second occurs towards the end of a specific phase in the project-cycle, when a new phase is being planned, or at other key stages of an intervention. Such interim assessments may be combined with lighter, more frequent periodic reviews of impact, say, on an annual basis. As the Wajir study shows, 'before' and 'after' studies between which a long time has elapsed are unlikely to reveal much about the sequence of cause and effect, nor will they permit 'impact tracking' to occur, which would allow an almost continuous integration of new and adapted indicators during implementation. His lack of continuity particularly applies in areas of high uncertainty, for example regarding security, and great fluctuations, for example in rainfall. Thus ongoing impact monitoring is vital in order to gather evidence about causality and to adapt to changing circumstances. The frequency with which it needs to occur during implementation will clearly depend on the context and how stable it is.

Lastly, there are 'terminal' evaluations which occur soon after a programme has finished or several years later. As the ENDA case study reminds us, extra care must be taken to (re)-gain people's confidence when the research team is going to a community where a project has not been running for a number of years — even if the researchers are from the same agency which originally supported the project.

Figure 2 in Chapter 1 on the case studies illustrates where each of the case studies 'fits' in terms of timing.

Seasonal issues

It is important at what time of year information is collected, not only because people's answers to some questions will change during the year, but also because their availability and willingness to respond will vary with the seasons. For example, BRAC had to delay field work during Ramadan, the Muslim month of fasting. While the 'hungry season' in Ghana is a critical opportunity for understanding people's coping strategies, it is also a time of great stress and peaking labour demands. Involving people in lengthy interviews or workshops at this time of year, even at times suitable to them, may not only lead to poor quality information but can be ethically dubious.

Particular activities may also show different results in different seasons, which can affect the impact assessment process. For example, in order to conduct an assessment of a well-digging component of their work, researchers in the CYSD study visited well sites in the summer, when the water table was at its lowest. They found out that the water-lifting devices they had introduced could not lift water efficiently at this critical time of year due to the low depth of water in the wells. If they had visited at another time of the year the problem may not have been so obvious. In order to overcome some of these problems, BRAC collected certain items of information (on consumption of and expenditure on non-durable goods) twice — once in the lean season and again in the peak season — in order to take into account seasonal fluctuations.

The question of seasonality is also important if baseline data or previous surveys are to be compared with new information. This is particularly the case if questions you include questions such as 'how many times a day did you eat in the last week?'. If this sort of information is not compared to equivalent periods of the year it will be pretty meaningless. It should also be remembered that even if similar periods are compared, fluctuations in rainfall, the economic situation, or social conditions may be much more likely to explain any differences than the project that is being assessed.

What day of the week and time in the day to use for assessment

Times that are most convenient for villagers may be least convenient for researchers and vice-versa. Some of the studies made particular efforts to overcome such problems.

- Researchers must recognise that there is a gendered aspect to people's time availability and that researchers must make special efforts to talk to women. A team of women who carried out an evaluation for Oxfam in Tigray observed that women there had no words in their language for leisure.[2]

- The research team should identify when people might be available for interview or workshops and arrange them accordingly.

- Particular days in the week, festivals or social events should be avoided.

- Researchers should make observervations and engage in conversations in informal surroundings (at a well, in markets, at tea stalls, in bars) without interrupting people's daily routines or meetings. In some cases, interviewers can help interviewees with their work, for instance by sitting with them and picking stones out of grain for cooking.

Despite such attempts to be considerate, several of the studies indicate that time availability for both researchers and respondents, particularly women, was a real issue and in some cases this led to the studies being simplified, particularly time-consuming methods being abandoned (see next chapter), and the worth of group meetings which only the 'time rich' could attend being questioned.

Summary 3.7 shows some of the key questions that need to be asked about the timing of different elements of impact assessment work.

Summary 3.7: Some questions related to the timing of an impact assessment process

- What stage of the project-cycle is the most appropriate to reflect on and analyse impact?

- How regular does the collection of impact data need to be to cope with changing circumstances and the difficulties of attribution?

- What season or time of year makes most sense for the collection of impact data? Does certain information need to be collected during more than one season?

- Are there particular days of the week , or times of day, that should be avoided when collecting impact data? Who might be excluded if certain times of the day (or night) are chosen to carry out interviews or meetings?

Where there is no baseline

The importance of having a starting position from which to measure change is perhaps one of the most common points made in impact assessment texts (Oakley et al. 1998). Within the case studies we find a variety of situations: where no baseline study had been systematically carried out (CORDES, Pakistan), where a baseline study or survey had been done but was inaccessible or unavailable (CYSD), where a baseline study did exist but did not contain all the necessary information to assess impact (BRAC, Wajir, Ikafe, Proshika), and where the impact assessment exercise was self seen as a means to establish a baseline for the future (Ghana).

Therefore all the studies, in one way or another, had to reconstruct the past. This not only underlines the need for baselines, but also illustrates what their limitations are. There are two main factors that make baselines a problematic tool. First, it is impossible to predict all the information that might be needed because information needs will change over time. This may occur because of changes in the environment (for instance, drought affected the ENDA-supported projects in Zimbabwe and the Wajir programme in Kenya), or as a result of changes brought about by the project. For example, in Matson the success of the community in resisting council-house sales encouraged them to get involved in improving other aspects of their lives, such as child-care or mental health, for which no baseline existed. A third reason why the require-ments for baseline information may change is that a better *understanding* of the information is actually needed, or a better understanding of ways in which it can be collected. For example, Proshika discovered that their original way of collecting information on the physical abuse of women was grossly underestimating its incidence. Any baseline using this data would therefore have been a very poor guide. As a result, they adopted different means of exploring this issue, moving away from individual interviews using questionnaires to greater use of participatory and group methods.

Lastly, there may be a different demand or divergent standards for baseline data. In one organisation, where the research team 'pointed out the shortcomings in the reporting and the lack of data in the files, former project staff objected. Most of these staff members claimed that they had the baseline data that we were looking for'. However, when the researchers did come across this information they felt it 'was largely in anecdotal form' and inadequate for impact assessment purposes.

The second difficulty with baselines is that there are major difficulties in not just the collection of relevant information but also in the analysis, storing and recovering of that information at a later date. In some cases, researchers effectively stumbled across crucial information by accident, often by meeting with former project staff who pointed them in the right direction but even in these cases they still had problems.

The researcher met the first anchor person ... and learned that a detailed household survey was conducted ... [b]ut the inferences from the survey were not converted into a report. Some of the survey sheets were found from the Project store. Efforts to trace the remaining sheets from the heap of old files proved futile. (CYSD case study)

Those case studies which had useable baseline data were able to make comparisons that recall or retrospective techniques (designed to help people remember the past situation and compare it to the present day) would struggle to achieve. For example, information collected from BRAC members when they enrolled allowed meaningful comparisons to be made between their status before joining BRAC and after a number of years. In addition it allowed BRAC to compare well-being indicators for members of various durations of membership. They were therefore able to determine that there was 'a significant positive relationship ... between the net change in members' involvement in income-generation activities and increase in membership length' as well as in their control over assets.

One of the weaknesses with recall methods is that people look back at a situation with the benefit of hindsight. As we saw earlier in the section on indicators, the CYSD case study revealed that women looking back at their relationships with men reached different conclusions than they would have done at the start of the project. If changing attitudes, awareness, and perceptions are important elements of impact that are being assessed, then this should be borne in mind.

In order to overcome some of these problems, a number of the case study programmes such as Wajir and BRAC have identified 'panel groups' or 'cohorts': a group of individuals or households who are tracked over the lifetime of the programme. They provide a 'rolling baseline', which allows changes in people's lives and priorities to be identified on a regular basis, and their views and opinions on project performance to be known. As was noted above in the section on indicators, this sort of approach also makes 'impact tracking' possible, which can help gather better evidence of cause-and-effect relationships between a given project and significant changes in people's lives.

Certain lessons that need to be taken into account for baseline data collection are included in Summary 3.8.

Summary 3.8: Key lessons for baseline data collection

- Aim to collect only those data that is seen to be particularly relevant to assessing the outcome of the project and that will be difficult to identify through recall or baseline reconstruction methods (see below).

- Aim to collect only as much information as the organisation actually has the capacity to analyse, organise, and store. Don't be tempted to match the kind of data and analysis that a larger organisation might collect.

- Recognise that it is impossible to predict all the information that might be needed and that any baseline will need to be updated.

- Explore the possibility of creating 'rolling baselines' by following the progress of a particular number of people or groups throughout the course of the project.

- Investigate the possibility of using new individuals, groups, or communities which become involved in a programme as a baseline for comparison with existing participants.

- Ensure that collected data is properly recorded, filed, and stored. Make sure that the organisation knows where these files are held and what they contain, and that there is an adequate system for retrieving the information when it is needed.

Baseline reconstruction

How can the lack of baseline data be corrected? There are three main sources which proved useful in reconstructing baseline data in the case studies: project documents and records, other organisations, and key informants (whose knowledge was elicited through interviews and participatory recall methods).

Baseline information from project documents and records

As we saw in the earlier section 'What information already exists?' several of the case studies needed to review existing project documents and records in order to prepare a consolidated summary of the project. This included background information and baseline information that not been used in combination before. For instance, the CYSD study found a 'situational analysis' which was prepared during the second phase (1992-93) of the project particularly useful, although by that time the project had already been going for four years. They also found case-study reports of self-help groups and traditional birth attendants which had, for example, specifically explored women's status and health practices before the project intervention. These project documents also proved very useful for reconstructing baseline information, but although they provided important qualitative information, supporting facts and figures were often found to be missing.

Baseline information from other organisations

Some of these supporting facts and figures may be available from other organisations. CYSD used statistical records from a wide variety of official agencies, including village schools, health centres, local government departments such as tax and forestry, which went back to before the project had begun. Although this was time-consuming (it took almost 15 days to reconstruct data on children's school attendance at seven village schools) it did allow key comparisons to be made with the situation prior to project intervention. Similarly, data on cropping patterns and intensity was readily available from agricultural centres.

Although CYSD recognise that the authenticity of government records is sometimes questionable, they are an important source of information base which can be used in conjunction with others. They also provide important insights into how official functionaries and organisations are likely to perceive trends.

It should be remembered that official information may not be available to other organisations (or it may take some time to get hold of it), and decision-makers may not use it to inform their policy and practice. In the Matson case study in the UK, the team asked official agencies to confirm trends on crime, health, and employment identified by the community by supplying relevant statistics. It became clear that there were problems with the comparability of the data over a period, because of a change in the way that data was collected, and that key staff within those agencies actually had great difficulty getting hold of this information. It also suggested that statutory authorities' perceptions of change were not actually based on an analysis of the quantitative data they collected.

Baseline information from key informants

School teachers, agricultural extension officers, chemists, traditional birth attendants, tax officers, health workers, community activists, former project staff, and the men, women, and children within communities have been invaluable sources of information in the case studies. Simple questions about comparing different years, or the situation before and after a project intervention, have provided very useful quantitative and qualitative information relatively quickly. This information relates to changes in the project environment as well as to changes more directly associated with the project in question. It is striking how many exercises in the case studies could have asked respondents to compare perceptions about current project performance or the current situation with the past but did not. For impact assessment — which is essentially about change — this comparison is critical.

On the other hand, ENDA found that they spent perhaps too much time and effort trying to reconstruct events that took place during the implementation of the project. At the time this was felt to be important if they were to follow the change model they had adopted. In retrospect, they felt that it was unnecessary to search out all of the details of project implementation. Those case studies which started simply by identifying the areas of change seen as significant by different stakeholders, and then exploring these in more depth, seem to have been more successful in reconstructing meaningful baselines.

CORDES developed a very systematic process of reconstructing baselines and then relating these to the current situation and to the evolving context. This method is based on what they term a 'triple diagnostic', asking the communities involved to answer the following questions:

- What was actually done?

- What were the objectives or motives which led us to do this?

- What was the impact on the community and what were the positive (helpful) and negative (constraining) effects of the context?

This line of questioning allowed communities to reflect on whether the original objectives had been met and whether the project, or other external factors, had brought about the change.

How to deal with attribution

One of the critical questions that impact assessment traditionally sets out to answer is what caused any identified change. For most projects this means trying to determine if the changes that have occurred would have happened anyway, and the degree to which an observed change can be attributed to a given project or programme. This is notoriously difficult.

Control groups

One of the ways in which the case studies have dealt with the problem of attribution is through control groups. The control group method requires a comparison between a population that has been targeted by a particular intervention and one that has not. Ideally, this assessment should be done before an intervention occurs and again afterwards, in order to determine if there is any difference between the two populations in question.

During its first impact assessment exercise in 1993, BRAC selected a control group from villages which no programme had yet reached, but which had similar traits in terms of land-holding to villages supported by BRAC. They hoped to be able to compare the well-being of these two groups at a later date during the 1996/7 impact assessment and thus deduce the difference between progress made by BRAC and non-BRAC members. However, BRAC's experience 'shows that getting a true comparison group is a tough problem' (BRAC 1998). First, during the three-year period between the two studies, 39 per cent of the comparison group households had dropped out from the list because they participated in NGOs or for other reasons. Second, even if they were not directly involved in other projects, several comparison households lived in villages where NGOs intervened. They may therefore have experienced a 'spillover' effect from these interventions, especially in the areas of health-care, sanitation provision, and reproductive behaviour, which all have an impact on material well-being. Third, it became clear that although comparison group households were similar in terms of land-holding to those benefiting from the BRAC programme, they differed in terms of age, sex, occupation of the household head, and education levels. This is significant, since the 1996/7 impact assessment found that initial land-holding and occupational status (self or wage employed) of the household head were the two major indicators influencing asset accumulation, apart from BRAC inputs. Last, although some attempts were made to control these factors (by applying multivariate econometric regression analysis, so as to separate out the different initial endowments of the comparison households and the contribution of external effects) it is recognised that there are major difficulties in quantifying many important socio-cultural aspects which may be critical factors[3].

Table 3.9: Comparison between BRAC and non-BRAC members
Source: BRAC case study, 1997

	BRAC members	**Non-BRAC** members
Poverty		
Below the poverty line	52%	89%
Living in extreme poverty	22%	37%
Assets	Higher for BRAC households both in 1993 and 1996. In 1996, 50% higher net worth (asset plus savings less outstanding loan)	
Rate at which asset value increased 1993-97	22%	84%
Savings	Twice as high as non-BRAC members	
Health		
Households using sanitary latrine	24%	9%
Rate of contraceptive use	40%	27%
Food	Average per-capita calorie consumption and total food and non-food expenditures were significantly higher	
	Higher food stocks, consuming more vegetables, fish and meat	Higher food deficits
	Low seasonal fluctuation in monthly food expenditure (3%)	High seasonal fluctuation in monthly food expenditure (18%)

BRAC therefore advises that the comparison group be treated with caution; on occasion, they have questioned the validity of retaining the comparison group (Mustafa et al. 1996). Table 3.9 outlines some of the data that emerges from the comparison between the control group and BRAC members. Although it clearly points to BRAC members being better off in terms of material poverty, assets, and food security, some points remain unclear because of the dilemmas cited above. One is the starting position of comparison members — were BRAC members better off in the first place? Another is whether changes during this period were associated with BRAC's inputs – indeed, the much faster rate of growth in asset value among non-BRAC members opens up a number of questions.

Non-project respondents

An alternative to establishing a control group at the beginning of the project is to do so at the time of the retrospective assessment by identifying non-beneficiaries and asking both project and non-project groups to recall their situation from a date before the intervention occurred and compare this to their current situation. Both the Wajir and Proshika case studies adopted this approach.

A good example from the Oxfam-Wajir case study in Kenya is illustrated below. In this case, households in project and non-project sites were simply asked to score out of ten their quality of life and ability to withstand drought, ten years ago and now. The average response for each group is shown in Table 3.10 and indicates marked differences between project sites, where people perceive things to be improving, and non-project sites, where people perceive things to be getting worse.

Table 3.10: Perceptions in changes in quality of life over the past ten years by 200 pastoral households in project and non-project sites (on a scale of zero to ten)

	Project		Non-project	
	Ten years ago	Now	Ten years ago	Now
Quality of life	4	6	6	4
Capacity to withstand drought	3	7	7	3

Source: Wajir Economic Impact Assessment Report

In the Proshika study this approach produced a number of findings which suggested that among those supported by the programme literacy rates, use of family planning, participation in local institutions, and economic assets were all higher, and the number of dowry marriages and infant morality rate lower compared to non-beneficiaries. However, there seemed to be little difference in immunisation and divorce rates, and in the use of organic farming methods — despite the project's emphasis on environmental awareness.

This retrospective method of comparing groups in and outside the project, rather than a 'before and after' control-group comparison limits the risk of wasting energy by collecting data that is subsequently considered almost useless because control-group members drop out. In addition, this approach may be more appropriate in areas where there are fewer NGO or governmental interventions and thus less danger of 'spillover' effects from other interventions. Yet this method does not overcome some of the problems associated with the 'before and after' approach such as being able to attribute differences precisely to specific variables, and to find strictly comparable groups. However, there is potential for greater comparison by further disaggregating the groups in question. So in Wajir for example, responses to questions about milk consumption (a critical element of well-being in pastoral areas) were not only explored from the point of view of project and non-project sites but also in terms of wealth and age.

Table 3.11: Average number of times milk is consumed in a day by 200 rich and poor households in project and non-project sites

	Adults		Children	
	Rich	Poor	Rich	Poor
Project sites	0.21	0.15	0.8	0.5
Non-project sites	0.18	0.09	0.7	0.5

Source: Wajir Economic Impact Assessment Report

This breakdown of results allows better comparison of different groupings across project and non-project sites, indicating that the frequency of milk consumption of poor adults in project sites is approximately 65 per cent greater than the frequency of milk consumption of poorer households in non-project sites. However, there is little difference in milk consumed by children in project and non-project sites. Such an approach allows for a greater understanding of who is receiving the greatest benefit from a given intervention.

In another approach, CYSD used a community they had just started working with as the control group. They found that because of this relationship, people were co-operative. In effect, they were using work carried out with this group in programme identification (through PRA exercises) as a baseline and as a comparator with existing groups and communities. This process allowed questions to be asked about levels of awareness on topics which CYSD had been aiming to change, for example about the use of neem pesticide or the availability of maternity allowances from primary health-care centres. The team also used direct observation to make comparisons; for example, they noted the lack of income-generation production units in the control village compared to project sites.

CORDES adopted a similar approach by comparing three communities which had worked with them for different lengths of time and at different levels of intensity, and measuring the various impacts achieved. Interestingly, CORDES also brought these groups together so that they could compare their own findings and draw their own conclusions.

The methods adopted by CYSD and CORDES overcome many of the ethical problems associated with the conventional control-group approach, although CYSD were concerned that the groups' expectations might bias results. The team feared that because the group was about to become involved with them, they would perhaps exaggerate their poverty and problems in order to be assured of future support. When the community were informed of the idea, they were reported to have questioned how they could be compared to the operational villagers. According to them, the targeted population had had opportunity to learn and act under the continuous guidance and with the assistance of the project functionaries, whereas they had not (CYSD, p.88). Of course, this is precisely the reason why they do in fact provide a useful basis for comparison, although the question with why such groups might want to get involved is an important one.

In fact, this motivation of the respondent is a critical issue for all types of impact assessment. As David Hulme notes

A 'rational actor' confronted by an impact assessor asking standard I[mpact] A[ssessment] questions ... would soon tell the interviewer where to put his/ her survey instrument. Fortunately in the world of practice more polite responses are the norm but the issue of how to persuade respondents to spare the time for an interview, and provide accurate and honest answers, is an important one that is rarely mentioned in I[mpact] A[ssessment] methodological statements.
(David Hulme 1997, p.19)

So although beneficiaries may put up with an endless stream of questions — because they understand that it is part of the price they have to pay for being involved with an NGO — they may answer questions in a way which they feel is most likely to ensure continued support. However, control groups may have even less incentive to co-operate (as they are by definition liable to remain excluded) or a greater incentive to exaggerate their needs (in the hope that someone responds). Some suggest that a reward, bribery, or payment of some form should be considered, as is the practice in the UK or USA when market researchers convene focus groups (Hulme 1997).

Lastly, impact assessments also need to take into account what effects a project has had on groups which were intended to benefit but did not. These differ from non-project respondents who are deliberately excluded from a particular intervention, but in effect also function as a control group. For instance, the Ghana study revealed that certain clan groups within the villages studied were systematically excluded from a number of development projects supported by local NGOs. However, one muct be careful in making this sort of comparison, because impact is not neutral: the project may actually have had a negative effect on some people's lives, which makes the comparison with those who have benefited less clear. Moreover, the reasons why certain groups may have been excluded — on the grounds of gender, ethnicity, or age — are precisely what makes them different from those groups that did benefit, which again makes the comparison problematic. This does not undermine the importance of understanding these possible negative impacts or processes of exclusion — quite the reverse — but it does suggest that as far as attribution is concerned, the existence of marginalised groups may not tell one much about what might have happened if the project in question had not occurred.

Using secondary data and other key informants

While it may be considered too difficult, too costly, or unethical to use control groups or non-respondents it may often be possible to use other sources of information about project and non-project areas or groups. As mentioned in the section on reconstructing baseline information, key informants and other organisations can sometimes provide this information.

CYSD for example collected information on land under paddy cultivation, vegetable, pulses, and oil seed cultivation from government agricultural offices, for areas in which they were working as well as for neighbouring areas. This threw light on the relative differences between the area where they had been promoting changes in agricultural practice and those where they had not.

The Ghana study on the other hand deliberately decided not to attempt to prove cause and effect; instead, they sought 'confirmation of attribution from different stakeholders in order to cross-check our analysis'. Data collected from individuals and communities about trends and project impacts was compared with anthropological studies in other communities in the area, a World Bank participatory poverty assessment, and other relevant data. This allowed some comparison between trends which were visible throughout the region, likely to be attributable to broad economic, environmental, political, and social phenomena, and changes which seemed to occur only in the communities in question, 'bucking' the trends elsewhere.

By looking for other explanations

Another important, connected, means of exploring attribution is deliberately to explore other possible explanations for an observed change or a difference between various populations or communities. For example, Cordes ensured that one key element of their 'triple diagnostic' method was to assess the contribution of external factors in promoting or inhibiting observed changes. In their case study, CYSD discovered many factors, which they called 'interference effects', that revealed why project impacts in one community varied from those in another. These included political interference, drought, crop destruction by wild animals, inter- or intra-village conflict, and donor-driven factors. CYSD undertook an 'external influence study' to understand these issues in more depth. This allowed them not only to compare a project village and a non-project control village, but also to understand why, for example, a project may have had a significant impact on people's lives in one village while it had much less impact in another. This in turn can help in estimating the degree to which differences in a project's context contribute to its success or even failure.

In another instance, BRAC had an indication during their first impact assessment exercise in 1993 that village-level infrastructure, and the distance from metalled roads in particular, played an important role in the economic performance of the communities where the village organisations they supported were located. They recognised that if they did not take this into account in the follow-up study in 1996, they could exaggerate the impact of programmes in villages with good economic infrastructure and possibly underestimate it in villages with poor infrastructure.

BRAC attempted to 'control' this and other factors by developing village profiles based on standard data, and derived from key informants in each village covered by the household survey.

The data include distance of the village from nearest city and metalled road, number of households, existence of socio-economic infrastructure such as haats, bazaars, educational institutions, health centres, NGOs, electricity, and so on, and access to various socio-economic institutions. (BRAC case study)

Although it is difficult to apportion the degree to which project or external factors contribute to a given change, it will add to the credibility of any impact study if the most obvious possible alternative explanations for observed changes are at least referred to and added to the balance of evidence gathered as part of an impact assessment process.

Summary 3.9 describes some of the key lessons learned in dealing with the critical issue of attribution.

Summary 3.9: Key lessons in dealing with attribution

- Apart from the ethical questions related to the use of control groups in a 'before and after' assessment method, there are a number of operational problems which usually make this approach impractical.

- The method which seeks to compare the situation of project beneficiaries and non-project respondents will usually be more appropriate.

- If non-project respondents are groups that the NGO is planning to work with in the future, then not only are some of the ethical dilemmas associated with this approach lessened, but the data gathered can also be used a baseline for that group.

- If non-project respondents are groups that the NGO does not plan to work with in the future, it seems incumbent on the NGO to make the information available to other appropriate development agencies which may be able to provide support and to consider compensating the respondents in some way.

The importance of cross-checking

Impact assessment is in the end a matter of judgement. For that judgement to be as valid as possible, and to be seen to be as valid as possible, the evidence that is gathered needs to be cross-checked. The search for attribution outlined above is one means of cross-checking information. However, cross-checking or 'triangulation' (a nautical term describing a navigation method which uses three points on the horizon to calculate a position) is important for many other purposes in impact assessment. Although some of the elements of impact assessment will involve discovering incontrovertible facts, much has to do with contrasting sometimes contradictory opinions, judgements, and feelings. Some of these apparently contrasting views may in fact be consistent, if seen from a different perspective, whereas some may really conflict.

The case studies used three main methods of cross-checking: by research method, by researcher or assessor, and by respondent or source of information.

By research method

The next chapter looks in detail at the range of tools and methods used in the case studies. Here I will simply note that the case studies drew upon six main, overlapping families of methods: secondary data review, surveys, individual and group interviews, discussions and workshops (sometimes using participatory tools and methods), case studies, and observation. The larger, more complicated studies drew on all or nearly all of these, whereas the smaller studies used maybe only two main methods.

Studies used different sequencing of methods. For example, ENDA undertook a questionnaire survey before holding focus-group discussions; however, they subsequently felt that the opposite might have been better because the questionnaire could have focused on specific issues raised by the discussion groups. BRAC on the other hand conducted a field study before the survey was undertaken in order to find out what impact BRAC field staff and members of village organisation expected the programme to have, and what they considered likely indicators. This gave valuable guidance for the study and also meant that the researchers tested the draft questionnaire several times to make sure that information on the indicators could be collected. The questionnaire was then followed up by further qualitative and case-study work on women's empowerment.

This combination of qualitative and quantitative methods is an important element of cross-checking.

Used before a quantitative survey, for example, qualitative enquiry may help with formulation and pre-testing of questionnaires, since a good questionnaire requires comprehensive advance knowledge about the system being studied and rigorous preparation. Qualitative enquiry may also generate hypotheses worthy of investigation, or help to narrow down the questions that more detailed surveys should focus on ... Qualitative enquiry may also be useful after a formal survey to follow up interesting leads ... and adds depth and context. (Moris and Copestake 1993)

It is important to stress the importance of direct observation by those conducting interviews, surveys, or participatory research exercises. This was brought out forcefully in the Ghana study when the research team noticed that a number of houses on the edge of a village had not been included in the map drawn by some of the villagers. When this was remarked upon, villagers revealed that these households had been excluded because they were from a minority ethnic group, and therefore not part of the community. It was only through astute observation, the willingness to cross-check those observations with other information, and by probing the contradiction between the two that new information was revealed.

By researcher or assessor

Another way of cross-checking results is by different researchers undertaking the same or similar research or interviews and comparing results. In the case studies, this was done in some instances during village-level PRA exercises: researchers split up, conducted parallel exercises, and then compared results. However, different researchers will always get different results because of who they are, how they behave, how they ask questions, and so on. This is particularly the case with female and male researchers, and 'insider' or 'outsider' researchers, who are liable to differ in their ability to ask certain questions and have them answered.

In the Pakistan case study, Oxfam programme officers, following in-depth discussions with beneficiary groups, graded the projects and local partners according to agreed criteria. These gradings were done independently by different programme officers and then compared. For instance, one of the criteria that Oxfam wished to assess was the 'participation of the community' in a number of projects run by different partners. The project officers agreed the following scoring system for levels of participation.

0: Beneficiary community has no awareness of project partner's activities.

1: Beneficiary community is aware of project partner and has some information or makes some 'contribution'.

2: Project partner consults beneficiaries; some meetings are held; some 'contribution' made.

3: Beneficiary community has some responsibilities at one project stage or there are more regular meetings; some 'contribution' made.

4: There is significant beneficiary involvement at different stages; they have significant responsibilities; some 'contribution' made.

5: The community works in more than one sector; takes initiatives; is able to mobilise resources.

The different graders' assessments were then recorded to make variations in scores clearly visible. There were three graders: A, B, and C (see Table 3.12). Where scorers felt unable to make a judgement, this was indicated by a question mark. For example, the assessors A and C seem to differ in their views on women's participation in project 2; only one scorer has assigned scores to projects 6 and 7; and scorer B was unable to make a judgement on project 3. Thus any independent observer can ask why A and C came to such different opinions or check whether the assessment of a certain project is based on a single person's view.

Table 3.12: Assessment of women and men's participation in seven projects in Pakistan

Project	1		2		3		4		5		6	7
Grader	A	B	A	C	A	B	A	B	A	B	A	A
Women's participation	0	0	3	5	1	?	0	0	2	2.5	3	2
Men's participation	1	?	?	1	1	?	0-3	?	2-3	?	0	2

One of the main tests of rigour in conventional scientific enquiry is that of 'objectivity' and 'confirmability': different observers must be able to agree on a phenomenon, and it must be possible to ensure that research results are not due to the researcher's bias. However, it is increasingly realised both inside and outside the laboratory that the very act of measurement may change the result. It is extremely difficult, if not impossible, for the researcher to remain distant or independent from the process he or she is researching. Therefore, it is important to be clear about the possible bias of individual researchers, and variations between researchers, and to try to diminish these, while recognising that it is impossible to eliminate them entirely. The reliability and credibility of the research is therefore also dependent on the transparency and detail of the record of research methods used. Peers should be able to trace and question the process of research undertaken. For example, the table above from Pakistan indicates how results of qualitative grading can be recorded in a way which makes it clear who was involved in which assessment, when disagreements between assessment occurred and, importantly, when assessors felt unable to make a judgement.

By respondent or source of information

One of the most common forms of cross-checking used in the case studies was by using different informants or sources of information. The first level of cross-checking was within communities, and the second between communities and other informants and stakeholders.

Cross-checking by respondent within communities

At a very basic level, this cross-checking simply involves, as in the Cordes case study, verifying if what had been proposed actually happened and whether it happened in the way that was intended. This validation formed an important step in their method of assessment. In other studies, the use of well-being ranking and gender analysis pointed to the importance of understanding differences between various groups within communities. Wealth, gender, age, ethnicity, and religion are often important elements in understanding these differences.

In the Ghana study, many women stressed the importance to them of income that they earned from selling produce grown on their own small plots of land. Men however, when asked about household income and the division of labour in the household, did not mention this activity or source of income at all. If the interviews had only involved men (which is not unusual in some surveys) this information would probably not have been revealed at all.

Not only can new information be revealed by finding additional respondents, but differences in priorities can also emerge through cross-checking. Table 3.13 reveals the preferences of different groups in a community in Andhra Pradesh, as discovered by a recent impact assessment undertaken by Action Aid.

Table 3.13: Preferences for change in Andhra Pradesh, India

Priority	Adult men	Adult women	Male youth	All
1	Housing	Land, irrigation, and crops	Land, irrigation, and crops	Housing
2	Land, irrigation, and crops	Housing	Education	Cattle
3	Cattle	Savings and loan	Health	Land, irrigation, and crops
4	Education	Cattle	Wage employment	Savings and loans
5	Savings and loans	Education	Savings and loans	Education
6	Clothing	Clothing	Cattle	Health
7	Leadership		Plantations	Clothing
8			Housing	
9			Self-employment	

Source: Action Aid impact assessment research

This research reveals important differences in priorities between different groups, but it also raises several questions about how group priorities are determined. Although it is unclear how this happens, the column for 'All' suggests that male priorities tend to win out (housing emerges as first priority, although women rank it second and young men eighth). It also suggests that negotiation does change priorities (cattle emerges as the second priority although none of the groups ranked it higher than third) and that women and young men together still have difficulty in getting their priorities recognised (despite both groups ranking irrigated crops as first priority, it slips to third place in the group listing). Young men possibly have most difficulty in getting their priorities recognised: wage employment does not figure in the group's list.

Groups within communities not only are likely to have differing priorities and views, these may in fact conflict. For example, the CYSD study revealed that women in several communities had initially been discouraged from saving in a group account or joining self-help groups, because their husbands perceived this as a threat to their domestic authority. Those who did join faced hostility from their husbands for extended periods. This hostility has been overcome in some cases, as economic benefits have increased and project staff have deliberately targeted 'awkward' husbands. This is a good example of how cross-checking views and attitudes within communities not only has to do with building consensus or agreeing priorities but can also be about understanding threats or obstacles to achieving impact which need to be taken into account and, if possible, countered.

However, it must be recognised that there are limits to the amount of time that people are willing and able to spend on cross-checking; there may even be a law of diminishing returns. In other words, it is crucial to prioritise what information must be cross-checked, which sources need to be involved, and to set realistic time-frames for doing so.

Cross-checking by comparing information from communities and other informants

Through visits to schools and discussions with teachers, CYSD discovered that although school records had indicated that enrolment was improving, the average attendance level was only 50 per cent of the enrolled students. These students were engaged in household duties such as looking after younger children when parents are working or rearing livestock. Taking the school records at face value, without cross-checking the findings with teachers, could have led to a very misleading impression about what was actually happening. It could also have led to an inaccurate assessment of the quality and impact of schooling if, for example, literacy levels had been calculated according to the numbers of enrolled children.

Tax officials, revenue departments, and forestry officers also proved useful key informants, not least in indicating whether official data and records could be trusted. In addition, some of these informants had been working in the project areas for much longer than the NGOs in question. Revenue officials in Orissa, who had been working in the area for the past 15 years, were able to describe changing trends in villages which they attributed to CYSD intervention, as well as providing vital information about the proportion of land in the project area owned by outsiders. This helped CYSD understand the importance of distress land sales by tribal communities, and of the encroachment on tribal lands.

Health workers can be key informants with important insight into local communities, not just related to health projects. For example, discussion with residents in Matson, UK, revealed that breathlessness was one of the most commonly cited health problems. A local chemist confirmed that prescriptions for asthma were very common, which in turn led to suspicions that damp in unrefurbished households was one of the possible causes of asthma. In this case, the key informant not only confirmed what people had said, but was also able to give a more precise definition of the problem and point to its possible causes. In terms of the impact assessment, this information helped to understand the potential secondary impacts on people with refurbished houses and those without.

Dealing with contradictions

Nearly all the case studies report the difficulties and challenges of dealing with contradictory information that emerges. In some cases, these contradictions could be explained quite easily. In others, they provided new insights that led to further lines of questioning. As noted in the CYSD study it is important to

study the logic behind such contrast and how best this can be interpreted. If it is not possible for different people to agree on the interpretation of certain findings it may be better to record the different views, rather than attempt to reach a consensus. (CYSD, p.30)

Cross-checking is an important means of exposing bias, specific interests, and power relations. Deliberately seeking out the views of a wide variety of people with different views is an important tool in assessing impact. As Moris and Copestake note,

[this] approach to data is much like that of investigative journalism. Assume bias is present, but allow for it by recognising explicitly a respondents' interests and by cross-checking statements with neutral observers or those holding opposite views ... for example ... [q]uestioning both buyers and sellers, wholesalers and retailers, about the same transaction (e.g. interest rates on

trade credit) often yields an upper and lower figure. By asking who is lying and why, important insights into relative market power may be gained. (Moris and Copestake, pp.48-49)

Summary 3.10 lists some of the main lessons about how to cross-check findings and some of the key issues that emerged from the case studies.

Summary 3.10: Key lessons about cross-checking findings

- Mixing qualitative and quantitative methods is a vital element of cross-checking. You need to consider what sequence of methods makes most sense.

- Direct observation is an important means of checking if there are discrepancies between what people say (or do not say) and their actions.

- Using different 'assessors' or stakeholders to review the same issue can reveal areas of consensus and difference. Agreeing at the outset which criteria to explore, or using a single reporting format can simplify comparison at a later date.

- Making the methods by which information was collected clear and transparent allows third parties or peers to cross-check the process of enquiry.

- Differences in power and status within communities — especially relating to gender, wealth, age, and ethnicity – make cross-checking between groups even more important. Using well-being ranking and gender analysis can be an important part of this.

- Key informants who know a particular region or group of people very well — health workers, local officials, teachers, and so on — can be an excellent source of information and can also verify information from other sources.

Summing up: the problem of aggregation and synthesis

This chapter has explored how the case studies went about designing their impact assessment processes, what preparatory steps were taken, how they coped with baseline data and indicators (or the lack of them), as well as how they tried to deal with the difficulties of attributing change to a given intervention. I have also described how the studies approached the need to cross-check findings and sometimes to record differences in views and opinions rather than attempting always to reach a consensus. This leads me to one of the trickiest problems that impact assessment processes have to take into account: how to summarise and present findings in a useful and relevant form, or forms, which do not lose the richness, diversity, and complexity of the story. It is important to address the question of synthesis at the design stage of an impact assessment, so that data collection and analysis can take its form into account.

Feedback

One of the ways to ensure that any synthesis of findings does not miss or misrepresent important views is to cross-check them with different stake-holders, through field presentations or workshops, and by circulating draft findings and reports for comment. This has happened or is planned in nearly all the case studies and has involved the following forms of sharing findings.

Community feedback: Findings can be communicated through verbal presentations and workshops, although it is unclear whether any of the case-study participants will be translating reports or findings into appropriate local languages.

Presentations and workshops with staff: This approach allows both the research team and local staff to review findings and learn more about methods of impact assessment.

Multi-stakeholder workshops: These can involve beneficiaries, staff, donors, other NGOs, bi- and multilateral agencies, government, and academics.

All these methods have been important in cross-checking findings, generating new insights, communicating results, and in helping different stakeholders understand differing opinions and views. Perhaps the most striking example of the importance of eliciting feedback comes from the Proshika case study. After conducting a large household survey, the results were separately communicated to programme partners from village organisations, middle managers, and senior managers. First, each group was asked to present what they expected the results to be against the key indicators of the study; then the actual results were presented and the divergence analysed. As a result, the findings for five of the 13 indicators were seriously questioned, which led to the issues being further explored. Follow-up qualitative and participatory research not only confirmed the major differences which the feedback had identified, but also revealed why the questionnaire process had produced the results in question.

However, workshops, in particular those involving many stakeholders, can also spark off conflict which it may, or may not, be wise to provoke. For example, the meeting of a wide range of stakeholders in Ikafe at the end of the field work resulted in heated debate. During the review, the disquiet of some of the representatives of the host population lead to threats of violence against Oxfam staff; indeed, some bullets were fired at the Oxfam compound just after the review. Although most people involved believe that this was the result of the 'normal' insecurity in the area it indicates that in situations where high levels of tension exist, bringing all parties together may be risky.

The report

Most impact assessments produce a report (or reports). Its structure can help summarise information in ways that do not sacrifice too much and which can also facilitate feedback. First, it is important than any intervention is properly contextualised. As I noted in Chapter 2, impact assessment essentially analyses how a given set of actions combines with the context to produce change. The report should therefore explain how the political, social, economic, and environmental climate influences the outcomes of a given project and how people perceive its benefits. Second, the report should distinguish between data, analysis, and recommendations, and clarify whose analysis or recommendations they are. This allows readers to agree with the data or analysis while contesting the recommendations or vice-versa. Third, as explained in the previous section, it is important that the report retains and presents any important differences in opinion or analysis from different stakeholders or even within the assessment team. Fourth, the report should present disaggregated data for relevant groups, even if this shows no differences between them. Disaggregation by gender, age, and well-being — although it was not done in most of the case studies — should almost certainly be done in every case. Other dimensions of difference such as ethnicity, clan, religion, or sexual orientation may also be important in some contexts.

Last, the use of case studies and people's own words can not only breathe life into the analysis, but also exemplify more forcefully what change means to individuals and communities, and what it feels like to experience it from day to day. It should be remembered that this may need to be interpreted for those who not familiar with the context.

Other means of communication

Although none of the case studies used video, radio, cassettes, or comic books to communicate the results of the research or to complement the main report, these methods are increasingly being used in the development field (Braden 1997).

Recent Oxfam experience in the UK and East Africa suggests that video in particular has real potential not only to enrich dry reports, but also for individuals and groups to represent themselves and the changes they have gone through, as well as communicating their feelings to others. With adequate and relatively cheap training, video has the added advantage of being a tool that communities can use to track and record change over time in a quite simple and cost-effective manner. It should be noted that synthesising several hours of video tapes is certainly no less, and possibly a little more, difficult than several hundred pages of data. However, groups and communities which synthesise and edit the material themselves, have added control over how they would like to portray themselves and their achievements.

In large organisations, the problems of aggregation are even more acute. I explore this in more depth in Chapter 7.

4

Choosing tools and methods

This chapter explores the 'families' of tools and methods used in the case studies: surveys; interviews, workshops and discussions; direct observation; participatory research; and case studies. Drawing on the lessons learned in our impact assessment studies, I draw some conclusions about their relevance and utility in a range of contexts and for various purposes. The final section also looks at how two of the case studies explored the relationship between costs, benefits, and impact.

Choosing appropriate tools and methods depends on the purpose and focus of the impact assessment, its context, the capacities and skills of those involved, and the resources available. One of the major skills needed by those involved in impact assessment is the ability to find an appropriate combination and sequencing of tools and methods. None of the tools presented below, *on their own*, is likely to be sufficient in determining impact, cross-checking findings, and dealing with attribution.

Surveys

A survey is simply a method of establishing a comprehensive overview of a given situation. Surveys are most suited to answering questions such as *what? how many?* and *how often?*. Although they can be used to answer *why?* questions, they tend to be less useful in doing so. They are therefore often used to gather basic data about a group of people (their age, sex, occupation, and so on). Surveys generally use a questionnaire and seek standard, quantifiable data from a representative population. If the number of people or groups being studied is small enough (generally less than 100, depending on the number of questions) a survey can cover the entire population. Two main types of survey which were undertaken in the case studies: large-scale questionnaire surveys covering respondents across several communities, and smaller-scale mini-surveys of the populations of a limited number of communities.

Large-scale questionnaire surveys

Four of the case studies (ENDA, BRAC, Wajir, and Proshika) used large-scale questionnaire surveys varying from 200 to 1,800 respondents. Between four and 60 enumerators administered the questionnaires face-to-face with the respondents. Although in all the studies the household was the main unit of assessment, one of the studies also targeted individual women.

Content

Each of these case studies took slightly different approaches to the survey. ENDA felt that because of their lack of baseline data they needed to use the questionnaire to identify the situation prior to project implementation and subsequent changes.

However, the team also felt that it was important to try and capture the project processes that had taken place using the questionnaire. This way it was felt that we could obtain a general perception of the project and not just the perceptions of the key informants. (ENDA case study report)

However, as a result the questionnaire was long and, possibly because it tried to collect too much information, 'the objective of trying to quantify impact still eluded the team'. They subsequently found that '[m]ost of the data that was collected using the questionnaire supported the findings of the focus-group discussion' which they undertook later. 'We feel that for the effort that was put into the questionnaire, the added value ... was not much greater than the focus-group discussions'. In retrospect, the team felt that although questionnaires may be a useful tool to assess the extent of impact it might have been better to run a shorter questionnaire after discussing possible indicators, defined by the community through the kinds of participatory methods subsequently used by the team (see section below).

The BRAC, Wajir, and Proshika studies, which had quite solid baseline data, focused their questionnaires much more tightly on presumed impacts. They also collected information to help assess whether the changes they identified could be attributed to the projects in question. The Wajir study deliberately set out to assess three levels of analysis (see Table 4.1). Level one relates to significant changes in pastoralists' welfare, as assessed by levels of food aid received; quality of diet; perceptions of changes in quality of life; child mortality; and capacity to cope with drought. Level two explores changes in livelihood which might explain the impacts on welfare described in level 1 and which relate to the outcomes of the project, such as reduced animal mortality; increased reliability of water; improved law and order; and the rate of return of new investments provided through credit and restocking. Level three examines the changes in the quality of and satisfaction with delivery of services which might explain the changes in livelihood and welfare; these can be considered as another lower level of outcomes. The areas addressed by the questionnaire are specifically chosen to trace the hierarchy of the project's objectives set out in a logical framework at the outset of the project, mainly covering outcomes and impacts.

Table 4.1: Cause-and-effect relationships between the Wajir project and pastoral welfare, in relation to the hierarchy of project objectives

Hierarchy of objectives	Indicators of objectives
1 To enable pastoral communities to live in peace, without fear of starvation or ill health, while minimising their dependence on food aid and other forms of welfare support	• Lower food aid requirements • Better quality diets • Reduced seasonal peri-urban destitution • Pastoralists perceive an improvement in their quality of life and their capacity to survive drought • Lower child-mortality rates
2 To strengthen pastoral livelihoods by establishing and/ or supporting sustainable local institutions	• Fewer animals die • Water supplies during the dry season are more reliable • Exchange rates between livestock or livestock products and essential household commodities improve • Private and public property rights are maintained • Pastoralists obtain income from a range of new sources
3 To improve the delivery of essential services (health-care, education, water) by establishing sustainable institutions	• Herders use quality drugs at correct dosage rates • Pastoralists sell animals and animal products at xx% of the price obtained in Nairobi • Prices for grain and other essential commodities do not rise more than xx% above Nairobi prices and remain stable • Pastoralists send their children to school and are satisfied with the quality of education • Water supplies are correctly maintained to avoid breakdown or siltation in the dry season • Food aid, credit, and other inputs are efficiently distributed to those most in need

The BRAC questionnaire was conducted primarily to collect quantitative data to determine the impact of their Rural Development Programme on its participants, with special reference to their material well-being, and their level of poverty in particular. However, they also included social aspects of well-being such as literacy and educational level of households, housing status, and some aspects of health, sanitation, and family planning.

Both BRAC and the Wajir impact assessment team consulted with field staff and, in BRAC's case, some village organisations in the process of developing expected impacts and indicators which became the focus of the questionnaires (see Table 4.2).

Table 4. 2: Main areas of questions asked in Wajir and BRAC household surveys

Wajir	BRAC (RDP)
• Demographic and household characteristics	• Demographic and household characteristics
• Wealth ranking: rich/ poor	• Land holding and other assets
• Quality of life	• Housing status
• Food aid received in past 12 months	• Food stock
• Milk consumption per day over past 12 months	• Health status
• Numbers of meals per day	• Family planning/ contraceptive use
• Child sickness and mortality	• Sanitation
• Water supplies	• Credit and savings
• Income and expenditure	• Household expenditure and consumption
• Conflict situation	• Coping with crisis
• Capacity to cope with drought	• Women's ownership of and control over household assets
• School attendance and satisfaction	• Women's access to income-generating activities
• Future aspirations for children	• Women's mobility
• Animal health/ drug treatment	• Training from BRAC
• Herd profiles	• Reasons for dropping out of the programme
• Herd movements in last drought	
• Role of pastoral association	

The Proshika survey focused on what they call two 'generic types of empowerment', economic and social. For them this emphasis on empowerment impact has 'a subtle but significant difference from the usual meaning of impact': while it assesses actual changes in the economic and social circumstances of the people it supports, it also assesses their capacities and potential to improve their circumstances in the future.

Preparation and pre-testing
No matter how well an agency knows an area or population, there is always a need to pre-test the questionnaire in order to ensure that the questions are understandable, that they are put in a suitable way, that the length of the

interview is appropriate, and that respondents will be available. The questionnaire can then be modified before it is administered to a wider group. Addressing problems and mistakes at this stage is not only much easier and cheaper, but can make the difference between a successful or unsuccessful exercise. Given the time and expense usually involved in questionnaire surveys of this type, it is well worth investing a little at the outset to get it right.

BRAC researchers tested the draft questionnaire several times to make sure that it was right for collecting information on indicators. Several revisions were made: for example, they found that it was difficult for respondents to recall income, whereas they could remember expenditure more accurately. However, they also found that although people could quite easily recall large expenditures over quite long periods (such as buying bicycles or radios) the period of recall for small purchases, particularly of non-durable food items, was much shorter. As a result, a question on consumption expenditure was repeated on three consecutive days, asking people to recall expenditure over the previous 24 hours. It was also recognised that expenditure varied greatly over the year. As a result, 'data on consumption and non-durable expenditure were collected twice — once in the lean season and again in the peak season in order to consider seasonal fluctuation in consumption and expenditure' (BRAC case study).

Respondents

The choice of respondents is clearly a critical part of the design of a survey study. The case studies used a mixture of random and purposive sampling (see Chapter 3). In the Wajir, Proshika, and BRAC cases, random samples of direct beneficiaries and non-beneficiaries were made in order to compare these groups. Care was taken to select households in similar zones and/ or with similar characteristics.

In the Wajir case study, one of the key questions was the degree to which observed changes in the Wajir area were due to the pastoral development project run by Oxfam. They therefore undertook stratified or systematic sampling, illustrated in Table 4.3. Two hundred households were selected by first dividing the area into zones. Centres in each zone were then clustered to ensure an approximate balance with respect to distance from markets and different agro-ecological zones. Five centres were selected from these, three in project areas and two in non-project areas. In each of the five centres, 20 pastoral groups (living more than 8km away from the market centre) were randomly selected for interview. Within each group two households, a richer and a poorer one, were interviewed. In project sites the sample was further stratified according to membership of pastoral associations (about 50 per cent of the sample were members). In addition, a purposive sample of 224 interviewees was selected in order to explore the impact of specific restocking and credit projects.

Table 4.3: Number of households sampled in Wajir case study

	Members of pastoral association	Non-members of pastoral association	Total interviewees
Project sites			
Khorof Harar	20	20	
Riba	20	20	
Wargadud	20	20	
			120
Non-project sites			
Duntow		40	
Batalu		40	
			80
Purposive sample			
Families with restocked herds	40		
Women involved in credit scheme	184		
			224
Total	**284**	**140**	**424**

BRAC, on the other hand, also had to take into account the previous impact assessment exercise (IAS 1) that they had undertaken. This had identified 'panel members', which were BRAC member households, and 'comparison members', who were not members of BRAC used as a control group. For the follow-up study, BRAC took random samples from panel members, from other BRAC members, and from comparison members. Given the wide geographic spread of the programme, BRAC also needed to get a reasonable balance across the country without spreading its resources so thinly as to make the exercise an expensive logistical nightmare. Therefore, of the 1,250 BRAC sample households which were randomly selected, 500 were from districts served by ten area offices which had also been included in the first assessment, and 750 households covered by 15 other areas offices (see Table 4.4).

As in the Wajir study, BRAC studies also deliberately included specific groups of people in their sample about whom they wished to discover more. In this case, they were curious about 200 members who had shown very high performance.

Table 4.4: Sampling frame from the BRAC case study

	Members of BRAC		Non-members
	Panel members from ten areas	Non-panel members from 15 areas	Comparison members
Randomly selected	500	750	250
Purposively selected successful cases		200	
Total	1,450	250	

Selection and training of enumerators

Undertaking a large-scale questionnaire survey which involves face-to-face interviews normally means having to hire interviewers. The numbers of enumerators or interviewers needed will depend on the scope of the survey, how long it lasts, what geographic area will be covered, and what logistical support is at the disposal of the impact assessment team. Within the studies, enumerators undertook on average between three and five interviews per day over two to four weeks. The total number of interviews per enumerator varied from about 20 to 60. If enumerators are expected to undertake repeat interviews over a period, as was the case with BRAC, the number of interviews that can be conducted will be limited. Still, BRAC managed to carry out 1,700 interviews, all of them repeated, compared to 424 interviews in Wajir and 240 in the ENDA study.

In cases where findings may vary over time (for example, because of seasonal variations) care should be taken minimise the time-gap in the collection of data. For example, BRAC's emphasis on collecting accurate consumption data, which vary over time, meant that many small survey teams had to work simultaneously across a geographically dispersed area. This posed some problems, notably putting high pressure on the research team to supervise the data collection effectively.

In three of the case studies which used questionnaires, the enumerators were chosen from the project areas to make sure they were accepted by the community, and to avoid language problems. Proshika contracted out their survey to a local research organisation 'to ensure impartiality'.

At the outset, between two days and one week was spent work with the enumerators on the following areas.

- briefing about the projects being assessed;
- sampling techniques;

- developing, testing, and refining the questionnaires and data-recording sheets, and translating them into local languages;

- interview techniques, especially how to probe for apparent inconsistencies. In the Wajir study this included some training on the basic techniques of ranking and seasonal calendars (see section on participatory methods) which were included to assist in quantification and recall;

- logistics, management; and supervision.

Analysis

Simple statistical techniques were used in the Wajir and ENDA studies to analyse the data collected. This generally involved calculating average results for various categories of respondent (rich and poor, adults and children, men and women, project and non project members) and presenting this as before and after data — see the example in Table 4.5.

Table 4.5: Perceptions of the relative reliability of water supplies now compared to ten years ago in Wajir

	Ten years ago	Now
Project site	3	7
Non-project site	7	3

Note: Average scores reported by 200 pastoral families

The Wajir, Proshika, and BRAC studies assessed the statistical significance of the results obtained. They particularly explored differences between project and non-project sites in order to determine the likelihood that these could have been caused by chance, rather than the projects. Their conclusion could then be applied to wider populations. In the Wajir study it was possible to calculate, for example, what the economic impacts on the 1,788 households in the project area were, if the statistically significant findings for the 200 households interviewed were true for the whole population (see the section on costs, benefits, and impact at the end of this chapter). Table 4.6 illustrates how this analysis was done. The average animal losses per household were given a financial value, which was calculated for both project and non-project sites. This established an average difference between these areas of £265 per household. If this applied to all the estimated 1,788 households living in the area, the lower mortality rates would thus translate into an estimated district saving of £473,820.

Table 4.6: Economic impact analysis of changes in animal mortality in Wajir

	Project site		**Non-project site**		**Difference**
	Mortality rate	Annual loss per household	Mortality rate	Annual loss per household	Annual loss per household
Camels	20%	£273	31%	£402	£129
Cattle	17%	£126	32%	£249	£123
Sheep or goats	18%	£49	25%	£68	£19
Total		**£454**		**£719**	**£265**

The BRAC study attempted to go one step further by employing more sophisticated statistical analysis such as multiple regression to try and isolate the effects of single variables on material poverty. They had to hire trained staff for data entry and cleansing and coding data, while processing and analysis was done by staff from BRAC's Research and Evaluation Division. This sort of analysis 'is enormously demanding in terms of data requirements, technical expertise and costs. It will only be feasible on very rare occasions' (Hulme 1997, p.7). BRAC themselves note that although these tools were used to separate the contribution of external factors from that of the project, this 'might not suffice because socio-cultural aspects can not be quantified'.

Having said that, exploring correlations within the data did reveal interesting gaps between the exceptional performance of some groups and lower achievements of others, which had not previously emerged.

[I]n identifying factors which influenced the differences in the level of success between the two groups [exceptional and less well performing groups] it was found that 61 per cent of the successful household members were involved in village organisation management against only 14 per cent for the other BRAC members. ... [Other] factors contributing to significantly higher level of performance [are] involvement in village organisation management, close kinship ties in the village organisation, involvement in BRAC training and enjoyment of special loan privileges. (BRAC case study)

Cross-checking results
All the case studies cross-checked their survey findings with information gathered in other ways, for example through participatory methods. In the

Proshika study, as described in Chapter 3, a systematic attempt was made to cross-check findings with a sample of the respondents, project staff, and senior managers. Each of these groups was asked to compare their expectations of the findings with the actual results. Nearly half the findings were questioned and further participatory research was carried out on specific issues.

Mini-surveys

Large-scale surveys can be inappropriate or one may have inadequate resources. In these cases an alternative is what some have called mini-surveys, covering a limited number of people or communities. These can be particularly useful if basic information is lacking.

Summary 4.1: How to gather quality data through questionnaire surveys

- Compensate for respondents who may drop out. Some respondents will be unavailable during the survey period, so it is often worth 'over-sampling' to compensate for this. In the Proshika study, 30 per cent more households than necessary were initially selected to make sure that they would have a margin for this contingency.

- Be aware of problems observed during data collection which might bias the results. For example, in the BRAC survey it was observed when collecting consumption data that in some cases household members took their meals outside the household. In order to prevent a potential distortion of data, missing data were replaced by average figures.

- Ensure that the questionnaire focuses on key issues. Questionnaires are most useful in answering questions such as *how many? what? how often?* and *when?*. (*Why?* and *how?* questions are often better answered by less formal or structured methods.) Discussions with project staff and beneficiaries before these key questions are framed can enhance the focus of the survey. Consider to what extent the questionnaire not only seeks to identify what change or impact has occurred, but also seeks to verify the degree to which project outcomes might plausibly have led to those changes.

- Include questions that allow comparison of issues before and after project implementation. Simple ranking of people's perceptions — for example of a change in their quality of life, relative satisfaction with different service providers or NGOs, capacity to cope with crisis or security — allow comparisons to be made across groups and simple statistical analysis to be done.

- Give careful thought to the choice of the number and type of respondents. Particular consideration must be given to how representative a sample is of a given population, and a combination of project and non-project sites should be chosen. It should be borne in mind that a scattered location of respondents may make the exercise very expensive and place additional stress on field survey teams.

- Recognise the importance of pre-testing and refining questionnaires. Before the survey is implemented, care must be taken in the selection of enumerators and their proper training and briefing.

- Ensure adequate cross-checking and feedback. This not only verifies findings but can also reveal problems with the survey method.

Three of the case studies carried out some sort of mini-survey covering a single village (Ghana), a limited number of villages or communities (CYSD), or a number of staff members (Matson). These were done in different ways and involved questionnaires and participatory exercises. The objectives were to get a relatively rapid, but comprehensive, overview of the activities, opinions, and attitudes of given groups of people.

In the Ghana study, mini-surveys were conducted in each of the three villages involved in the impact assessment. They were used to explore the degree to which various household members were involved in activities promoted by outside agencies (NGOs, government, and others), through interviewing small groups of villagers or using existing project records. This method is dependent on acquiring an accurate list of village households and determining which member was involved in what activity. This proved quite difficult because household listings tended to be incomplete for various reasons (see section below on social mapping and wealth-ranking), project records were poor or ambiguous, and it was sometimes difficult to locate individuals within specific households.

Despite this it was possible, through a process of cross-checking during follow-up visits, to develop quite a comprehensive picture in each community of who was involved in which activities, and who was not. When cross-checked with other information — relating to well-being and ethnic and clan membership — a clear pattern of inclusion and exclusion emerged. A disproportionate number of socially dominant and economically better-off households were involved in development activities when compared to poorer households. This issue of exclusion has since become an important focus for discussion when the NGOs involved in the study reviewed the preliminary findings.

In the CYSD study detailed household surveys were undertaken in three of the 21 villages covered by the study in order to cross-check and quantify changes identified previously, for example from secondary sources. This confirmed for example that a substantial increase in land encroachment for paddy cultivation had occurred and that some households were increasingly involved in income-generation activities. The mini-survey also allowed a more detailed understanding of how and why these processes were occurring.

In the case of Matson, a short self-administered questionnaire was used towards the end of the study to get a 'wider cross-section of views from the staff than what was gleaned through conversations and interviews'.

Thus, small-scale or mini-surveys can be used at different stages of the impact assessment exercise for a range of purposes. In Ghana the survey was used to generate a general picture of a whole community on a specific issue, which the researchers could then explore in more depth. The mini-survey in this case acted as a means to ensure that any further interviews and research would include the views not only of the 'included' but also the 'excluded' population.

In both the case of CYSD and Matson, mini-surveys were used to confirm findings derived from other, more qualitative, research methods and to deepen their understanding of specific issues. In the Ghana study it enabled the researchers to gauge the *scale* of a phenomenon (the exclusion of some households from NGO activities) that had been identified by other methods.

Mini-surveys offer a useful alternative to large-scale ones, but because of their very nature care should be taken when generalising from them to larger populations. Many of the lessons noted under the large-scale survey section apply to mini-surveys as well. It should be remembered that it makes little or no difference to an interviewee if they take part in a mini-survey or a large-scale one. The onus is therefore on those designing the survey to ensure that every effort is made to keep the interview as short and as focused as possible, and that the quality of the results obtained mean that people's time was not wasted.

Interviews, workshops, and discussions

Simply talking, and listening, to people is probably the most common and useful way of assessing impact. This does not mean to say that it is easy. In the case studies these discussions happened in a variety of ways: individually and in groups; formally and informally; using pre-defined questionnaires, semi-structured interviews, and workshops; and simply by chatting. This section looks at two main areas: individual interviews; and group interviews, discussions, and workshops.

Individual interviews

As mentioned in the above section, face-to-face interviews using questionnaires were undertaken in a number of case studies. Most studies also carried out less structured interviews (sometimes called semi-structured interviews) with a wide variety of informants, as well as engaging in chance opportunities to exchange views and opinions with others.

Table 4.7 outlines some of the main distinctions between surveys and semi-structured interviews, although in practice they are often not as clear-cut as the table suggests.

Table 4.7: Advantages and disadvantages of structured surveys and semi-structured interviews

Structured survey	Semi-structured interviews
Design completed, questions defined, and duration set before interviewing starts	Design continues during interviewing phase; questions are identified and modified during the course of interviews and between interviews; duration varies
All informants usually selected before interviewing starts	Informants can be identified progressively, making use of findings from previous interviews
Identical questions for all respondents	Questions or topics tailored to different informants and stages of enquiry
Informants chosen as representative sample	Informants chosen to explore a range of different types of knowledge and perspectives
Data reduced to understandable patterns using statistical analysis	Findings reduced to understandable patterns using qualitative analysis
Findings validated by calculating the likelihood of the patterns observed being due to chance rather than specific factors	Findings validated by cross-checking and triangulation
Most suited to answering what? how many? how often? questions. Can answer why? or how? questions but tends to be less effective in doing so, as these answers are often difficult to quantify and compare	Most suited to answering why? and how? questions. Can answer what? how many? how often? questions but answers will usually not be valid for a wider population

Adapted from Woodhouse (1998)

The Matson study particularly emphasised the semi-structured interview approach; it deliberately set out to discover from a wide variety of people their perceptions of change in the community. The researcher used three basic questions to structure these interviews, which otherwise were open-ended: 'What are the changes that have taken place in Matson?' 'Has the quality of life improved or not over the years?' 'What do you think caused those changes?'

In order to carry out the interviews, the researcher needed help to identify a good cross-section of the community. In this case, an advice worker at the One Stop Shop[1] on the Matson estate used his rich understanding of the community to draw up a list of categories of residents to be interviewed: older people, youth, lone parents, long-standing residents and newer residents, residents who did not use the services offered by the project, board members of the project, project staff, other service providers, local businesses, and statutory service staff.

Project staff members were then asked to identify names of people who they thought would be willing to take part, taking care to ensure a balance between men and women. The advice worker painstakingly phoned each potential interviewee and set up meetings. By the end of the study, 28 formal interviews were conducted, half of them with men and half with women. However, some groups were more difficult to engage than others as Table 4.8 reveals.

It is important to note that efforts were made to contact groups which had proved difficult to involve in the formal interviews, such as non-project users and busy officials. The researcher stressed this:

there were also innumerable conversations with the staff, board members, and the residents who 'dropped in' at the project. Notable among these conversations were ones with the Matson bus driver over a cup of coffee at the end of his shift, with an elderly woman who volunteered to help me post my letter at the post office, with members of the Phoenix Club[2], with a resident who had just moved into Matson and was looking for change to make a telephone call ... But a major source of getting a feel of life in Matson was from the children. Having been invited to talk to the children at Robinswood school on India, which I coupled with a few magic tricks, I made some good friends among them ... hanging around the community shop I invariably bumped into them and got talking about India, Matson and magic!! Not necessarily in that order. (Matson case study)

The Ghana study also emphasised semi-structured individual interviews, carried out. repeatedly over a one-year period. Their selection was made following participatory research in the community where a wealth-ranking exercise (see section below on participatory tools) had been conducted. This allowed a sample of individuals to be chosen who represented distinct, locally determined, well-being categories. The sample selected deliberately included a greater proportion of women and individuals from poorer households (Table 4.9).

Table 4.8: Interviews conducted in the Matson study by stakeholder

Category	Number of interviews	Comments
Residents	13	Interviewees represented all the sub-groups; five of them happened to be either staff or board members.
Non-users	No formal interviews	Many casual conversations at the bus stop, post office, telephone booth, chemist, and so on.
Board members	4	
Staff	10	Interviewees included volunteers and one student placement.
Local business	1	
Other service providers	5	
Statutory service staff	No formal interviews	Opportunities were taken at various meetings and functions arranged for other purposes to engage these and other officials, including city and county councillors, the local Member of Parliament, social service managers, housing officers, and so on.

Table 4.9: Breakdown of individuals selected for repeat interviews (Ghana study)

Village	Navio		Yiziiri		Demon	
Wealth-category	Men	Women	Men	Women	Men	Women
A (better-off)		1		1		1
B	1		1		1	
C		1		1		1
D	1	2	1	2	1	2
E/F (worse -off)	2	2	2	2	2	2
Total	4	6	4	6	4	6

These interviews aimed to explore people's perceptions of poverty and well-being and to trace how these have changed, to examine the effectiveness of those organisations whose work affects their lives, and to record their assessments of the sources of any change identified. Individual interviews have proved to be particularly useful in drawing out:

- sensitive information on intra-household relations, for example changes in gender relations within the household or between wives in polygamous households, and sensitive information regarding income, credit, and so on;

- differences and similarities between men and women, as well as between individuals from better-off and worse-off families, in terms of their perceptions of change and what they value;

- the impact of sudden shocks such as illness or theft on vulnerable people, and how these can dramatically affect their well-being;

- the importance of seasonality and the relationship over the year between food security, income and expenditure, and illness.

- Interviews complemented and helped to cross-check information obtained in other ways, for example through community research work, as well as revealing critical issues which, although raised before, had not been emphasised strongly enough, such as child and infant mortality.

Reflections on individual interviews

The importance of interview skills and attitude
The selection, training, and management of people who regularly conduct face-to-face interviews and discussions as a central part of their work is often inadequately thought about and resourced. The quality of the information generated through interviews is dependent on the relationship that interviewers manage to develop with the respondents, and on the following attitudes, behaviour, and skill:

- sensitivity to the respondents' mood, body language, and time constraints, and to the different cultural norms that may shape these;

- understanding that questions can be asked (and answered) in diverse ways;

- ability to really listen to answers, and to probe and cross-check in a thorough but sensitive manner;

- taking notes in a discrete, non-threatening way which does not interrupt the flow of conversation;

- using humour and personal experience to bring up sensitive issues or to challenge a response.

These skills are even more important for those conducting semi-structured interviews, where the interviewer must show a lot of initiative, compared to enumerators in large-scale surveys, who have less scope to ask spontaneous questions. Rather than selecting impact assessment interviewers only according to their technical competence or sectoral expertise, candidates' inter-personal skills should be given equal weight, perhaps by conducting 'mock' interviews. Clearly, the respondents' gender, ethnic identity, and language also plays an important part in determining the sex and background of the interviewers — although there are advantages and disadvantages to involving 'insiders' and 'outsiders' in impact assessment processes (see Chapter 3 on 'Who should be involved ?').

As noted above in the case of enumerators, skimping on training and briefing can be a false economy, given that the quality of data will be, in large part, determined by the interviewers' skills and behaviours. Those conducting semi-structured interviews within impact assessment processes may require training in how to ask questions that help determine what has changed over time; how significant or valued different changes might be; and why and how such change has occurred. This may need to be combined with basic interview training regarding behaviour, body language, dress, and basic listening skills; when to use open and closed questions; how to probe and cross-check; and how to record and evaluate the interview.[3]

Last, interviewers must be given time and space to reflect on their experience and to share it with other colleagues. Managers should help them make this space and encourage such exchange.

Overcoming assumption and bias

Everybody holds certain assumptions and biases depending on their own experiences, upbringing, and training. Interviewers are no exception, and have to try deliberately to minimise the weight of their biases. Often, these have a clear gender dimension; for example, male interviewers can be unaware that they are only communicating with other men. It should also be borne in mind that interviewees make (sometimes false) assumptions about their own communities. In the Ghana case study, discussions with the interviewers led to the following conclusions and precautions.

- Interviewers can assume that respondents are able to estimate farm size, rainfall, yield, income and expenditure, and so on. However, this data should be cross-checked through observation, visits to fields, and with other information collected during the interview. For example, since farm size, yield, consumption, and income are all related, are the responses to these questions consistent? Is the estimate of land farmed, sacks produced, amount of production sold, amount of food bought consistent with the number of months during which food is available and the number of meals eaten daily?

- Interviewers should use their own knowledge and findings about a community to understand responses better, not to confirm assumptions and prejudices. For example, some development workers assume that spending money on funerals or other social activities is wasteful. They might therefore seek to discover what proportion of household expenditure is spent on this perceived luxury and make judgements about the household's willingness to invest in 'productive' activities. In fact, discussions with communities that probe this issue further often reveal how important such expenditure is, not only in conforming to social norms and customs, but also as an investment in community and social relations. These relations help to create the bonds and trust or 'social capital' that hold families and communities together and allow them to make claims upon each other.

- In writing up interviews, interviewers should be as faithful as possible to the answers given and aim to quote an interviewee's exact words in order to minimise the degree of misinterpretation. If interviewers add their own analysis and interpretation, this should be made clear.

- If there is more than one interviewer, it may be worthwhile to conduct a number of interviews together at the beginning of the process in order to harmonise the content and style of the interviews and to offer critical feedback to each other.

Probing and cross-checking

One difficulty in assessing impact is that you quickly notice that 'facts' are not necessarily reliable. People exaggerate (or lie). Even sincere people make mistakes, or cannot remember things accurately. So you have to ask every question to different people, to judge what the truth is even about simple figures. It is worth the effort. Also, your relationship improves with people if they find you are happier to know the truth [rather than being] told something they think you want to hear. (Pakistan case study)

Individual interviews often allow confidential and sensitive information to emerge, yet also increase the possibility of interviewees exaggerating, lying, or using the interview for their own purposes. This does not mean that individual interviews should be trusted less than other kinds of interview, which also have disadvantages (see below), but as discussed in Chapter 3, the interviewer needs to be aware of bias, and ask who might be exaggerating or lying, and why. This can provide important clues to the interviewees' interests and relations with other groups or individuals, and the project being assessed. Respondents may not want to seem impolite by saying that they do not know the answer to a question, or they may see the interview as an opportunity to negotiate with those doing the survey, for example to provide more or different types of support.

In the Ghana study, contradictions seemed to emerge regarding the responses of individual men and women about women's involvement in farming activity. Probing further with the respondents, and with other stakeholders, revealed that these differences could be explained in a number of ways. In one region, among one ethnic group, the gender division of labour was indeed such that women did not farm their own plots. In others they did, but men did not consider it worth mentioning because they either considered it as 'gardening' or as such a small-scale activity that it did not warrant a mention in comparison to men's 'family farming'. For women on the other hand, this activity was a vital source of independent income, and it therefore figured very highly in their accounts of income.

Probing and cross-checking inconsistencies or exceptions is critical. If something does not fit with other findings, it usually needs to be explored further, rather than ignored.

Being opportunistic and curious

Both the Matson study and the Ghana study demonstrate the importance of seizing unexpected opportunities to chat with people whose views might otherwise be missed. Interviewers' preparedness to 'hang about' in informal settings, such as drinking sorghum beer, proved very beneficial. The CYSD study provides another example: during an informal conversation at a tea stall the researcher came across a man from a certain village who was highly critical of the project being assessed and of the project staff. The researcher inquired further, and his informant offered to respond in more detail if the researcher met him at home. There, he explained how a member of another local NGO had persuaded some villagers that his agency could do more for them than CYSD. This had led to a split among the villagers and resulted in CYSD withdrawing from the area. However, this other NGO had done nothing for the village, causing great resentment. This information led CYSD to discuss this issue with the other NGO and local leaders, and helped them understand the background to what had looked like general political interference. This sort of information was the result of a deliberate strategy of hanging around and observing (see section on 'Exploring Relationships').

Summary 4.2: Key lessons about individual interview

- Training and managing interviewers. The selection of interviewers and researchers needs to involve not only assessing technical knowledge but also candidates' behaviour, attitudes and inter-personal skills. Within impact assessment processes, special training in interview methods and recording findings may be required

- Overcoming assumption and bias. Interviewers should assume that respondents can answer certain questions and then cross-check the answers, rather than assuming ignorance. They should use their knowledge about a community to understand responses better, not to confirm assumptions and prejudices.
- Probing and cross-checking. If a piece of information contradicts other findings it should be explored further.
- Being opportunistic and curious. Interviewers should be prepared to 'hang about' in order to seize unexpected opportunities to chat with people whose views might otherwise be missed.

Group discussions, workshops, and interviews

Group processes are a commonly used method at all stages of impact assessment. Bringing people together is often a cost-effective way of eliciting several people's views at the same time, which can also generate new insights and provide a forum for questioning and cross-checking individual opinions. However, care must be taken to ensure that the views of more powerful individuals do not dominate. This section explores some of the most widely used group exercises carried out in the case studies: village meetings and community workshops; focus-group discussions; and multiple stakeholder workshops.

Village meetings and community workshops

Village meetings and community workshops were undertaken for different purposes in a number of the case studies. In some they were used early in the process to introduce the work, and to gather general information about the community, its socio-economic environment, and the changes that had occurred over time. In others, it was used after individual interviews and surveys had been completed, to cross-check and feedback information and to explore impacts on the community.

The Ghana study, for example, undertook a series of community discussions in three villages, using a number of PRA exercises over a two- or three-day period. The information gathered was used to establish a village profile and to develop a sampling frame for selecting individuals for interviews. In this case researchers believed that community discussions were required to understand likely divisions within the community, as much as to gather general information. Understanding these divisions — by wealth, gender, age and ethnic/ clan identity — clarified whose opinions the follow-up work needed to capture in order to get a rounded view of perceptions of change in these communities. During the course of the community discussions, the facilitator often divided participants into male and female groups in order to explore particular issues and to capture likely gender differences from the outset. This is obviously easier to do than for other, less visible differences such as wealth or clan membership.

These follow-up interviews with individuals were also used to cross-check findings from community discussions and to explore key differences within households (for example, between men and women, but also related to age and marital status). This helped researchers better to distinguish which kinds of information genuinely seemed to represent a consensus about the community, and which were more contested

The CORDES study involved a series of community exercises which involved almost all the village residents. They also brought together communities to discuss their relative difference. This was interspersed with more focused discussions with specific interest groups within the villages.

In the ENDA study a concern was raised that although interviews and questionnaire surveys identified impact at the household level, they did not articulate it at the community level. The team had discovered, for example, that those people directly involved in a seeds project could clearly articulate its impact. However, members of the community who received seeds from other farmers did not attribute changes in their life to the project, although the seeds had originally been brought into the community by the project. ENDA therefore thought that community workshops could be a forum for gathering data on the broader changes that had taken place in the community, and as a means to feedback findings to the community as a whole.

The experiences in the case studies point to a number of practical lessons in carrying out community research.

Preliminary site visits: These can be a vital part of preparing a community meeting.

The preliminary site visit served two main purposes. It allowed the impact assessment team to conduct interviews with the old local field staff. The visit was also used to become familiar with the community leadership. This bonding was an important preparatory step for the participatory work that was to be conducted during the next phase of the [impact assessment] project ... The impact assessment team were also able to note the logistics of working in the areas and have an appreciation of the conditions under which the project was undertaken. Having visited the area the team felt more confident that they could adequately discuss the project with former staff and have new insight into the project. (ENDA case study)

In addition a visit like this can ensure that future meetings are conducted at times that are convenient for the majority of community members, women in particular.

Key informants and gate-keepers: These individuals provide an introduction to and entry point into communities. Know-who, rather than know-how, is particularly important if a project has ended some time ago, or if the researchers are new to a community. In ENDA's case, former staff were the key informants.

[I]t was possible to get an entry point into the community [through them, which] is an important part of getting to know the community in Zimbabwe— people are more at ease if you know people they know. People are also more willing to talk to you if they know that you have already had a similar discussion with people they know. (ENDA case study)

Useful information on community history: In nearly all cases where this was explored, community meetings provided this, particularly on events of special significance (see section on time-lines below). Community history offers important information on the role of external actors and how this was perceived, as well as on significant collective experiences.

Exclusion of women, children, and other groups: Particular groups can be excluded either because they are absent from the meeting, or because they are present but do not participate. Both the Ghana and CYSD studies report that village elders, and sometimes active male youths, tended to dominate general meetings. Researchers can divide the group into different categories, or ask groups that did not participate to review and modify the work of the larger group, but this is not always possible or desirable. How exclusion is dealt with to a great extent depends on the degree of inequality between groups and how they cope with differences of opinion and conflict. This will vary enormously from place to place. However, as Table 4.10 illustrates, this is an important issue to bear in mind when considering the appropriateness of community discussions or workshops.

Focus-group discussions

One way to avoid some of the problems outlined above, and to explore specific issues in depth, is to hold a focus-group discussion. Focus groups are small (about six to 12 people) and either made up of existing groupings of people with similar interests or identity (for example, those receiving credit from Cordes; women involved in the Wajir credit scheme; or Oxfam-supported rose growers in Pakistan) or specifically chosen to represent a variety of opinions and backgrounds. Although some of the same types of problems as in community discussions may occur — such as dominant individuals dominating the discussion, the risk of this happening is reduced if the group shares a similar background and interests. A moderator or facilitator normally helps to keep the discussion on course, to clarify areas of agreement and disagreement, and to ensure relatively equal participation from all.

Table 4.10: Advantages and disadvantages of group discussions, particularly at the community level

Advantages	Disadvantages
• brings together a sum of knowledge greater than any individual insight, generating new insights and mutual learning	• can allow dominant voices to be further legitimised and the voices of the less powerful to be ignored or undermined
• opportunity for group or peer checking and verification	• can make the marginal and less powerful seem to consent through silence or presence
• can raise problems not hitherto recognised as common, and lead to discussion of quite sensitive issues	• can drive sensitive issues underground
• can lead to consensus-building and conflict resolution as differences are explored and discussed	• may produce unprioritised 'shopping lists' • may expose, but not deal with, conflicts or further polarise people
• can create synergy and new ideas through debate and dialogue	• may simply recycle entrenched views
• can be fun	• can be boring and frustrating • methods can dominate over content
• can cost less than individual interviews	• may be seen as a necessary 'ritual' that must be gone through in order to get aid or support
• may take less time than undertaking individual interviews and then cross-checking results	• may waste people's time even if it saves that of the interviewer or facilitator

The BRAC case study used focus-group discussions (with six to ten key informants) to explore impacts on women's empowerment, both for individual women and their family. The group discussed women's involvement in income-generating activities, their ownership and control over assets, perceptions of their own well-being, their economic dependence on their husbands, and their mobility.[4] The findings were used, where possible, to complement and cross-check quantitative data from the household survey.

The CYSD study also made extensive use of focus-group discussions, recognising that village meetings were unsuitable for providing personal information (say, on family-planning methods or intra-household relations) or insights into sensitive issues (village conflicts, vested interests, politics, caste or class relationships, and so on). Focus-group discussions with members of a women's self-help group were felt to be one of the most efficient method in understanding their views on changes in women's empowerment.

For example, one discussion involving 20 women from two villages (Jamena-Munda Sahi and Konkali) explored differences in daily work patterns, changes in work distribution between males and females, and overall differences between the females of 1987 and today's females (see Table 4.11). The participants were asked to identify the reasons for these changes. Participants found this easier than answering questions such as 'what difference has the project made to your lives?'. The results can be considered a mix of project outcomes and impact, as well as changes brought by wider social change in India. However, it does provide a basis for starting to understand what change is the women in question consider significant, as well as to what they attribute that change.

Table 4.11: Perceptions of changing roles of women in Jamena-Munda Sahi and Konkali, India, generated by focus-group discussion

The females of 1988	The females of today
• no compromise on the duties assigned to females	• take more care in children's education and health, are keen to immunise their children, and attend pre-natal check ups
• not much care given to pregnant ladies and children	
• less freedom to express their views in public in comparison to today's females	• have more daily labour available for them
	• more concerned with having a clean environment and good health
• had one pair of sari as their only dress	
• not allowed to go out alone at night	• more concerned about safe drinking water
• suspicious and afraid about outsiders	• now wear sari and blouse
• not enough food for women after serving other family members	• males are now mingling with females in common places

Table 4.11: Perceptions of changing roles of women in Jamena-Munda Sahi and Konkali, India, generated by focus-group discussion (continued)

The females of 1988	The females of 1988
• female education not considered important	• are now engaged in productive ventures like paddy processing and vegetable cultivation
• more dowry received by the female in comparison to the present dowry	• now cultivate kitchen garden and therefore eat nutritious vegetables
• males took decisions in family planning, expenditure, and marriage of daughters	• increasing importance of female education
• all females were having arranged marriage in the traditional way	• are saving money for the marriage of their children (the amount of male dowry has come down and marriage expenses have gone up)
• had faith in traditional witches and quacks	
• were afraid of doctors, injections, and medicines	• more cases of love marriages are observed among today's tribal females
• used to practice traditional family-planning methods with herbal medicines	• are adopting modern family-planning methods
• did not have freedom to decide the number of children	• have more freedom and participate in community work
	• now have unity among themselves after the formation of self-help group (SHG), and the freedom and acceptance of the community to sit together in village meetings and express their views
	• in some cases males are coming forward to join hand with females in household duties
	• increasing need among the SHG members for liaising their SHG with group ventures

These examples, and other experiences in the case studies, reveal some further interesting points related to focus groups.

Focus-group discussions can stimulate analysis which promotes critical reflection on past changes and generates ideas for the future. In the discussion above, women expressed the view that males still consider females subordinate and that some men in the village were trying to disturb the work of the self-help group, precisely 'because it has put a check on the subordinate position of females in decision-making and freedom of expression'. The women then discussed ways of dealing with this. Although some of the women went away 'unhappy because the meeting was not able find a solution for checking male dominance in their society', this example illustrates the potential of focus groups to produce new insights and ideas.

Focus groups do not have to be confined to community groups. Project staff, donors, other NGOs or interested parties can constitute a focus group to explore impact from their perspective. In the CYSD study, for example, a focus-group interview of project staff investigated factors that, according to them, had reduced the impact of their work. This revealed that frequent changes of project staff had severely undermined continuity, disrupted innovative schemes, and reduced staff morale.

Focus groups can help reconstruct baselines and project histories. In the ENDA and CORDES studies, focus-group discussions were found to be a very effective way of discovering what had been done in the community during project implementation. Members of the group could recall a number of events and workshops, and the names of people who worked on the project. In most cases people could recall when the first meetings were held and who introduced the project to their area. In addition, as in the CORDES study, they were often able to identify the gap between what had been planned in terms of impact, and what actually occurred.

Focus groups can help to determine and assess progress against indicators. Focus-group discussions can occur at any stage of an impact assessment process. The CYSD study used them to determine indicators for specific activities, and found them effective.

[P]articipants expressed that this [was] the first time that they [were] critically analysing ... their own development in a group. They also were convinced about some changes and impact in their life style which they had not realised before. (CYSD study)

The Pakistan study also used focus groups to explore impacts and to rank them in order of priority (see section on ranking below). They made particular efforts to ask people about negative and positive impacts, and to explore what the discussion of past impacts suggested for indicators for the future.

Focus groups can help in dealing with sensitive topics. Along with other qualitative methods such as individual in-depth interviews, focus groups have proven useful tools in addressing culturally and politically sensitive topics that people may consider threatening, such as reproductive and sexual health (Jaswal and Harpham 1997).

Care must be taken about the length of focus-group discussions and the range of topics covered. Some of the studies talk of discussions lasting up to four hours and still not completing certain tasks. Experience suggests that even in the most stimulating circumstances, attention starts to wane and people get tired after about 90 minutes. If discussions are to last more than 90 minutes, make sure that people know this before the start, and consider breaking up the session to have drink or food. Do not overload the discussions; it is better to complete a few questions in depth than to rush through many superficially, leaving participants dissatisfied with the outcome.

Table 4.12 summarises some of the main advantages and disadvantages of focus-group discussions.

Table 4.12: Advantages and disadvantages of focus-group discussions

Advantages	Disadvantages
• relatively efficient: more people's views can be obtained than in one-on-one interviews	• only a limited number of key questions can be asked
• provides quality control through people's interaction	• needs very good group-facilitation skills
• allow people's views to develop in exchanges with others	• requires good note-taking
• allows an assessment of agreement or disagreement on a given issue	• may reinforce existing power relations within the group or be dominated by a small number of individuals
• can occur at any point in impact assessment process	
• can be used with several stakeholders	
• did not have freedom to decide the number of children	

Multiple stakeholder workshops and meetings

A number of studies brought together several groups to reflect on the impact assessment work and exchange opinions. In most cases this was done towards the end of the assessment in order to encourage feedback, to cross-check results with a wider group, to communicate the results to individuals or groups who had not been involved up to that point, and to debate what implications the results had for the future.

In the course of the Ikafe review process in Uganda — described in more detail in the next chapter — two multiple stakeholder meetings were held, each involving more than 80 participants. The first was held at the end of the initial field work and the second four months later, following further field research. It was held in order to hear how key policy-makers reacted to initial findings and to involve groups which had previously been prevented by insecurity in the area from participating. These meetings were felt to be necessary because of the complexity of the programme and the diverse range of actors in the situation, listed in the following.

- The refugee population which had immediate practical needs as well as long-term concerns about their uncertain situation;

- The host population which, although willing to provide shelter for their 'brothers' from Sudan, wished to benefit from the infrastructure being installed for the refugees as well as preserving their own security, cultural identity, and in the longer term, their land;

- a range of elements of the Ugandan Government such as civil servants and ministry officials, teachers, local councils, and the army (whose primary interest is national security and law and order in this volatile and tense region);

- the United Nations specialised agencies which have specific mandates regarding care of refugees and food distribution;

- NGOs which, although they have more flexible mandates, in this case were supporting specific parts of the programme in the areas of health-care, education provision, water and sanitation, community and refugee organisation, agro-forestry, and land allocation. These included Oxfam's local, refugee, and international staff, local and refugee staff from Action Africa in Need, and the Jesuit Refugee Service's local and international staff.

The findings of this case study had emphasised that the problems raised by different groups were all connected and therefore needed coherent solutions, which particularly required better co-ordination between different actors. The review process had built up this analysis over time, and had, to some extent, strengthened the capacity of both the refugee and host communities to articulate their concerns to government and aid agencies. This moment of response by policy-makers and senior agency representatives allowed some explanation as to why certain problems and misunderstandings had arisen. Refugees and the host population understood that problems which they had blamed on individual agencies (particularly NGOs) were often due to wider problems that the NGOs could not solve on their own, and gained some understanding of what might be done to solve some of the problems raised.

In the Matson and Wajir studies, workshops were also hosted for a range of stakeholders towards the end of the impact assessment process. Both proved very useful in raising important issues, particularly about how various agencies need to work together to achieve impact.

As with focus groups, this process requires very experienced facilitators with experience of dealing with potential conflict. The whole purpose of multi-stakeholder workshops is to bring to the surface differences of opinions as well as agreement. Less dominant groups may need to prepare carefully in order to put forward a clear and consistent point of view, perhaps through a chosen representative.

However, in situations where there is a degree of tension or suspicion between groups, a meeting of this type would be counter-productive and could worsen relations. A great deal of thought should go into the possible implications of multiple stakeholder meetings for the future relationships between the groups concerned. If there is strong doubt about the likely outcomes, and if adequate facilitation and conflict resolution skills are unavailable, it may be better to avoid this type of meeting.

Summary 4.3: Key lessons learned about group discussions, workshops, and interviews

- Be aware of divisions and power relations within the group which may require breaking up the group into smaller groups or complementing group work with discussions with individuals. If you think that group work is liable to reinforce existing power relations it may be better to avoid it.

- Be aware of those unlikely to participate in group meetings and seek out their views. Carefully consider the timing and location of meetings so that it is possible for key groups and particularly women to attend.

- Under the right conditions group work can encourage new insights, mutual learning, foster solidarity, and build consensus. For impact assessment teams, it can be particularly useful for reconstructing project histories and the context in which projects evolved, as well as for cross-checking findings generated by other methods.

- Group work of this sort requires sophisticated facilitation and conflict-resolution skills.

Direct observation

Although it is likely that direct observation played a part in all studies, only some of them specifically refer to observation as a method of impact assessment and to the results obtained in this way. In only one study (Matson) was direct observation the primary method of assessment.

We saw earlier the Matson study's emphasis on talking to people in a variety of ways and settings. In the following, Stan Thekaekara's describes three spheres of activity in his participation/ observation methodology.

Talking to people: attending various meetings provided the opportunity for conversations with 'officials'— which included city and county councillors, the local MP, social service managers, housing officers and the like.

Being a part of whatever was happening on the project: This involved spending time at the different sites, occasionally manning a reception desk, answering the telephone (a great way to get an inkling of the kind of relationship between the project and the residents— it was obvious that most of the residents were not only on a first-name basis with the staff but invariably were very clear about who exactly they needed to speak to in order to sort out a problem).

Sitting in on whatever meetings were taking place: There were different kinds of meetings that I attended. Meetings of the Board and sub-committees of the Board; review meetings of staff; meetings of city and county council bodies; meetings of Tenant's Associations and the Tenant's Federation; meetings with other Neighbourhood Projects, meetings of the Matson Forum, and meetings of the Neighbourhood Project Network. Some activities were followed through by attending all meetings relating to it that took place during the two months— for example a new initiative of the Project to try and provide foster carers from Matson. (Matson case study)

Building trust and rapport

A distinction is usually made between participant observation, where the observer shares in at least some of the activities or discussions that are being assessed, and assessments where the observer deliberately does not become involved in the situation under assessment. In reality the distinction between participant and onlooker is often somewhat blurred, because the onlooker's mere presence can influence the proceedings. The onlooker can therefore inadvertently 'participate' in changing the nature of what is being observed, and conversely, there may be times when the participant observer will be less involved in ongoing activities. In most of the studies there were occasions when participant observation was adopted, such as joining in informal discussions as they arose, and others where onlooking was more emphasised.

In either case the studies indicate the importance of observers being present, so that people get used to them and build up a degree of trust and rapport, but also the importance of trust and rapport as a pre-requisite for making observation a useful tool for impact assessment. In this sense observation, and particularly participant observation, is a means to build trust, as well as being dependent upon its creation.

The other element stressed in the case studies is how observation and engagement offer researchers a better understanding of the context in which a given project or programme is undertaken. For example, in the ENDA study

[d]iscussions were held with community groups wherever the team encountered the people. These groups of villagers were found at boreholes, gardens, shopping centres or on the street. The team had no influence on the composition of the groups. Meeting these groups had the immediate benefit of allowing the team to become familiar with the communities, an essential element for the participatory workshops that were to be held later on.

Cross-checking

Observation can be a useful way of cross-checking information. In the CYSD study, information on agricultural practices which the project had promoted suggested that some farmers were ceasing to use these practices, despite early involvement in the project. Direct observation of farmers' practices and cropping patterns confirmed this, which in turn led to informal conversations with farmers to discover why this was the case. This helped to identify different types of farmer and the particular constraints they face in adopting new agricultural practices, as well as their attitude to the support provided by the project.

Exploring relationships

Observation is a particularly effective tool in assessing the quality of relationships between individuals or groups. Both the Matson and the NK/GSS studies specifically used observation methods to explore the relationships between community organisations and their members, between the community and other actors (NGOs, government authorities, or donors), and between community leaders and other members. Researchers participated in or observed meetings between these groups and recorded the following:

- the degree and quality of participation of individuals and groups, including who was not participating or not even invited;

- the way in which different parties treated each other, and their ideas;

- the way in which conflict or disagreement between groups was handled;

- the degree of independent decision-making in various groups;

- the body-language of the participants and the physical setup of the meeting;

- the informal interactions before, during, and after meetings and during breaks.

Such techniques of observation are also particularly useful for observing relations within the household, and between different parts of a community, for example in relation to patronage, dependency, or ethnicity.

Gaining new insights

Observation can help to gain new insights or to discover things that people may not wish to reveal in interviews, or may be not asked about in surveys. For example, some of the village meetings organised in the CYSD study

had to be stopped ... due to interference by drunkards. These people had consumed liquor (made by mixing poisonous chemicals) which is prepared in the village itself. Later through informal conversation with some females it was learned that about 30 per cent of the males in this village spend 15 to 20 rupees daily on consuming liquor.

Through spending time with villagers, the observers got to know about a particular issue which they then followed up. Although the purchase of alcohol was likely to have an effect not only on family income but also on levels of domestic violence, the issue had not been raised as a possible obstacle to improved well-being or women's empowerment in formal meetings and interviews.

Lessons learned about direct observation

Like all other methods there are advantages and disadvantages to observation as research tool, some of which are summarised in Table 4.13. What is perhaps different is that observation is normally a part of all other methods and tools. Good interviewers, for example, will carefully observe the non-verbal signals that a respondent may give and adapt their questions in light of this; they will observe the environment in which an interview is conducted to see if there are signs that confirm or contradict what the interviewee is saying. For instance, in the Ghana study respondents stated that food security this year was much worse than last year. This was brought home to the interviewers when they observed how much more time than normal small boys in the village were spending hunting bats, small birds and rodents — a sign that the season was indeed very poor.

Table 4.13: Advantages and disadvantages of direct observation

Advantages	Disadvantages
• can help to build trust and rapport between observer and group	• dependent on level of trust between observer and observed
• enables an understanding of a programme's or project's context	• resource-intensive and therefore limited in terms of sample size
• allows observer to be open and discover things no one else has paid attention to	• observer can affect results
• allows observer to see things which are so obvious to people that they may not report them to others	• dependent not only on observation skills but also on inter-personal and communication skills of observer
• can enable observer to learn things that participants are unwilling to share in interviews	• open to bias and observer's selective perception
• enables cross-checking of perceptions and opinions voiced in interviews or surveys	• can be limited to external behaviours if the onlooker approach is adopted and is not used in conjunction with other methods

For the purposes of impact assessment, observation will particularly mean keeping one's eyes open to changes that are occurring within communities and between groups of people. It will also mean exploring the unexpected or unusual, and the unsaid. An example from the Matson case study gives a flavour of this:

In a supposedly high-crime area I was surprised to find that the Project's One Stop Shop on Matson Avenue does not pull down heavy steel shutters at night. This, in spite of valuable computers and other things within. Instead a fragile wall of glass forms the shop front, completely covered with decorations in the form of job advertisements, painstakingly stuck on every day by John Boe and his colleagues Fe Clarke and Ciaran Murphy. When I asked them why they ran such a risk their reply was: 'All the kids hang out here at night — they hardly come by during the day. If we want them to see the jobs, then night it is.' What they did not say and bears thinking about is how people react to this kind of concern coupled with trust.

Because of his knowledge of the context (high crime rate) the researcher spotted something that did not fit with what might have been expected. In observing this, and then probing further, he gained valuable insights into the relationship between the project staff and youth in the area and started to understand some of the many reasons why unemployment and crime on the patch were declining.

Summary 4.4: Lessons learned about direct observation

- Direct observation although often critical for building rapport and trust, for cross-checking results, for generating new insights, and for exploring the impact of processes on relationships between people and between groups, is often not adequately thought about or referred to as a method of assessing impact.

- Like interviewing, the importance of observation demands adequate training and preparation. Any training or preparation needs to include discussion and advice on what and who to observe; how to observe — as participant or onlooker, overtly or covertly; when to observe — at particular events, times of the day, or seasons; and how to record and communicate observations made — in notes, on tape, on video.

- Direct observation can be resource-intensive, can affect results, and is open to bias. It needs to be used in conjunction with other tools.

Above, some of the main lessons about direct observation as a tool for impact assessment are summarised.

RRA and PRA/PLA tools

As noted in Chapter 2, participatory tools and methods have been part of most agencies' impact assessment approaches for several years. They were used extensively in the case studies, during group and individual interviews, in discussions and workshops. Most teams used the more extractive RRA tools (rapid rural appraisal) rather than the more participatory PRA or PLA (participatory rural appraisal/ participatory learning and action) tools. This section explores some of the specific tools used. It should be remembered that semi-structured interviewing usually forms a critical component of participatory research and readers are referred to the section above.

Many of the problems associated with individual and group interviews, described in earlier sections, are relevant here. The tools and methods presented below should always form part of a discussion or interview, and are therefore subject to the same concerns relating to the possible exclusion of some groups or to sanctioning the views of dominant groups. This is particularly the case in group exercises that provide a public forum which some may wish to exploit for their own ends.

Time lines and historical profiles

A time line, or historical profile, used during an impact assessment can help to capture broad changes in an individual's or a community's life. It can also stimulate discussions on how those changes occurred and what effects they had on people's lives. This is normally done by asking people to recall important events in the past and then to reconstruct history by adding other events and processes of change. This can be done using stones or symbols to represent specific events or using pen and paper. For example, the ENDA study concluded that

[t]he communities readily remembered droughts, and they could articulate the year that the drought occurred. Events could therefore be related to these periods. People in Zimbabwe also remember that independence was in 1980 and [this] is used as a standard reference point.

An example of the historical profile and contextual analysis produced at a workshop in Chivi is presented in Table 4.14. It indicates that 'the communities were able to distinguish clearly between the activities of the different NGOs and also indicate the years in which these NGOs were most active'.

Time lines have several uses during impact assessment. First, they allow a project to be situated in a longer historical time-frame. They can indicate the role and significance of other actors (NGOs, civil servants) and factors such as rainfall or important political events. Third they can give an indication of positive and negative impacts and how these have changed over time. For the purposes of impact assessment, these issues are particularly important as they can help with a lack of baseline data and the problem of attribution (as discussed in Chapter 3). In addition they can allow any given project to compare how its impact is perceived in relation to others, and how its activities combined with those of others to achieve certain impacts.

Time lines are usually, but not always, a good way of getting to know a group or community in a relatively unthreatening way, indicating an interest on the part of the researcher in the community's own history. This may not be the case where mixed groups hotly contest historical events and how they are interpreted. In zones of recent conflict, and in communities where there is liable to be more than one interpretation of history, care should be taken in resurfacing potentially conflicting views. In such cases it may be preferable to undertake this exercise with particular sub-groups and to then compare results.

Table 4.14: Historical profile and contextual analysis for Madamombe (Chivi North)

Year	Event	Change	Impact (change in lifestyle)
1984	Danida assistance	Built a dam	Gardens sprang up and more water for cattle
	Madamombe clinic built	Health-care services easily available/ accessible	Better health for the community
	Secondary school built	More education for the people	Increase in knowledge base
1985	Tapped water available	Clean water	Decrease in the incidence of disease
	Toilets available	Better health	Conservation awareness increased
1987	Introduction of ENDA	Lessons on how to grow indigenous trees	Fewer malnutrition cases reported
	Drought	Yellow maize introduced by DANIDA Food for Work	Less privileged were cared for

Table 4.14: Historical profile and contextual analysis for Madamombe (Chivi North) (continued)

Year	Event	Change	Impact (change in lifestyle)
1989	Surveyors pegged out the road		
	Donors came to the community	People given items of clothing	Less privileged were cared for
1990	Zvishavane water project	Dams, wells, and fish ponds built	Clean water easily accessible
1991	Drought	Cattle, crops, and trees died	Shortage of drought power, money and water; increased diseases and soil erosion
	Drought relief	Food crisis eased	No people died
1992	AIDS epidemic	Increase in people dying and number of orphans	People are now more morally conscious
1993	Tarred road built	Increase in road traffic	Transport load reduced
1995	Government grain scheme		Sustenance for community
1996	Floods, ground frost	Crops destroyed, trees damaged	Food shortage; fewer trees
	Post office and suggestion box	Banking available	Life made easier
	Public call box	Means of arresting thieves, easy communication	
	Hospital expansion	Better health-care facilities	

Ranking

There are many ways of ranking or ordering data. In the case studies, some of the most commonly used techniques, or the most interesting for the purposes of impact assessment, were wealth ranking, problem ranking, impact ranking and performance ranking.

Wealth or well-being ranking

Ranking by wealth or well-being seeks to discover the criteria by which individuals or groups describe a given individual or household as more or less wealthy, or well-off, than another individual or household. It aims to gain a picture of who is better-off, or worse-off in a given group, and why. This is usually done by gathering the names of the individuals or households to be ranked on separate cards and then asking individuals or groups to place each card in piles with others of similar well-being. Questions are asked during, or at the end of, the process to try and determine more precisely the common characteristics of the various piles that emerge. The example from the Ghana case study in Table 4.15 indicates the kind of analysis that can emerge from this exercise.

The results of wealth ranking can be used in several ways for impact assessment purposes. It can allow a direct assessment of the degree to which different strata of a community are involved in a given project and thus what likely impact may have occurred. In the Ghana study, this revealed that particular groups and families seemed to be involved in all activities and others, usually the less well-off, were not. It therefore also provided a sampling frame from which to select individuals for interview who represented different levels of well-being in the communities concerned.

Second, by understanding the key criteria that people use to determine well-being, researchers can gain insights into the problems faced by people with different levels of well-being. It can point to a project's negative effects; for example, the promotion of a particular agricultural activity which demands high labour input may bypass families which see lack of labour capacity or a large number of dependants as a critical reason for their poverty.

Third, asking what changes have occurred in the situation of individuals or households over the past few years (which can be done by asking people to re-sort the piles to the situation ten years ago), can point out changing patterns of well-being and the reasons for increasing well-being or impoverishment. In the Ghana study it became clear that even for 'richer' households a sudden illness or theft of cattle could have a dramatic impact on levels of well-being.

Table 4.15: Well-being ranking in Navio, Upper East region of Ghana

Ranking	Better-off				Worse-off
Criteria	A	B	C	D	E
Income?	Satisfactory (salary)	Yes Satisfactory (farm income)	Insignificant	No	No
Food availability	All year round, plus surplus for sale	All year round, no surplus	Available for a greater part of the year, about eight months	High proportion of dependants Food deficit	
Land	Larger plots, fertile land		Smaller plots, less fertile		Not fertile
Own fruit trees?	Yes	Yes	No	No	No
Own livestock?	More cattle, sheep, and goats	Fewer cattle, sheep, and goats	Sheep, goats and poultry	Goats and poultry	Poultry
Number of wives	More than one		One	One	One
Number of households in category	11	8	8	13	19

Dated April 1997

Fourth, wealth ranking can provide an important baseline for the future and offer a basis for prioritising areas of desired future change. Given that the lack of baselines was a particular problem for some of the case studies, well-being ranking provided some of them with much need information. Last, the mechanics of wealth ranking, in particular pile-sorting, can be used for many purposes such as comparing different villages, groups, or types of organisation. In Ghana, this technique was used to distinguish between the different members of the Northern Ghana Development Network. In other studies, such as the Action Aid Impact Assessment[5] work in Vietnam, wealth ranking has been used with government officials. However, the studies faced a number of difficulties with this method.

Getting the initial list of individuals or households. It can sometimes be difficult to gather an up-to-date list of individuals or households in a community. Even where such lists exist from censuses or local government offices, they may be inaccurate and are rarely up-to-date. In the Ghana study, where such lists did not exist, social maps[6] were drawn from which lists were then developed. However, in some cases further research revealed that some households had been deliberately excluded by those drawing the map because they were not considered part of the community. Once again, cross-checking and keen observation can help to minimise such problems. Experience from other parts of Africa[7] suggests that involving women, who may be better informed about the community, is critical, as is being aware that certain categories of people often tend to get 'forgotten': older people, disabled people, and the families of women who are second or third wives in polygamous households.

Unwillingness of people to categorise or label neighbours and friends. In some, but not all, cases people were unwilling to classify their neighbours by wealth or well-being. In some studies (CYSD) the issue was therefore depersonalised, so groups were asked to describe the characteristics for example of a 'wealthy man'. This is consistent with other experiences of participatory impact assessment, such as the evaluation of Calcutta Slum Improvement Project[8], which asked respondents to think of the slum population according to categories of well-being and then to assess the approximate income range for each category as well as the proportion of the population that fell into each.

Problems of defining households and associated gender relations. The household has usually been the main unit of analysis in wealth ranking, which creates several problems. Definitions of what constitutes a household vary between places and groups. Moerover, the household is not a static entity: its membership may change suddenly or over time; at times people may include relatives who have migrated or children who are being temporarily looked after, at other times they may not. But perhaps the most problematic aspect is that ranking households tells us little or nothing about well-being within the household. Women often prioritise different aspects of well-being than men and, if care is not taken, their views may easily be ignored or subordinated to those of males. The result can be a wealth ranking of households which reflects only men's criteria of well-being, and which conceals differences in well-being within those households. Getting men and women to rank households separately is one way of overcoming the first problem and can reveal important differences and similarities — this may be preferable to having one mixed group doing the ranking, which was the case in most of the case studies.

In order to understand differences in well-being within the household, other tools and methods such as individual or focus-group discussions are probably more appropriate. Although one of the studies planned to undertake well-being ranking of some individuals within households, this proved to be extremely difficult, because the problems getting an initial list of individuals were even greater than getting one of households, and people were even less willing to label individuals' well-being than that of households.

Problem or preference ranking

Problem or preference ranking is simply a means of understanding people's priorities. This technique usually involves asking people to list their problems or preferences for change, which are then ordered in some way. This can be done by simply ranking them from most important to least important. A more sophisticated method is to weight problems by assigning them a score – for example, by asking participants to distribute a certain number of stones, beans, goat droppings or points (whatever is handy or understandable) between the items listed. This gives a better understanding of the relative priority between different problems. Table 3.16 provides an example from an Action Aid study in Andhra Pradesh in India, in which the ranking was done by men, women, and young people, separately and then together. This indicated how important it is not to assume that these groups have the same problems or priorities.

Impact ranking

This is a variant of problem ranking developed in the Pakistan study. In this case, groups of project beneficiaries were brought together to identify a full range of positive and negative impacts, using a checklist of possible dimensions of impact (see Table 3.2 for details). Then, either individually or as a group, people were asked to rank those impacts by order of importance and explain their decisions.

In one of the projects in the study — a micro-credit project supporting women's goat-rearing activities which had been assessed as successful in terms of its economic impact[9] — the women involved felt that the impact of the project on other aspects of their lives was as strong, or stronger. For instance, women valued the new decision-making powers they had gained and their ability to offer a goat at the festival of Kurbani Eid.

When we meet together, we talk about the project and about our goats. We discuss when to sell them and how we can get a good price. Other money in this house goes into man's hands. We use this money to buy jewellery, dishes, and clothes. Men don't ask us how we spend our money.

Before we did not sacrifice goats; now we sacrifice them. We give them, and now God will give us something. Before, we worried that God would be angry at us for not sacrificing. There is a benefit at Ramadan times too. Before, we cooked black tea. Now there is milk, so, to open our fast, we can cook tea with milk. (Pakistan case study)

In addition to these specific examples of impact, the Pakistan study recorded how individual group members ranked wider dimension of change. Table 4.16 shows the results from one exercise in Ravat Goth, Pakistan (for an explanation of the categories see Table 3.2).

Table 4.16: Individual impact rankings in Ravat Goth, Pakistan

Name	First	Second	Third
Amnud	Religion	Relationships	Participation
Qaim Khatun	Knowledge	Participation	Relationships
Hakim Zaid	Relationships	Knowledge	Art
Kareemat	Life	Knowledge	Participation
Shahzadi	Knowledge	Participation	Relationships
Mumtaz	Participation	Knowledge	Life
Sabahi	Participation	Knowledge	Life
Zadi	Knowledge	Religion	Participation
Sabi	Religion	Relationships	Participation
Sakina	Life	Religion	Relationships

Table 4.16 indicates that even among a small group of women from the same community, receiving the same support for the same activity, different value is assigned to the impacts achieved. So although we can say that most of the women considered the knowledge they gained from the project either the most or the second most important impact, for three participants (Amnud, Sabi and Sakina) the impacts on their spiritual life, relationships, participation, and life (in the sense of health and material security) were all valued more than the knowledge gained.

In this case participants had to rank impacts according to predetermined categories or dimensions. While in theory this makes comparison easier, it also groups dimensions in ways which may not be evident to participants. In addition, the very fact that the data can then be averaged runs the risk of creating scores which squeeze out the diversity and difference which the individual scores retain. If both are presented in the report, the reader at least has the chance to interpret what had been lost in the aggregation process.

Performance ranking and satisfaction matrices

The performance of development organisations or government services, and the degree of satisfaction with a given project or agency can also be ranked or scored. As others have noted:

When hogs, figure skaters or bodybuilders compete, judges assign cardinal scores to subjective criteria: quality of coat for hogs; artistic impressions for figure skaters; and muscle tone for bodybuilders. Grades for academic papers are another familiar example: a professor's subjective evaluation of a humanities paper is given a cardinal score. In each case these subjectively assigned scores are added, averaged and tabulated in ways only appropriate to cardinal data. This means that judging requires training to achieve this level of inter-subjective agreement. For instance judges of livestock contests are occasionally judged on the degree to which their subjective judgements conform to those of established judges. (Insham, Narayan and Pritchett, quoted in Alkire 1999)

As this quote suggests, there are agreed standards upon which subjective judgements are based. This agreement has often been lacking in qualitative assessments undertaken by NGOs. Oxfam staff tried to overcome this by discussing what was meant by, for example, empowerment or participation, and how it was observed, before judgement was made about the impacts of a number of different projects. In the Pakistan case study, as we saw in Chapter 3, Oxfam programme officers agreed a scale for scoring participation which ranged from '0', indicating no awareness of project partner's activities by beneficiary community, to '5', where the community is working in more than one sector, taking initiatives and is able to mobilise its own resources. First individually, then together, they scored the projects and organisations involved in the impact ranking process, based on agreed criteria for each variable.

However, people will have their own (often differing) views about projects and organisations with which their communities are involved. It is therefore usually not possible or desirable to achieve the same sort of agreement. However, it is possible to compare how satisfied a range of groups are with a given situation. The example below comes from the evaluation of the Calcutta Slum Improvement Project mentioned above. In this case, residents from six slum areas separately identified key criteria for a satisfactory environment and then scored their level of satisfaction with each from 1 ('not at all satisfied') to 5 ('very satisfied').

The groups were asked to list criteria by which they defined the slum environment. These were written on cards which were placed along a vertical axis. Afterwards, a horizontal axis was drawn with the numbers 1 to 5 along it ... [t]he group then placed seeds against each criteria. After completion, a discussion was facilitated where reasons for decisions were noted ... Criteria related to project interventions could then be assessed for how well they had been met, whilst new criteria gave an idea of possible future interventions or areas for community action. (Kar et al. 1997, p.85)

The results from the different slums was compiled into Table 4.17 which indicates overall levels of satisfaction across the slum communities, indicating areas of high satisfaction, for example with the electricity situation, mixed satisfaction with the provision of children's sports and games, and low satisfaction in areas such as unity and women's income.

Table 4.17: Satisfaction matrix from a participatory impact assessment exercise in Calcutta

Criteria	Extent of satisfaction				
	1	2	3	4	5
Road			2	3	1
Drainage	1		1	1	3
Tap water supply	1		2	2	1
Latrine		1	1	3	
Electricity				1	4
Primary health-care		1	1	2	1
Children's education	1			3	2
Children sport and games	1		1		1
Reduction in women abuse			1		
Reduction in alcoholism	1		1		
Cleanliness		1			
Women's income	1	1			
Women's awareness/ rights		1		1	
Economic earnings			1		
Political conflict		1			
Unity		2			
Children's safety		1			

Definition: 1= not at all satisfied, 5 = very satisfied

Numbers in boxes indicate frequency of response in different slums

Source: Kar et al. 1997

What is useful about this sort of approach is that it allows the reader not only to get an overview of the situation, but also to see where differences of opinion exist and which criteria are important in different slum areas. Community groups' expression of dissatisfaction — with children's safety, political conflict, or women's income — is made visible rather than subsumed into a picture of averages. This, along with other elements of the study, led the researchers to question whether existing project indicators should be changed to reflect more closely people's own satisfaction criteria. Further, it indicated that although most slums were relatively happy with the outputs that the project had delivered — such as roads, drainage, electricity, health-care and education services — there were also a number of other areas which affected people's overall quality of life (an improvement in which was one of the project's desired impacts) which they felt less good about – such as alcoholism, unity, and women's rights. This helps us to understand what change can be attributed to the project, and also what changes the project might seek to promote in the future.

Lessons about ranking

Overall, the types of ranking described above are powerful means of comparing a wide range of topics — well-being, problems, organisations, projects, impacts, performance, and satisfaction — not just by ranking these hierarchically, but by describing their relative importance. As we have seen, there are also ways of retaining the diversity of opinions that are gathered through ranking, and comparing and contrasting these to understand where different people and groups seem to agree or disagree.

However, I have also noted potential problems associated with ranking, particularly wealth or well-being ranking, and emphasised the danger that ranking data by its very nature allows the use of the standard array of statistical tools, which may be inappropriate or misleading. Ranking exercises are subject to the same problems (and benefits) outlined in the section on group interviews, notably the danger of manipulation by dominant groups, particularly men.

Chapati or Venn diagrams

Venn diagrams were used in the case studies to capture respondents' perceptions of the perceived importance of various institutions and of their relationship with them. They are sometimes called chapati diagrams after the circular Indian flat bread.

In the CYSD study respondents were asked to draw circles, the size of which represented the importance of each institution to them. The relationship with each institution was reflected by the distance between circles and the centre, which represented the respondents' group. So a circle placed close to the centre indicated a close relationship with that institution. The respondents were asked to do this for the current situation, and as it was ten years before, but the complex nature of the task made it quite difficult. The compromise was to specify the 'before' and 'after' relationship but not to include the relative importance of the institutions.

Figure 4.1: Chapati diagram tracing 'before and after' relationship of key institutions/ stakeholders with village Munda Sahi (CYSD case study)

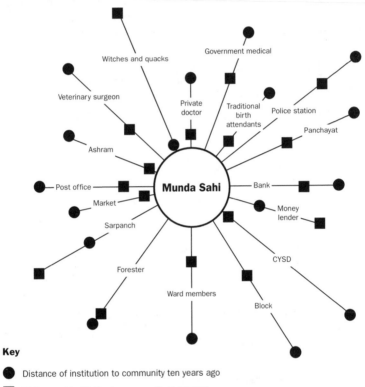

Key

● Distance of institution to community ten years ago

■ Distance of institution to community at present

The results are illustrated in Figure 4.1. For instance, the exercise revealed that in the health sector, traditional birth attendants and private doctors now had a closer relationship with the community; government medical centres remained quite distant; and 'witches' and 'quacks' now had a much more distant relationship. In the economic sector it seems that the market and banks are assuming greater importance in people's lives, while the relationship with money lenders is declining. This exercise and the discussion it generated allowed CYSD to explore with the communities not only the outputs of its health and credit activities, but also how these might have contributed to changing relationships and patterns of behaviour at the community level.

These diagrams can play a useful role in stimulating debate about relationships between groups, and the CYSD study indicates how this can include attempts to explore change in relationships over time — a crucial aspect of impact assessment. However, in other cases, such as Ghana, chapati diagram exercises were found to be confusing for people.

Impact flow charts

Flow charts depict the flow or direction of a particular activity or process. They typically start with an event or an action, such as planting a seedling or setting up a group, or a problem, such as lack of rain, and then explore the consequences. Usually this is done by asking 'what happened next?' or 'and what did this lead to?' or 'what effects did this have?'. The impact flow chart is the opposite of the 'problem tree' method which seeks to discover the causes or roots of a problem in that it investigates the effects of a problem or action.

The Ghana case study effectively used impact flow charts by asking men and women, separately, to cite the most important change event in their community in the past few years. The facilitator then encouraged them to explain the knock-on effects of this events through the use of a flow chart. The results are presented in Figures 4.2 and 4.3.

Figure 4.2: Impact flow chart of most important intervention in Yiziiri (men's opinion)

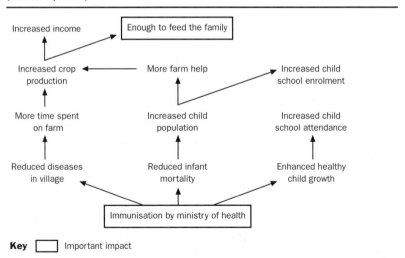

143

Figure 4.3: Impact flow chart of most important intervention in Yiziiri (women's opinion)

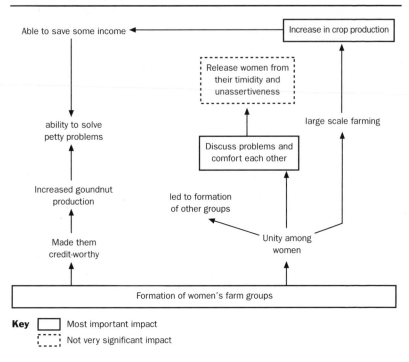

Key ☐ Most important impact
⌐⌐⌐ Not very significant impact

There are several interesting things to observe about this exercise, not least the differences between men and women's views of what is important. Women emphasised that the formation of their own group had provided them with a degree of unity and a forum to discuss problems, and that this allowed them to achieve things together; which had individual benefits in terms of economic gain and increased self-confidence. Men on the other hand stressed how the immunisation campaign by the Ministry of Health had improved child health. This had positive effects on education through higher school enrolment, but more significantly for the men, by increasing the availability of farm labour it contributed to higher production, income, and ultimately food security.

The impact flow charts also proved helpful in understanding how people saw the process and sequence of change, rather than how the project envisaged it, and where these two perceptions overlapped. For example, the women saw their unity as a key stepping stone to several other things, whereas the project placed much greater emphasis on the provision of credit. Being aware of such potential differences is crucial for impact assessment exercises: communities and NGOs may have agreed to various projects for different reasons, which may not be clear at the outset. This may become clearer if impact assessments include opportunities for various groups to explain the importance to them of the effects of a given intervention, in a way that is not 'led' or predetermined by the intervention's declared objectives. If an activity's potential unplanned consequences are not explored in this way, there is a danger of mistakenly identifying the obvious project inputs, such as credit in this case, as the critical success factor behind a given impact, when in-depth research makes it quite clear that the combination of credit and group formation was the determining factor.

Trend analysis

The analysis of trends and change over time lies at the heart of impact assessment. Some of the simplest examples of these tools are the 'before and after' or 'ten years ago and now' exercises illustrated in Table 4.5 and 4.11. These show perceptions of the changing reliability of water supplies in Wajir and perceptions of changing gender roles in Jamena-Munda Sahi and Konkali, India. Respondents were either asked to simply describe changes or asked to score them using simple 1-5 or 1-10 scales. Such exercises, used in several case studies, have proved simple yet effective in adding a dynamic element into the analysis.

However, comparing only two points in time in a 'before and after' exercise runs the risk of fluctuations between those points being concealed (see Figure 4.4). This can lead to exaggerating or underestimating changes that have occurred, and/ or being unable to distinguish between changes brought about by the project and changes caused by other factors. Other exercises used in the case studies therefore tried to capture trends using data over a number of years.

Figure 4.4: Showing how measurement at only two points can conceal large fluctuations between those years

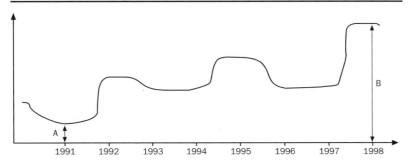

The example in Table 4.18 from Ghana illustrates how this can be done. Respondents assessed the relative improvement or deterioration of certain factors over time by assigning scores from 1 to 10 (the factors had been defined in the well-being ranking described earlier in this chapter, and in other exercises such as an historical profile). They assigned scores for every other year over the past eight years. What emerged from this exercise, despite the rather idealised characterisation of 1989, was the devastating effect of a serious conflict with neighbouring groups in 1993/4, which not only led to large-scale loss of life, but also seriously disrupted economic and social life. In 1997, NGOs and government made strong reconstruction efforts particularly in the health and education sectors, but very poor rainfall affected food security and water availability. Clearly if an exercise had simply looked at 1989 and 1997, the significance of the conflict and the recovery from it may not have been adequately taken into account.

Table 4.18: Trend analysis in Demon village, Northern Ghana

1989	1991	1993	1995	1997	Issues
10	8	6	4	1	Water
1	4	2	4	10	Health
10	4	1	1	1	Food security
10	8	1	2	8	Peace
3	4	6	6	10	Rainstorm [high winds]
10	6	1	1	2	Income
10	8	1	2	5	Sheanut processing
10	5	1	5	2	Fishing
10	6	1	2	3	Livestock
2	2	1	7	10	External interventions

Key: 10 = good, 1 = poor
April 1997

For the purposes of impact assessment, trend analysis can give an insight into change over time and suggest causes for fluctuations. This in turn allows researchers to include factors outside the project or programme in the assessment which have had a bearing on people's lives (in this case, conflict and poor rainfall). Situating a project in a wider context helps to minimise any exaggeration of, as well as underestimating, project impacts.

Trend analysis thus provides a useful tool in looking at change and attribution. However, it is clearly better suited to some situations, issues, and groups than others. Apart from obvious points — such as farmers being more likely to remember trends in weather or crop production over time than city dwellers — it is wise to remember the following.

People tend to remember best those things that are most important to them. Trend analysis should probably focus on these. For example, the Ghana study looked at trends related to the criteria which had emerged during the wealth-ranking exercise and which respondents themselves deemed critical to well-being.

People tend to be able to recollect particular memories when they can place them in the original context. Memories are often triggered when people recall the place they happened, the people who were present, or the political or environmental climate at the time. As the historical profile in the ENDA study indicates, drought years or the date of independence are common reference points. It is sometimes better to start trend analysis from these points and work forwards, or backwards, from them.

People tend to remember relative change rather than absolute change. They may also be more willing to disclose relative change. Rather than asking people what their income was this year and what it was last year, it may be more useful to inquire whether their income has increased compared to last year. Another method is to ask people to assign a score or weight to a given year's income and then to do the same for the following or preceding year, and so on. In this way, as in the Ghana example above, an insight can be gained into not only if a given year was better or worse for someone, but also relatively how much better or worse.

People may deliberately or accidentally not tell the truth or omit information. As noted in the section on interviewing, they may have very good reasons for doing so! The notion that people cannot or will not undertake this sort of analysis, or that their opinions are 'subjective' and therefore less valid, has meant that this often invaluable source of information has not been tapped. But its flaws do not invalidate the tool; they merely underline the importance of cross-checking (see Chapter 3) and seeking to understand why people might lie or exaggerate, and the need to build an atmosphere of trust and mutual understanding in which might truths can be shared openly.

Other participatory tools and methods

Other tools such as mapping, transect walks, pie charts and other diagrams, were also used in the case studies, although not as commonly as those detailed above. Some of the case studies used video material – CYSD, for example, looked at tapes which had been filmed in previous years to learn about changes in the density of forest cover.

Indeed the use of participatory video, role play, and drama in evaluation is becoming more commonplace (Braden 1998, Mavro 1997). Initial experience suggests that both can be useful in helping people tell their story, in ways that they wish it to be told. So in theory participatory video allows people to prepare, view, and adapt their representation of themselves and then communicate that to others, uncensored by intermediaries. Drama can allow people to express opinions and judgements about projects or organisations that they could or would not otherwise reveal. This is an area where much more can be done and learned.

Participatory tools — some issues and lessons learned

Participatory tools are increasingly being used in evaluation and impact assessments. At the same time a number of observers and practitioners are expressing doubts about the quality of some of this work, its potential to exclude certain groups, the way that it has become an orthodoxy or ritual to be followed, and the way that it can become dominated by tools, methods, and exercises at the expense of the content (Mosse 1994). The experience of the case studies suggests that there are some critical issues for ensuring the credibility of participatory research.

Recognising power and social relations. As the section on group interviews in this chapter suggests, participatory exercises in groups can neglect some people's views (for instance, women's or children's) and, moreover, validate and legitimate the views of dominant groups, thus increasing their power vis-à-vis others. Some of the studies revealed that minority clans or ethnic groups were excluded from meetings and even 'forgotten' during exercises such as wealth ranking. However, the studies also revealed that where careful attention is paid to this issue, participatory tools and methods can be used to reflect differences of power, opinion, and perception, as well as analyse the relations between different groups. This must be a deliberate strategy and part of the research from the outset.

Respecting people's time. Participatory exercises and especially 'community PRAs' can take up a lot more of people's time than individual interviews. This is particularly the case if a whole range of exercises is to be undertaken in a short intensive period, because this suits the researcher. The danger of this happening is particularly acute when the tools and methods start to dominate — the very diversity of techniques and exercises that have been developed compounds the problem. It seems, as a recent Action Aid confirmed (Goyder et al. 1998), that more thought needs to go into not only prioritising what information is particularly important, but also into choosing tools which are relatively efficient in providing it. The experience of the case studies suggest that one should focus much more clearly on those aspects of change which different groups perceive as most important, to compare and contrast these, and to explore the causes of those changes.

Combining participatory tools with other methods and sources of information. The dissatisfaction with conventional research and evaluation approaches, and the appeal of participatory methods have sometimes led to proponents of participatory methods failing to build on and utilise the many years of experience accumulated in the study of economics, science, sociology, and anthropology. This is in some cases due to the theoretical debates which lie at the root of the different disciplinary traditions, but may also be due to ignorance and prejudice. From a practical point of view, it is a waste not to be prepared to use other methods, to learn from them, or to use information collected by other methods. Such information provides important opportunities to cross-check and verify findings, to avoid wasting resources and time, and, equally importantly, to question the validity of data collected in other ways.

Developing clear standards and criteria for processes of participatory inquiry. A number of 'criteria of trustworthiness' have been suggested for participatory processes (Pretty 1994) which include length and depth of engagement of actors; persistent and parallel observation; cross-checking of sources, methods, and investigators as well as participant checking; analysis and expression of difference and negative case analysis; evidence of searching out different views and explanations; journals and peer review; and impact on stakeholders' capacities to know and act. The case studies covered in this book and recent findings from Action Aid's participatory impact assessment work recommend that one should also think about balancing the 'length and depth of engagement' with a process or schedule agreeable to both community groups and researchers, and make more efficient use of existing sources of information. Methods should evolve and be adapted based on a mutual analysis of their strengths and weaknesses; and one should monitor the extent to which the information gathered actually has an impact – for instance, whether it leads to change in the policies or practice of the project or organisation being assessed and whether it is meaningful to all parties.

Summary 4.5: Key lessons about participatory tools

- Participatory exercises in groups can ignore some people's views, and legitimate the views of dominant groups, thus increasing their power. However, if used with care, participatory tools and methods can reflect differences of power, opinion, and perception as well as analyse the relations between different groups.

- Participatory exercises can take up too much of people's time. Focus on those aspects of change that different groups perceive as most important, comparing these, and exploring their causes.

- Participatory tools need to be combined with other methods and sources of information. By using secondary sources and key informants time can be saved and findings cross-checked and verified.

- There is a need to develop clear standards for processes of participatory inquiry which balance the length and depth of engagement with a schedule agreed by both community groups and researchers; efficient use of existing sources of information; the development of methods based on a joint analysis of their strengths and weaknesses. One should also consider the extent to which the information gathered will have an impact, such as changing policy or practice of the project or organisation being assessed, and the extent to which it is meaningful to all parties.

Case studies

Case studies are not really a tool or a method, but rather an approach to gathering comprehensive, systematic, and in-depth information about a case of interest. They typically involve multiple research tools and methods, many of which are described above. Case studies can examine, among other things, individuals, communities, events, time periods, programmes, or organisations. Regardless of the unit of assessment, case studies generally seek holistically to describe that unit in depth and detail, to set it in context.

Case studies are particularly valuable where broad, complex questions have to be addressed in complex circumstances. In these cases the number of variables will usually be far greater than can be controlled for, so that experimental approaches, which seek to isolate the effects of different variables, are not appropriate. This is particularly pertinent for development and policy work, given the many parallel and interrelated factors which affect people's lives.

150

Case studies are also relevant where individual, rather than standardised, outcomes are sought. They are increasingly used in assessing health and education services and policies, and development agencies such as the World Bank and USAID are carrying out more case studies and synthesis (cross-case) studies. The following factors may make a case study approach more or less appropriate: if there is a high number of interrelated variables within an unpredictable and uncertain environment, and more individual outcomes, then case studies will be more appropriate. If there are few variables which are clearly related, a predictable and stable environment, and if you expect more standardised outcomes, then standard quantitative measures are probably more appropriate.

Case studies therefore, are generally used when one needs to understand a specific group of people, a particular problem, or a unique situation in great depth; where one can identify cases rich in information — rich in the sense that a good deal can be learned from a few examples — and where the complexity of the issues makes standardised approaches less suitable. Like many other approaches, case studies usually involve exploring several different, and competing, interest groups. As they may have different interpretations of events this often again requires cross-checking of findings. In many situations it will be necessary to combine case-study work with broader, less in-depth, surveys. This was the general approach adopted in the impact studies reviewed in this book.

In the BRAC study, for example, case studies were used to explore the qualitative changes associated with women's empowerment, and to find out more about households which had dropped out of the programme as well as those which had demonstrated exceptional success. For assessing women's empowerment, a random sample of 25 village organisations was selected for case-study work, while the dropouts and successes were chosen from relevant data collected through the household survey. This use of case studies allowed BRAC to understand the factors which influenced the different levels of households' success, such as close kinship ties and involvement in the management of the village organisation; higher levels of training; and enjoyment of special loan privileges. In collecting women's views of impact, qualitative case-study methods provided more in-depth information than the quantitative survey. This was particularly the case in deepening the understanding of how the programme had contributed to women's positive self-perceptions, increased their self-confidence as their dependency on male household members decreased, changed decision making at the family level, and increased women's mobility which enabled them to communicate better with the outside world.

CYSD also used a case-study approach to explore critical incidents which had influenced the impact of their programme. These included conflict between groups in a particular village, and two projects which had failed. In addition, they found that past case studies of particular individuals, villages, groups, or organisations proved to be among the most valuable documentation for reconstructing baseline data, because they provided detailed information, about the position of females, as well as about health practices and coping strategies before the project intervention. The study of the two project failures – which tried to introduce new, inappropriate, technology – revealed a high speed of project identification and implementation (due in part to donors' pressure), as well as a poor understanding of the technical and labour demands of the new technology.

Project staff attributed some of the causes of this problem to the fact that fulfilling their output target had become their primary concern, but also to poor advice from external consultants. These examples demonstrate how an in-depth case study can bring up facts relevant for the workings of an entire organisation, in this case suggesting the need to clarify relations with donors and consultants; to remedy weaknesses in project identification and appraisal; and to adopt and adapt targets and indicators in ways that discourage the uncritical fulfilment of inappropriate targets.

The Ghana study used a 'layered' approach to case studies. At the first level we have case studies of three local organisations. At the second level, case studies were made up of three villages where these organisations worked. Third, ten individuals were selected in each of the three villages. This approach tried to ensure that case studies reflected the wide variety of given groups, so that any similarities that emerged were likely to reflect core impacts. In this case this meant capturing the varied nature of the members of the Northern Ghana Development Network (NGDN); the agricultural and climatic diversity of the areas in which the Network operates; and the varied levels of well-being in the villages. Thus at each level (network, organisation, and village) information was collected in order to select case studies. This 'snowballing' technique recognises that the information needed to choose case studies may not be available at the outset of the research, but may need to be collected during the course of the assessment.

Table 4.19 builds on these examples from the case studies to illustrate the usefulness of different types of case study.

One should not forget how useful case studies can be in demonstrating and communicating impact, as well as for training processes related to impact assessment. Stories and examples usually make up an important part of an organisation's formal and informal communication as well as its decision-making processes. Case studies are a great device for explaining and illustrating complex and sometimes dull programmes. They can act as a

Table 4.19: Types of case study and their usefulness

Types of case	Usefulness
Unusual, extreme, or deviant cases (programme dropouts, failures, or successes)	Useful in understanding puzzling cases which seem to break the rules, and why certain people or organisations seem to achieve particularly good or bad results. Useful in understanding the reasons for exceptionally good or bad performance.
Typical or average cases	Useful in understanding the situation of most people, communities, and organisations. Findings may be replicable in other 'normal' situations.
Homogenous or similar cases (for example, looking at impact on a group of women of the same age, or looking at a number of credit projects)	Useful in looking at particular sub-groups in depth, which may be important when many different types of people or activities are involved.
Varied or heterogeneous cases (deliberately seeking out different groups of people, organisations, or types of programmes)	Useful in exploring common or distinct patterns across great variance. Common patters in such cases are likely to indicate core and central impacts of wider relevance, precisely because they occur across diverse groups.
Critical cases (may have wider relevance; can be used for broader purposes, such as innovative work or work with new groups; or may produce results which have high political impact)	Useful when a single case study can dramatically make a point; statements such as 'if it happens here it can happen anywhere' or 'if it doesn't work here it won't work anywhere' indicate that a case is critical.
Snowballing cases (one starts with a few cases and then selects others on the basis of the findings)	Useful when the information to select all case studies is not available or are dependent on a greater understanding of the situation.
Convenience cases (possibly the most common type where case studies are chosen solely because it is easy - the information already exists, the site is very close, and so on)	Generally a bad idea if these are the only or most important reasons for choosing case studies.

Adapted from Patton (1990)

shared starting point from which managers, trainees, and others can debate wider issues. This is vital if staff do not share common experiences or if there is a tendency for debates to become very abstract and theoretical. Good case studies can ground debates in reality, as well as providing empirical material to determine wider policy questions. Summary 4.6 makes some key points about the use of case studies for impact assessment purposes.

Summary 4.6: Lessons learned about case studies

- Case studies proved particularly useful to explore qualitative impact such as women's empowerment and self-confidence, and relationships within the household.

- Case studies were also useful in following up some of the results generated by other methods, for example in order to analyse particularly successful or unsuccessful projects or groups, and exploring why they had succeeded or failed.

- Case-study material, because it tends to cover single examples in depth, is particularly useful for illustrating and communicating impact to others; if chosen carefully, the study can have much wider relevance.

Costs, benefits, and impact

In recent years NGOs have been criticised for not doing enough to explore the relationship between the costs involved in what they do, and the benefits or impact that is achieved (Riddell 1997). The reasons normally given for this are that NGOs are resistant to this sort of quantification of complex processes, or that this type of analysis is too complex and difficult to undertake.

Two of the case studies (Pakistan and the Wajir programme in Kenya) attempted to explore the relationship between costs and benefits in some depth. Both divided project benefits into those that yielded clearly measurable economic gains, and those that were less easy to quantify but nonetheless made significant contributions to a secure livelihood and human development. In Wajir, quantifiable economic benefits included changes in livestock mortality; benefits brought about by restocking destitute families with animals; women's credit; savings brought about by the provision of animal and human drugs; and savings made through greater security in the area. In the case of the Pakistan study, three micro-projects were studied and compared: a goat loan project, a literacy project, and a rose cultivation project.

The Wajir study

In the Wajir study, most of the information for assessing economic benefits was collected by surveys of representative samples of project participants and non-project respondents, as described at the beginning of this chapter. This data was then used to compare families living in project and non-project areas and to calculate average savings per household in relation to differences in livestock mortality and expenditure on drugs. These average figures were then extrapolated to the total number of targeted families in the project areas, which permitted an overall calculation of project benefits.

For more targeted activities, such as women's credit and animal restocking, more specific surveys and focus-group discussions were undertaken with a sample of beneficiaries to determine economic costs and benefits. Average benefits of the credit scheme were calculated in terms of the return on loans disbursed and of savings accumulated; the economic benefits of restocking were calculated in terms of increase in the value of the stock of animals and of the additional income achieved through milk sales. A financial value was also calculated for livestock stolen in the area which the Wajir Peace and Development Committee had recovered. Table 4.20 describes the steps undertaken for each project component in order to arrive at the overall cost-benefit figures.

Table 4.20: Steps undertaken in calculating economic benefits of different components of the Wajir programme

Livestock mortality	1 Calculated average difference in mortality for 200 households in project and non-project areas.
	2 Calculated average monetary saving per surviving animal and thus per household per year.
	3 Extrapolated findings to all the 1,788 families targeted by the project.
	4 Calculated overall reduction in livestock mortality and the estimated annual saving to pastoral communities over the lifetime of the project (£473,582).
Restocking	1 Found out number and value of animals distributed per family.
	2 Calculated average number of animals per family at the end of years one and two of the project, as well as the number and value of animals at the time of the assessment.

Table 4.20: Steps undertaken in calculating economic benefits of different components of the Wajir programme (continued)

Restocking	3	Calculated average monetary benefit per family over the first two years of the project.
	4	Calculated the value of average additional milk sales from a family's flock.
	5	Calculated total benefits per family.
	6	Compared total benefits with initial input costs (income over and above the initial value of the animals purchased by the project).
	7	Calculated the total benefit of the project's restocking component based on the 500 families which have been restocked (an increase in livestock capital, over and above the original value of the donated animals, and milk production valued at £101,000).
Women's credit	1	Calculated average return on loans made to a sample of women
	2	Calculated average rate of return on the loans disbursed (102%).
	3	Compared this to initial capital disbursed (KES 4,662,000 disbursed to date generated KES 4,755,240 in one year).
	4	Calculated overall return (£44,000).
Drug savings	1	Discovered average expenditure on drugs per person per household in project and non-project areas through questionnaire survey.
	2	Calculated difference between the two groups (on average, households in project sites spend 42% less on drugs per person compared to households in non-project sites).
	3	Calculated average annual savings per person.
	4	Calculated overall reduction in drug expenditure in the project area (£9,726).
Wajir peace	1	Discovered amounts of stolen goods recovered by the Wajir Peace and Development Committee.
	2	Calculated value of these goods: records show that two land cruisers and one trailer, livestock and 2,000 guns have been recovered through the initiative.
	3	Calculated overall reduction in theft losses (£30,000).

Table 4.20: Steps undertaken in calculating economic benefits of different components of the Wajir programme (continued)

Overall analysis	1	Made assumptions about the likely future costs and benefits of the programme as a whole — based on current performance for years one and two, the programme plans, and likely inflation rates.
	2	Calculated future annual benefit of each project component, and the annual overall costs of the programme, for years three to ten of the programme.
	3	Predicted and added up the total present value of the economic benefits of each of the components, taking into account the effect of inflation for future benefits.
	4	Predicted the total present value for the economic costs of each of the components, taking into account the effect of inflation on future costs.
	5	Calculated a number of ratios of present cost-to-benefit value (total or net present value — total present value of benefits minus total present value of costs — was £1,305,663), a simple cost-benefit ratio (1:2.2) , and the internal rate of return (the rate of inflation that would be required to reduce overall benefits to the same level as costs – in this case, the IRR was 55%).

This process of calculating overall figures for those parts of the programme that lent themselves to this sort of analysis permitted a comparison of the key economic costs and benefits of the entire programme. The project team could then derive some commonly used ratios such as overall net present value, cost-benefit ratios and internal rates of return[10]. As these ratios were calculated for the lifetime of the project (ten years) and the assessment was undertaken in year three of the project, this demanded, like most assessments of this type, some rather 'heroic' assumptions be made:

- that the benefits measured in year two would be maintained at the same level over the next seven years;

- that as a result, there would be no absolute increase in benefits over the project's lifetime;

- that the capital available for credit would remain available at the same level;

- that the operational costs would fall in line with the programme plans.

In addition these sorts of calculations require predictions, among other things, about future inflation and how this will affect costs and benefits.

Despite these uncertainties the cost-benefit analysis helped to determine the relative importance of elements of the programme in terms of economic benefits (see Table 4.21). Combined with findings from the qualitative assessment undertaken, this can provide useful material for future planning.

Table 4.21: Proportion of economic benefits derived from different parts of the Wajir programme

Elements of the Wajir programme	Percentage of total economic benefits
Animal health	74.6%
Restocking	12.0%
Credit	8.2%
Drug savings	1.5%
Wajir Peace Committee	3.7%

Bringing together economic impact analysis, cost information, and qualitative information, also allowed the Wajir team to draw meaningful conclusions about those elements of the programme which were extremely difficult to measure, particularly the institutional development efforts.

The relatively high benefit:cost ratio, even under the some of the most conservative assumptions, point to an overall success of the project. Institutional capacity development, especially with respect to delivery of animal health services to pastoralists, makes the greatest contribution to the package of economic benefits that accrue to the pastoralists.

It is important, however, to note that the pastoralists only started to realise economic benefits during the second year of the project and that the greatest benefit will only be realised from the sixth year of the project. This brings to the fore a very important consideration in development programmes in pastoral areas. It is often necessary to consider the amount of capital investment needed to establish and/ or strengthen local institutions before they can be able to deliver the necessary services. It takes a lot of financial resources to remunerate personnel involved in capacity development, gain the community's confidence by responding promptly to their most immediate needs, travel to the project sites in order to get the institutions functioning, train the members of these institutions, invest in capital and monitor and evaluate all on-going activities. This initial investment in capacity development, though costly and less efficient, is often necessary if one considers future stream of benefits from the project even in the absence of the donors. (Wajir case study)

The Pakistan study[11]

The assessment team in Pakistan undertook similar analyses of three micro-projects. These included a goat loan project and a rose cultivation project, as well as a literacy project, where the economic returns were less obvious. The information collected on economic impact was recalculated according to different assumptions — about how women's work is valued and whether Oxfam's support costs are included in the calculation or not — and compared to participants' own ranking of benefits, to explore how they compared economic benefits to others (see the section on ranking above for more on the method used in this study). Some of the key economic results are found in Table 4.22.

Table 4.22: Comparative results of cost-benefit analysis in three projects in Pakistan

	Goat-rearing	**Khoj literacy**	**Rose cultivation**
Total Oxfam grant	63,400R	506,329R	16,764R
Participants' socio-economic status	poor women	poor women	poor women and men
Number of direct beneficiaries	140	66	10
Number of years of operation	5	3	2
Grant total per participant	453R	7,671R	1,676R
Annual income per participant	1,102R	190R	2,286R
Market viability?	Yes	No	Possibly
Plausible internal rate of return[12] including Oxfam costs	20%	-6%	-52%
Plausible internal rate of return excluding Oxfam costs	20%	-6%	36%

All costs in constant 1992 Rupees
Adapted from Alkire 1999

The conclusions for the goat-rearing project are relatively clear-cut: it is economically viable and seems a worthwhile investment. Interestingly, the women involved ranked non-monetary benefits higher than the impact on their income. They particularly ranked their self-confidence, the solidarity that came from working with other women on the project, and the knowledge they had gained in terms of goat breeding and marketing, higher than the economic benefits. Clearly there are linkages between these different benefits and untangling them is difficult — women's increased knowledge about goats may be reflected in the sale prices they receive. In this case at least some of the women's increased knowledge can, in theory, be given an economic value. However, the women themselves feel that there are other benefits which cannot be 'priced' in this way.

In the case of the Khoj literacy project, the economic and non-economic impacts go in opposite directions. From an economic point of view the project is not sustainable without continued support, but the non-economic assessment makes clear that the project has had a 'fundamental and transformative impact' on the women students. This was particularly the case in terms of their ability to speak out and to deal with physical abuse — the following quote from a graduate student is a typical example.

My mother and father did not allow girls to speak; they would beat us. Now I have learned to trust my own talk, and ability to judge that this is good and this is bad ... My heart has become strong. I can speak about my rights, can even slowly, politely tell my parents that they have done something wrong. We have begun now to talk with them abut the difference between sons and daughters, that we are equal. Literate people can solve their own problems. (quote from a literacy student in Alkire 1999)

One of the main reasons why the economic returns to the project are low is that even literate women find it hard to get jobs, because overall female participation in the labour market is so low (7.15 per cent in Pakistan's urban areas in 1993/4). The primary barrier to their participation is not so much low productivity, or lack of skills and entrepreneurship, which literacy might address, as their inability to work outside the home or to undertake lucrative employment in the home. The barriers to female employment are therefore largely due to social constraints and conventions — which participants are starting to question as a result of the method of literacy used in the project.

With this understanding one can make more sense of the fact that Oxfam's grant to this project was eight times larger than the grant to the goat-rearing project, and reached less than half the number of women. Indeed, it may be a much more strategic investment because it, and projects like it, can arguably contribute to changing social constraints which will allow many more women, including those who are already literate, to realise their potential in the labour market.

In the case of the rose cultivation project, the main issue in determining the project's economic viability is the cost of Oxfam's support. As we see from Table 4.22 the inclusion or exclusion of Oxfam's support in the calculations makes a critical difference. The conclusion of the cost-benefit analysis alone would be that

while the income generation activity for roses would be viable and indeed lucrative as an economic investment, and while this income would have significant social premium because it would have accrued to the poorest households in the village, the high cost of Oxfam support turned what would have been a highly positive social cost-benefit into a strongly negative one. (Alkire 1999)

However, while this analysis makes it clear that Oxfam should be increasingly devolving responsibility for the project to the women's group it does not capture why these costs were perhaps necessary in the first instance. The project history and qualitative assessments make this much clearer as they reveal the catalytic role of the female Sindhi-speaking Oxfam project officer (for example, in ensuring adequate technical feasibility) and her efforts to ensure that the group's organisational development was taken into account. The fruits of this labour are evident in the participants' perceptions who once again rank non-monetary aspects of the project extremely highly.

Conclusion on costs, benefits, and impact

As a result of these sorts of analysis NGOs may often be faced with a choice between efficiency and empowerment. If economic impacts could be improved without compromising the other impacts, as in the Khoj project, this would be the preferred path for the future. However, if the option was to support a successful income-generation project that did not have high impacts on knowledge, relationships, or empowerment, the choice would become starker and more difficult. The choice can be made arbitrarily or on the basis of 'gut-feeling'; an agency can decide to prefer one objective (income) over another (empowerment) as a matter of policy, and develop appropriate expertise in this area (this may in part also be determined by what other actors are doing). Lastly, a judgement or policy decision can be made to work with and support particular groups of people, for example, the poorest, and to identify with these groups the activities and impacts they wish to achieve, and develop a broad expertise (and range of contacts with other specialist groups) that would allow a flexible response.

Clearly while economic analyses of costs and benefits can be useful in making these sorts of decisions, 'there is nothing in economics which relieves us of the obligation to choose' (Robbins 1932, pp. 135-136, quoted in Alkire 1999). And indeed, as the Pakistan and Wajir case studies make plain, it is the *combination* of the economic analysis with a qualitative assessment of dimensions of change, which is likely to make those choices at least better informed, if not easier. Summary 4.7 outlines some of the key lessons learned in the case studies about trying to undertake a more systematic analysis of the relationship between costs, benefits, and impact.

Summary 4.7: Key points about economic impact assessment

- There is a need to distinguish between those elements of a project or programme for which an economic analysis makes sense and those for which it does not.

- Collecting data for project participants and non-project participants with similar characteristics can allow differences between the two to be calculated; care must be taken to dissaggregate this data, especially with regards to gender. Remember to 'price' people's labour and time.

- When assessing economic benefits, look not only at income gained but also at savings in expenditure.

- Where it is not possible to survey or talk to all participants, talk to a sample to arrive at an average value and then extrapolate this to all participants. The statistical validity of this is will depend on your sampling procedure (see Chapter 3) on the variance between the values discovered among the sample. Care must be taken to ensure that gender differences are not subsumed in averages.

- Compare the costs and benefits for different components of a project or programme if possible, as well as looking at the project or programme as a whole. Remember that the value of money changes over time; always use constant prices. If constant prices are not used, assessments of a project's future must take into account the effects of inflation on future costs and benefits (constant price figures, and inflation and discount indices are usually available from multilateral agencies or government statistical departments or finance ministries).

- When making assumptions about the future (or for example, about the opportunity cost of someone's time) it is often better to include a range of values or scenarios, for comparison. Don't forget top spell out that these are assumptions.

- Always remember that economic analysis on its own is incomplete and can be misleading. It needs to be combined with qualitative and non-economic assessments. Particular care is needed in comparing projects with very different economic and social elements.

Both economic and non-economic assessments are necessary for taking informed decisions. They do not, however, remove the need to make judgements and to develop policies which guide the choices that are made between rival objectives.

The previous chapter explored issues related to the design and preparation of impact assessment processes. This chapter has looked in some depth at the different tools and methods used to undertake impact assessment and drawn a number of lessons from the case studies. In the following chapters, I shall discuss how these lessons and findings apply to specific aspects of NGO work: emergencies, advocacy, and organisational self-assessment.

5

Impact assessment and emergencies

This chapter describes some of the specific characteristics of emergency situations and their implications for impact assessment. In particular, I explore the similarities and differences with the lessons learned in Chapters 3 and 4. The first section analyses some of the specific characteristics of emergency situations and the implications for impact assessment work. The second part looks more specifically at the design of the impact assessment process in emergencies, and the choice of tools and methods. Although none of the case-study projects were involved in large-scale acute, or first-phase, emergency work, some — notably Wajir, Ikafe, much of Cordes' work, and one village in the Ghana study — either developed out of an emergency situation and were medium-term responses to it or, in the case of Ghana, involved assessing impact in a community ravaged by a local conflict. The chapter therefore refers to relevant parts of these studies as well as other material on evaluation and impact assessment in emergency contexts. In particular, it draws upon an evaluation of Oxfam GB's work in Africa's Great Lakes region (Collins et al. 1998), other work undertaken on the subject by Oxfam (Dawson 1998), recent work attempting to draw together lessons about evaluating humanitarian assistance from across the sector,[1] and the work of the Sphere project.[2] The chapter concludes by drawing together the lessons on key indicators to be examined in emergency situations, on tools and methods, and some of the questions regarding the ethics and practices of humanitarian organisations which can affect their impact.

Recent years have seen greater scrutiny and a growing critique of humanitarian operations, following events in Somalia, Rwanda, and Bosnia. Rightly or wrongly, Northern NGOs have borne the brunt of much of this: they stand accused of being ineffective and dishonest about their achievements; of lacking accountability and the ability to learn; of acting as sub-contractors for major donors in a 'humanitarian industry'; of being a fig leaf for government inaction, or worse the vanguards for the creation of western-style civil society and liberal democracy; of having a poor understanding of the political economy in which they are engaged; and of having a vested interest in their own survival (African Rights 1994, Duffield 1996, 1997). This is compounded by a growing 'contract culture' where a focus on 'on the fulfilment of contracted inputs and outputs rather than on actual humanitarian outcomes' allows 'the industry to demonstrate contractual success even within spectacularly unfulfilled mandates' (Stockton 1995).

This barrage of criticism has largely focused on the 'dark side' of humanitarianism, as Hugo Slim points out.

[M]ore academic attention is being paid to the negative effects at present and it would seem somewhat urgent for NGOs to be able to assess and advocate the positive effects more clearly in the years ahead. Such assessment of the 'bright side' of humanitarianism must move beyond traditional quantitative indications of output (food and blankets given etc.) to a more subtle analysis of impact and outcome which can stand up to the increasingly rigorous analysis of the dark side of relief in war. (Slim 1998)

Characteristics of emergency situations

Assessing the impact of interventions in emergency situations demands addressing many of the points that have been made in previous chapters, such as being clear about the model of change being pursued, setting clear objectives and indicators, and collecting adequate baseline data. Many of the challenges described, relating for example to attribution and aggregation, are equally present in emergency situations.

However, emergency situations also have very distinct characteristics. If a humanitarian emergency is defined as any situation in which there is an exceptional and widespread threat to life, health, or basic subsistence beyond the individual's or the community's capacity to cope, the following characteristics usually apply:

- a high level of immediate needs in terms of security, health-care, or subsistence;

- increased vulnerability of some groups who are less able to express their specific needs (particularly women, children, refugees, and minority groups);

- weak local capacity to respond;

- a volatile, turbulent environment which may also be insecure;

- possibly the presence of multiple actors/ agencies, often deliberately or inadvertently pursuing different goals;

- a poor level of information on precisely what is going on and why.

Hallam and Borton[3], in their review of 'Good Practice in Evaluating Humanitarian Aid', also suggest that complex emergencies or conflict situations have an additional number of characteristics. In many civil wars — which make up the majority of conflict situations — the objective of opposition or rebel groups is to overthrow the government or to secede. The degree of recognition and status accorded to opposition groups is therefore a highly sensitive issue with implications for the role of international agencies, the legal basis for their operations, and the legal rights of affected populations. Civilians may be deliberately attacked and their way of life and means of livelihood undermined; rape and sexual violence are often common. Such attacks on communities often have the objective of instilling such fear in groups of similar background that they will seek refuge elsewhere, releasing territory for use by the faction responsible for the atrocities. Attacks may also be carried out on targets which play a special role in the cultural identity of particular groups, such as places of religious worship. Women are often regarded as bearers of a group's cultural identity, which affects how they are treated during and after war, and how they view themselves. They can become targets for abuse as a way of degrading a whole society or ethnic group.

Complex emergencies frequently last for several years, but within this the situation can be highly fluid. Fighting is increasingly causing civilian as well as military casualties, and threatened populations flee, creating more or less localised displacement crises. Chronic problems are therefore frequently intensified by acute situations requiring urgent responses. In both cases the degree of freedom enjoyed by individuals, and institutions such as the press and the judiciary is either severely constrained or eliminated. Actors involved in the conflict and those involved in trying to provide humanitarian assistance therefore operate in a context of severely weakened national accountability mechanisms.

This in turn means that conflict often results in the development of economic activities which would normally be classified as illegal or semi-legal, such as the exploitation of natural resources, drug-running, money-laundering, and trading in arms. Often these activities are controlled by, or taxed by, leaders of the warring factions who use them for personal gain or to continue the conflict. Commercial organisations based outside the affected countries may be involved. Such 'war economies' have enabled conflicts to be prolonged.

Humanitarian assistance can be diverted from the intended beneficiaries and controlled and taxed in the same way as 'war economy' activities. In many recent conflicts it has been difficult to distinguish between civilians and combatants. In many cases, the intermingling of combatants and civilians is a deliberate strategy of the warring parties. In this situation, humanitarian agencies are often unable to prevent assistance distributed for use by civilians and vulnerable populations being used by combatants and warring factions. We lack reliable evidence of what proportion of humanitarian assistance is diverted, but questions arise about the degree to which external assistance can fuel and prolong conflicts.

A large number of actors can be involved in complex emergencies, ranging from national relief structures, local NGOs, international NGOs, UN agencies, the ICRC, the IFRC, and the national Red Cross and Red Crescent societies. Increasingly human-rights agencies and monitors are also deployed in ongoing conflicts, as are organisations seeking to resolve the conflict. Humanitarian activities may run parallel to, or in concert with, peacekeeping operations, which may involve troop contingents from a variety of countries. The conflict may involve neighbouring states. The coordination of such a multiplicity of actors is a major challenge both to local authorities and external agencies. With such a wide range of actors, it is almost guaranteed that they will not share the same goals or even be at odds with each other.

Much of the recent literature on evaluation in emergency situations, because of events in Bosnia, Kosovo, Somalia, and Rwanda, has tended to focus on complex emergencies and conflict situations. However, it needs to be recognised that there are also important distinctions between various types of emergency. The distinction between 'man-made' and 'natural' disasters is often challenged, but it is clear that dealing with earthquakes, floods, hurricanes, or drought in areas free of conflict presents specific challenges. It is different from humanitarian work in conflict zones, and therefore holds different challenges for impact assessment. In addition one can distinguish between varying capacities within the world's regions to deal with disaster. Much of the literature on impact assessment and evaluation presumes an important, if not predetermined, role for international agencies and actors in delivering humanitarian relief and in developing policy. There seems to be much less literature and evaluation experience about assessing the impact of local response, local preparedness, and local capacity-building.

One can further distinguish between those emergencies that are periodic in nature and to that extent predictable, and those which are not. Floods in Bangladesh are a regular event and it is their severity, rather than the event itself, which is less predictable. In such circumstances, a risk analysis identifies those likely to be most vulnerable in advance of the emergency, and allows preparedness measures and plans for response to be put in place. In theory, the experience of previous disasters can be disseminated after the event and fed into the next response. In Bangladesh it is reported[4] that as a result of lessons learned, some agencies have recognised that in order to assist women and children, women staff must be included in assessment teams and provision for women made in places of safety. It is believed that this has reduced the number of women who have died, or suffered serious losses, in recent floods in Bangladesh.

Implications for impact assessment

The characteristics outlined above have several implications for impact assessment. The scale of need and the weakness of local capacity may mean, at least in the short term, that direct intervention 'high up the impact chain' is necessary, for example by providing food or water in order to prevent immediate loss of life. In the short term, building the capacity of a third party to provide food and water (in other words, providing support lower down the impact chain) may not be an option. Generally, the fewer the links in the chain the easier it is to assess whether a given input achieves an impact.

Discontinuous and rapid change makes planning and setting objectives more difficult. The need for a timely response can also limit the possibilities for adequate collection of baseline data and for participation, although both can be added to an intervention over time.

Different groups of people have different capacities to cope with crises as well as different vulnerabilities, particularly depending on their gender and age. It is essential to understand these when establishing impact indicators and assessing results. Recognising these differences and collecting baseline data for future assessments might necessitate diverting resources from ongoing operations, which might be considered an unacceptable luxury when there are lives to be saved.

The complexity of the emergency and the interconnectedness of the actions of multiple agencies may make attribution of impact particularly difficult. In this case, an impact assessment of a single agency's work will be less useful than an analysis of the combined actions of several agencies. On the other hand, the short impact chain in an emergency may, in some cases, make the attribution of impact easier than in long-term activities. For example, an agency's provision of clean water in a refugee camp can have an obvious, immediate effect on people's health and life chances, whereas it will be much more difficult to assess whether training a local team to provide counselling for refugees actually leads to reduced stress levels.

The insecurity, fear, and trauma of people affected by emergency situations may make 'telling the truth' not only dangerous but deeply disturbing. Especially in conflict situations, various groups will also have an interest in ensuring that their version of the 'truth' predominates. This has implications for participatory processes.

Local responses, preparedness, and capacity are often undervalued and sometimes undermined by external agencies. A comprehensive approach to impact assessment in emergency situations has to include the relative merits and impact of local actors vis-à-vis external actors, their impact on each other and the implications of this for a longer-term response, as well as the degree of predictability of the emergency in question.

These points have consequences for the design, choice of methods, and implementation of impact assessment in emergency situations, which I discuss in the following sections.

Design

Preparation

As stated in Chapter 3, being clear about the purpose of an impact assessment is the first step in designing an effective process. Being clear about who the assessment is for, what its boundaries and its focus are, what financial and human resources are available, and what timescale is envisaged are obvious, but vital questions. However, experience also suggests that the very nature of emergency situations makes answering these questions very difficult. Some therefore, have suggested that a preliminary scoping study or design phase may be appropriate, 'which allows the evaluator to identify potentially significant issues and prepare a more accurate schedule and budget for the remainder of the evaluation' (Hallam and Borton 1998). Again, as previously discussed, preliminary workshops involving a range of stakeholders may be an effective means not only of determining the purpose of a given study but also of designing one that is realistic.

Clarifying assumptions

All interventions make certain assumptions about how change happens, why it has occurred, and how it might occur in the future. Making these assumptions explicit and being clear about the 'logic' behind them is usually the first step in designing an assessment. This permits the kind of institutional and policy analysis which is increasingly recognised as an important part of impact assessment (see particularly Chapters 6 and 7).

What types of impact and indicators are to be assessed?

Impact assessment studies, particularly in complex emergencies, must recognise that objectives and strategies may well change in response to changing circumstances, that some objectives are often not stated or agreed by all parties in advance, and that unanticipated effects are usual. As the Wajir study concluded,

the impact on project beneficiaries' livelihoods and welfare often calls for the continuous integration of (new) impact indicators during the project implementation period. Only in this way can we know whether the project is having any impact on the beneficiaries. The constant integration of impact indicators ... is also necessary because of the uncertain and unpredictable nature of the project environment. (Wajir Economic Impact Assessment)

What this suggests, and as indicated in Chapter 3, the process of assessment and indicator development must:

- emphasise monitoring and 'impact tracking' in addition to adequate planning and evaluation;

- recognise the potential for differential impact on specific groups, particularly relating to gender and age;

- update and reformulate existing indicators, as well as introducing new indicators and dropping others, in the light of changing circumstances;

- explore significant changes which occurred as a result of the projects but which lay outside the initial indicators, and use this information to develop indicators for the future, as well as deliberately setting out to capture negative change and to seek out those who might provide this information.

Choice of Tools and Methods

Surveys

In Chapter 4 we saw how the use of large-scale household surveys can provide useful impact data if executed properly and if used in conjunction with other methods of data collection. The Wajir programme in north-eastern Kenya illustrates how surveys of this type can be used in what is essentially a long-term rehabilitation programme. However in large-scale emergency operations with a high degree of population movements, such as the Great Lakes crisis, it is unlikely that this sort of approach will be feasible after the operation, given that making contact with refugees and displaced groups and returnees will prove almost impossible.

However, this does not mean that impact assessment surveys cannot play a role during the crisis as a form of impact monitoring, or in post-emergency situations which do not involve large population movements. In Goma in the Democratic Republic of Congo, this role was performed at least partially by a number of epidemiologists who gathered data from a broad perspective, assessing potential risks and lapses in coverage and identifying emerging problems. This was identified as a major factor in improving humanitarian response in Goma compared to other sites where this role was largely absent (Borton et al. 1995, Collins et al. 1998).

In this case, impact data tended to focus on mortality and morbidity rates while individual agencies examined the quality and quantity of their outputs. In Oxfam GB's case, because of its role in water provision, the focus was on the quantity, quality, and accessibility of water. In some cases, where more qualitative feedback from refugees was gained, this proved important in helping the programme to evolve in different directions. For example, although there was a 95 per cent coverage of public latrines in Chabilisa camp in Karagwe, the population felt that public latrines were very dirty and unattractive to users. This was particularly acute because the population were unwilling to take responsibility to clean latrines that so many people used. As a result, teams of cleaners were employed, and the introduction of family latrines in some camps proved very popular and encouraged families to build and maintain them (Collins et al. 1998).

Clearly many of the lessons which relate to the management and implementation of surveys for impact assessment of long-term development work which are highlighted in Chapter 4 are equally relevant in emergency situations:

- focusing on a small number of critical issues;

- getting the balance right between exploring impact and verifying the degree to which project outcomes might have led to it;

- collecting data which allows comparison of issues over time;

- checking how representative the sample chosen is, and being aware of the need for dissaggregated data;

- pre-testing and refining questionnaires before the survey is implemented;

- taking care in the selection of enumerators and ensuring that they are properly trained and briefed.

Interviews, workshops, and discussions

Since documented information is likely to be unavailable, interviews, workshops, and discussions are an important part of assessing impact in emergency situations. These will probably need to involve a wide variety of stakeholders in order to reconstruct the context and project history, and to cross-check findings from a number of perspectives. Many of the advantages and disadvantages of group discussions or interviews compared with individual interviews highlighted in Chapter 4 are also relevant to emergency situations. For example, while bringing together people with different experiences and perspectives can help paint a picture of impact, in a conflict situation the ability of less powerful individuals or groups to express their views openly in the presence of others may be extremely limited.

On the other hand, the experience from the Ikafe case study in northern Uganda suggests that it is possible to strengthen the voices of some groups (in this case the host population and refugees) vis-à-vis others (aid agencies and local government authorities) through adequate preparation and a carefully designed and facilitated process. The exchanges in Ikafe provided rich food for thought for the agencies involved as their own perception of performance was contrasted with that of the refugees and the host population. These different perceptions are summarised in Table 5.1 which outlines the positive and negative impacts as described by Sudanese refugees, the Ugandan host population, and the aid agencies.

As the Ikafe experience demonstrates, different stakeholders may not share common objectives and may in fact seek contradictory impacts. They may use the political opportunity that an evaluation offers to advance their views and opinions, and to downplay those of other groups, leading to exaggerated responses and half-truths pre-dominating. An impact assessment team must be aware of that bias and ask who might be exaggerating and whose views are not represented and why, in order to understand the interests of different groups and their relations with others.

The Ikafe case study also brought to the fore the high levels of tension, trauma and stress that are present within stakeholder groups and between them. Embarking on a process which asks people to relive painful events and involves them in discussions with others who may have a different perspective requires extreme care and thoughtful preparation.

If impact assessments need to reconstruct history, often through interviews, there is a growing consensus that this should take place relatively soon after the event. However, it may also be necessary to make provision for the assessment of longer-term impact, for example in relation to psycho-social trauma, which may have long-term effects that take time to address.

Direct observation

Chapter 4 elucidated the role of direct and participant observation in building trust and rapport, cross-checking information, exploring relationships, discovering new insights, and in enabling a better understanding of an intervention's context. However, we also saw that the success of the method is dependent on existing levels of trust between observer and observed; that observers can affect the results they are observing; that it requires not only good observation skills but also interpersonal and communication skills; that it can be open to bias and selective perception on the part of the observer; and that it can be limited to external behaviours if the onlooker approach is adopted and it is not used exclusively. It is also a resource-intensive method.

In an emergency situation, it is clearly impossible to be a participant observer in the true sense, without being a victim of that disaster. Yet, as the evaluators of the Oxfam programme in the Great Lakes pointed out, boundaries between victims and onlookers can become blurred in complex situations.

Table 5.1: Different perceptions of project performance and impact in Ikafe

Group Perception	Sudanese refugee	Ugandan host population	Agencies including Oxfam
Positive	Situation improved since moving from Koboko; infant mortality decreased.	Local economy showed some improvement. Infrastructural improvements benefited some locals.	Infrastructure developed; food and water delivery, health-care and educational services set up which benefit all refugees and many locals, leading to improved nutritional status of refugees and increased food security. Seeds and tools delivered to most refugees who have been assisted with cultivation. Land allocation in process: strong boost for local economy.
Negative	Water and food provision irregular. Land often of poor quality. Seeds and tools delivered late. Alternative livelihood opportunities limited, and markets far away. Young not attending school. Lack of involvement of refugee council.	Not enough local people employed or contracts given to local contractors. More infrastructural development should have been located in the main local town instead of in the centre of the refugee settlement. Lack of consultation on land allocation to refugees, and violations of some sacred sites.	Lack of land and security problems hinder development of refugees' self-reliance.

> *During many of the Great Lakes emergency operations circumstances were often extremely harrowing and threatening. High levels of stress were, as a consequence, often unavoidable. The extent of psychological trauma suffered by many of the local staff in the Kigali office was so extreme as to be beyond the comprehension of the evaluation team ... One senior office manager lost 40 members of her family during the genocide.* (Collins et al. 1998)

Agency staff, particularly local staff, do share, at least partially, the horror and the risks inherent in an emergency situation (whereas external assessors usually come in after the height of a crisis). Thus staff are observers whose views and experiences may be very pertinent in understanding impact and the process by which it occurred. By the same token, however, their very close involvement in possibly traumatic circumstances also means that they may find it difficult to distance themselves from the events. As noted in Chapter 4, observation is a skill that needs to be developed and rewarded, a theme I shall return to in Chapter 7.

RRA and PRA/ PLA tools

Many of the participatory research methods covered in Chapter 4 can be useful for impact assessment work in emergency situations. Some examples are given below of tools which would seem to be of particular relevance, given the characteristics of emergency situations.

Time lines and historical profiles

Time lines and historical profiles, or matrices, can be useful means of reconstructing the context and programme operations that occurred. They can also be used to gain an overview of the actions of various agencies, enabling assessors to understand overall impact. The example from northern Ghana in Table 5.2 illustrates the perceived relationship between the outbreak of a bout of ethnic conflict and the actions of the government and international and local NGOs. It traces the activities of local and external agencies and also records a number of key events over the past 40 years. This was done by asking a group in the community to recall key events and local and external activities over time. As with other techniques of this kind, time lines are a means to provoke and focus discussion. The actual output or diagram is usually much less important than the dialogue and insights that it stimulates.

In this case the method helped to reveal the limited involvement of government, and local and international NGOs in the area until the conflict of 1994/95. It also provokes a number of questions as to appropriateness of the overall response in meeting emergency needs and in terms of the likely long-term response to the structural issues which provoked the conflict.

Table 5.2: Time line of Demon village, northern Ghana (April 1997)

Year	Key events	Activities supported by local organisations	Activities supported by external agencies		
			Government NGOs	Ghanaian	International NGOs
1960			Set up primary school		
1988	Famine Windstorm				
1989					Two boreholes
1990		Formed welfare association			Built day nursery
1991				Set up women's group	
1992		Organised youth association		Distributed cashew seeds Started credit scheme	
1993		Organised men's *susu* group			
1994	Ethnic conflict	Formed farmers' association	Started night schools		Distributed corn seeds Renovated primary school Provided fertiliser
1995	Ethnic conflict Windstorm Flooding		Provided fertiliser	Peace and reconciliation work Started revolving fund Set up women's groups	Provided farm inputs Supported resettlement Started revolving fund Set up feeding schemes for school
1996	Windstorm		Delivered Food Aid KVIP	Started revolving fund Distributed cotton seed	Provided roofing sheets for chief's place
1997				Set up structure for livestock	Financed blocks for teachers' building

Scoring and ranking

Although in an emergency it is important to quantify absolute numbers of for example, the displaced, the dying, or the prevalence of disease, one must also understand changes in knowledge, attitudes, and perceptions. Although these may be difficult to quantify, it is not impossible.

The Wajir case study managed to quantify and compare perceptions of relative change. Two hundred pastoral families were simply asked whether they felt the conflict situation was better or worse than ten years ago and to score the situation ten years ago and now, using up to ten stones (with one signifying 'bad' and ten signifying 'good'). In both project and non-project sites, the situation ten years ago was assigned three marks, compared to an improvement to seven marks now. So the perception in both areas was that the situation had improved, whereas other parts of the impact assessment had revealed important differences in the welfare of respondents in project and non-project sites. Comparing these different findings allowed the assessors to propose that the greater perception of security, which was felt in both areas, could not explain the other differences observed in the project and non-project sites. This strengthened the argument that the observed changes were due to the programme they were assessing. This example illustrates how this sort of scoring can provide important insights into people's perceptions of change over time. It also shows how, by comparing the perceptions of different groups, questions of attribution can be addressed.

However, practitioners should always remember that this sort of scoring provides an understanding of relative, not absolute, change. In the above example, people generally feel that the situation has improved, but we cannot be certain that there is any agreement between respondents about what the score of one or ten means as these were not defined in advance. Average figures may conceal great variations between respondents' answers, particularly if some groups are likely to face different threats to their well-being and security than others. For example, women and children's perception of their own personal security in emergency situations may differ dramatically from that of men.

One way of ensuring that the views of different groups are represented is to undertake a well-being ranking, where a number of key informants help determine the characteristics of a range of groups (see Chapter 4 for more details). Although these types of ranking normally focus on material well-being and assets (for example, as illustrated in Table 5.3) it is possible to include political vulnerabilities related to, say, ethnicity or religion, as well as other aspects of identity such as gender. These issues will be of particular relevance in monitoring the situation of those most vulnerable, and in assessments of differential impact.

Table 5.3 is based on a well-being ranking exercise carried out in four refugee communities in Ikafe, Uganda, with a range of informants, most of whom were women. It indicates that people who were employed by aid agencies or who owned enough capital to start small businesses were considered among the most well off, while those without assets or sufficient labour to farm, or who are physically disabled are considered the least well-off. This sort of information can be very useful in setting a sampling frame for continued monitoring of the programme's impact on different groups.

Table 5.3: Well-being ranking from Ikafe refugee settlement, northern Uganda

High well-being	Average well-being	Low well-being	Very low well-being
People employed by an international agency in Ikafe/Imvepi	Families with enough labour to farm the land that has been given to them	Those with no capiatla to engae in any petty trading activities	Those who have sold all their assets
People with enough capital to run a small business (a hotel, restaurant, and so on) in Ikafe or Imvepi	Those who have a small amount of capital to trade (selling beer, fish, tea) in the refugee settlement	Those families who are short of labour (due to ill health, disability, death)	Those who consumed seeds and sell all non-food items in order to buy food
	Those who have a technical skill (mechanic, bicycle repairer, carpenter, teacher) and can earn money from this activity	Those who have been transferred to areas where land is infertile	Those who are physically disabled and can not sell their labour
	Those who own some livestock (goats, a cow, some chickens)		Those families who don't have labour even to farm the land they have been given access to (for example, unaccompanied orphans, weak widows, disabled people)
	Those who are strong (able to construct their own house, latrine, and shower shelter) and can sell their labour to Ugandan nationals		

Chapati or Venn diagram

Emergency situations can involve a multiplicity of stakeholders pursuing different interests, and understanding who they are, how they relate to each other, and how they are perceived, is an essential part of the impact assessment process. One way of gathering this sort of information relatively quickly, and stimulating discussion on the issue, is through the use of chapati or Venn diagrams, as illustrated in Chapter 4.

Figure 5.1: Venn diagram of relationships in the Ikafe programme according to Oxfam managers

Dated April 1996

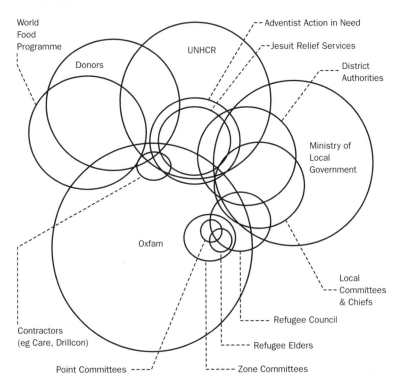

Note: The diameter of the circle indicates relative (perceived) influence or importance; the overlap indicates (perceived) intensity of contacts

The example in Figure 5.1 from Ikafe illustrates Oxfam managers' perceptions of the relative influence and inter-relationship between the substantial number of agencies and groups involved in the programme. It was part of the early work done during the impact assessment process; along with other methods it helped establish the key actors who needed to be involved in the assessment, as well as Oxfam staff members' perception of them. The refugees' relative lack of power compared to Oxfam, UNHCR, the donors, and the local government is clearly brought out in this diagram, and was a major concern for the assessors who had designed an assessment process that deliberately sought refugees' views.

Flow charts or mind-maps

Chapter 4 showed how flow charts, and the comparison of flow charts prepared by different groups (by men and women in Figures 4.2 and 4.3) can help deepen understanding of cause-effect relationships and reveal secondary impacts that may not have been intended. Given the turbulence of emergency situations, the high likelihood of unexpected impacts, and the fact that hard evidence may be lacking, flow charts can be a useful tool in promoting discussion about impact. (Like other participatory tools, they need to be used in conjunction with other methods.)

The example in Figure 5.2 from Ikafe reveals the complexity of the host population's perceptions of change brought about by the influx of refugees, and the project designed to support them. In addition it provides a holistic understanding of the context which can become a starting point for distinguishing between change that can be directly attributed to the project, such as increased employment, and change that can generally be attributed to the refugee influx, such as greater insecurity. It also provides space for exploring unexpected or unintended impacts — in this case, these included the violation of cultural sites and the perceived decline in moral standards — to be considered alongside those that were expected, such as better social infrastructure.

It also illustrates the degree to which local people and refugees in Ikafe attributed many of the things happening in their environment to the project. As one of the team involved in the study stated,

... the Sudanese refugees and local Ugandan people seemed (themselves) to want to attribute everything to the project intervention. This was mainly because they though that their lives had been negatively affected since they had been moved from Kiboko to Ikafe (rather than the Oxfam activities per se). (Ros David, personal communication)

This in turn can become a bone of contention with staff who feel that the views of the refugees, and host population, about the project do not refer to those issues over which the project, and project staff, have any control.

179

Figure 5.2: Ugandan host population's perception of impact of refugee arrival and programme responses by aid agencies

Adapted from Ikafe case study

Employment
Generally positive, but some groups feel discriminated against:
- Action Africa in Need employs 48 Sudanese and 34 Ugandan staff;
- Jesuit Refugee Service employs 2 staff from Arua and 8 from Aringa;
- Oxfam employs 3 international and 339 local staff, 30% of whom are refugees.

Social services and infrastructure
Nearly all positive impacts through the provision of
- 3 schools (1 for refugees);
- 6 grinding mills;
- 79 boreholes and 9 shallow wells;
- 2 hospital tents and 3 dispensaries;
- 175km manually built roads and 56km machine built roads.

Insecurity
Negative impacts related to
- crime (9 armed robberies);
- traffic accidents due to increased traffic flow and the speed of vehicles;
- the spill-over into Uganda of the Sudanese civil war and the SPLA movement;
- social conflict such as mistrust of police, bad communication, destruction of cultural sites, and high but unmet expectations.

Local people's perception of the impact of Sudanese refugees arriving in Ikafe

Local economy
Generally positive impact:
- trade has brought more money in circulation and improved the consumer market;
- local contractors are being used for road maintenance and for purchase of materials;
- there is increased tax revenue from NGO staff and from local markets.

Land use
Mostly negative impact, although there has been some protection and environmental education. Degradation has occurred due to increased bush burning and tree cutting. Moreover, there is less cultivable land for host population, and less hunting ground is available.

Socio-economic integration
Mixed impacts. On the positive side, the influx of refugees has led to cheap labour availability which as increased productivity and income. But it has also led to cultural disintegration through intermarriage, the violation of cultural sites, and a decline in moral standards which has led to a rise in the number of unmarried mothers and cohabiting.

The Ugandan host population in Ikafe identified six main areas of im[....]
the diagram, most of which are seen to have both positive and negative
elements. The first relates to employment by the aid agencies, in terms of
absolute numbers and in terms of the employees' origins: Were those
employed refugees or local Ugandans? Which district (for example, Arua) and
group did they belong to (Aringa or Terego)? The second are of impact refers
to the generally positive changes in the local economy, notably the general
increase in the amount of money circulating because of the aid agencies'
presence. The third category outlines the mainly negative perceptions of
changes in land use brought about as a result of the settlement, including
increased environmental degradation and reduced land for hunting. Fourth,
the host population identified changes in socio-economic integration, in
particular negative aspects such as declining morality, cultural disintegration,
and violation of sacred sites. They saw some positive elements in the
availability of cheap labour. The fifth element indicates the wholly negative
perceptions of declining security through increases in crime, road accidents,
social conflicts, and the movement of rebel troops. Lastly, people recognise
impact related to better social services and infrastructure including roads,
dispensaries, wells, grinding mills, and schools.

Trend analysis

A 'before and after' analysis referred to in the example of perceptions of
relative change in security in Wajir, can be of limited value in rapidly changing
emergency situations, because there can be great fluctuations. In order to
understand rapidly changing circumstances impact tracking or monitoring
needs to be carried out, and programmes adapted as a result.

This can also be done retrospectively, as in the time line from Northern
Ghana in Chapter 4, where villagers reviewed change over a number of years,
and assigned scores relating to key elements of their livelihoods. This kind of
exercise can provide an insight into perceived changes in people's quality of
life over time, and suggest causes for these. This then allows for factors
outside the project or programme to be explored, situating a project in its
wider context and helping to minimise any exaggeration, or underestimation,
of project impacts.

Lessons relating to participatory tools

The call for greater involvement of 'affected populations' — local actors and
organisations — in assessing impact is increasingly made, complemented by a
recognition of the need to assess the different impacts that projects can have
on groups such as women, men, children, and older people. In addition, the
views of those who did not benefit from the assistance should be deliberately

sought out as they may reveal problems with the agencies' targeting of beneficiaries. The case studies, and Oxfam's experience in the Great Lakes region, reveal that the potential for involvement varies at different stages of the emergency. In the Great Lakes crisis, obstacles included being obliged to work through camp authorities, many of whom were implicated in the genocide as members of the pre-war Rwanda government, and working in fragmented and divided communities in Rwanda itself (Collins et al. 1998). As Christopolos points out, a naïve approach to participation in situations of great abuse of power can be counterproductive.

Agencies that claim to follow a pluralistic view may also end up acting in a relativist manner due to a naïve borrowing of concepts and working methods from liberal democratic structures and transposing them to contexts where crude and unobstructed abuse of power abounds. There is no effective technique to empower someone who has a gun pointed at his head. Simple populist rhetoric— let the people decide— creates easy prey for those immoral characters who wish to manipulate situations to their personal benefit ... Accountability to beneficiaries and local institutions must be based on listening to the voices of the people in the camps, the burnt out villages, the ruins. Participatory approaches have a major role to play here. Caution is called for, however, to ensure that faith in methods does not blind us to those who will abuse them. There is no special technique that we can apply to vaccinate ourselves against the manipulation of participation to immoral ends. (Christoplos 1998)

People affected by trauma, political and sexual violence, threats and social dislocation may not only be scared to talk, it may be positively dangerous for them to do so. Therefore approaches to participative research and evaluation need to be modified and adapted. This may mean among other things:

- ensuring that a range of stakeholders is involved in the process of sampling,

- being aware of the political ramifications and risks of the assessment, and how these affect the credibility of the findings in the eyes of various stakeholders;

- seeking advice about who to talk to, and how to go about it, from trained trauma counsellors as well as those who genuinely represent these people;

- ensuring the confidentiality of interviews and interviewees;

- avoiding particularly traumatic and distressing areas of discussion;

- cross-checking information by using a variety of sources and methods (see below).

Despite these real difficulties, it is usually possible to increase the involvement of local people. In terms of impact assessment, this often brings out critical information. For example, Oxfam's water provision programmes in the Great Lakes region usually monitored the quality of water at source, rather than at point of use. By monitoring at point of use and talking to users, assessors found out that in some camps there were major variations in the quality of water consumed due to how it was carried and stored. This led to improved practices, such as adding chlorine to water tankered to site, and a jerry-can cleaning campaign (Collins et al. 1998). In Tanzania, focus-group discussions with men and women in two camps revealed that long queues at water-collection points contributed to attacks on women.

These examples illustrate that — even if opportunities for the full involvement of local people may be limited due to the political and safety situation — a better understanding of their situation and constraints can provide important feedback for project design and management. In turn, these limited initiatives can expand over time as and when it becomes possible. Given the fact that key groups are consistently *not* involved in programme design and implementation — particularly women, older people, and children — it is even more crucial that critical attention is paid to their involvement in impact assessment processes. This means being constantly aware of, and exploiting, the changing opportunities that exist for their involvement, and devoting adequate resources and time to it at the outset.

Case studies

As we saw in Chapter 4, case studies are not really a tool or method but more an approach that is particularly useful in complex situations where a large number of variables are inter-related. This makes the case study approach especially suited to emergencies. They necessarily involve many of the tools and methods described above.

Case studies in emergency situations often fall under the critical case type described in Chapter 4. Although emergency situations are usually unique they often produce intense managerial and organisational stresses that test the robustness of existing systems to the limit. In this sense emergency cases often have wider relevance and can throw light on critical organisational and policy issues which have high political impact. For this reason undertaking analysis across a number of case studies can be particularly important in drawing out generic lessons, and in supporting processes of institutional learning.

The importance of cross-checking and feedback
As explained in other chapters, cross-checking or 'triangulating' findings is of paramount importance. In emergency situations, which may be even more

dependent on qualitative methods of data collection, and where the manipulation of information may be even more in evidence, it becomes even more vital. As detailed in Chapter 3, cross-checking can be done by deliberately using a variety of types and sequences of research methods, researchers, respondents, or sources of information.

Since contradictions in findings may be even greater in emergency situations, the impact assessment design may have to be adapted in order to cross-check them as they emerge. Those managing impact assessment processes must therefore incorporate a high degree of flexibility in their design and be open to share their findings and give stakeholders the opportunity to respond:

[D]espite every effort to obtain all relevant information, there will be information which the team did not find, think to find or gain access to. There will inevitably be information that has been misinterpreted by the evaluators. The process of distributing the draft reports for comments and discussion is an integral part of evaluation. (Dabelstein 1996, p.291)

Criteria and indicators

The experience of the case studies and recent literature on the evaluation of humanitarian work underline the importance of adapting and reformulating indicators in the light of changing circumstances. However, four key area of change require evaluation in all contexts. These are:

Mortality and morbidity rates. These are particularly useful indicators in the first phases of a crisis or in refugee camps and other settings where the risks of widespread disease and contagion are high.

Coverage and differential impact. Agencies need to know who has and who has not been covered by a particular intervention, and what the impact is on different groups particularly men and women, young and old, displaced and host populations.

Protection and security. It remains a major challenge to resolve the issue of intervening, or persuading others to intervene, in ways which can enhance peoples' right to security in emergency situations. Changes in the levels of sexual violence and rape, destruction of homes and property, and population movements are likely indicators of the general security situation. Again, particular attention must be paid to human-rights violations of vulnerable groups which may not only include women, older people, children, and ethnic minorities but also males of fighting age. Faced by violent conflict and human-rights violations, various sections of the population will have different vulnerabilities. Women may be targeted for rape to undermine a community (Uganda, Bosnia), men may be raped as a tactic of terror (Sierra Leone), young girls may be taken as sexual slaves by fighting forces, and young boys coerced into fighting and abused as part of the initiation (Liberia), males of fighting age may have to move from house to house never sleeping in the same place twice for fear of being press-ganged (Bosnia), ethnicity may become a cause of violence (former Yugoslavia, the Great Lakes region), and the elderly may no longer receive the customary social respect and care.

Sustainability or 'connectedness' with longer-term issues. This describes the extent to which humanitarian work is undertaken in ways that support durable recovery; several areas of assessment within this have been suggested. These include

- net benefit — an assessment of the overall short-term and long-term cost and benefits;

- capacities and vulnerabilities — the degree to which long-standing individual, community, organisational, or even national vulnerabilites have been reduced and existing capacities increased;

- changes in gender dynamics — the degree to which positive changes that may have occurred have been maintained and reinforced or negative changes countered or reduced;

- peace, conflict resolution, and justice — the degree to which the programme has contributed to building understanding and social cohesion between conflicting groups, and reduced the tendency to resolve conflict through violence.

There is currently some controversy over the degree to which NGOs, in particular, can or should deliberately seek to build capacities, change gender dynamics, or promote peace during conflicts, or whether they should stick to a minimalist humanitarian relief role (Slim 1998, Duffield 1996, Macrae 1996). It seems unlikely that a categoric position either way is very helpful, although this does not negate the need for NGOs to understand the broader and longer-term consequences of their work, *whether they are intended or not*. However, it is often only possible to see broader impact with hindsight — predicting long-term or secondary effects in volatile situations is notoriously difficult. In the humanitarian arena, not responding to immediate threats to life on the — often hypothetical — grounds that it may contribute to prolonging a conflict is usually not ethically acceptable (Slim 1997). The provision of humanitarian assistance does not absolve warring parties and their supporters of their moral and legal obligations under International Humanitarian Law and the Geneva protocols. Nor does it absolve the international community from its duty to help bring conflicts to an end and to resolve the root causes that brought them about. In fact, it makes it even more important to gather evidence about the broader impacts of humanitarian assistance in situations where other actors do not comply with their moral and legal obligations. Not only will this help humanitarian agencies adjust their operations in the light of the findings, but, more importantly, it will contribute evidence to any potential process of legal redress. This sort of analysis can also illustrate the cost of the international community's failure to create a more 'rounded' political and economic, as well as humanitarian, response to complex emergencies.

Tools and methods

Emergencies in general, and complex political emergencies in particular, present severe challenges to orthodox approaches to choosing tools and methods. The examples cited in this chapter indicate how methodological innovation and adaptation to the specific contexts of emergencies can occur and result in important insights being gained. This is significant, given the recent findings by Hallam and Borton that

[c]urrent monitoring and reporting systems for humanitarian assistance programmes often do not take full account of the needs of ex-post evaluations and the effectiveness of the evaluation process is considerably hampered. (Hallam and Borton 1998)

Overcoming this requires improving monitoring systems, developing indicators and standards, and better information management. It should also be remembered that impact assessments may in themselves have little impact on organisational practices and policies if they are not followed up. It is necessary to set up a clear and systematic process, with a timetable and allocation of responsibilities for discussing and agreeing findings, implementing recommendations and changes, and adaptating policies and procedures. An agreed monitoring process for ensuring that this happens is also sometimes required: for example, in the case of the multi-donor evaluation of the crisis in Africa's Great Lakes Region, the Joint Evaluation Follow-up Monitoring and Facilitation Network (JEFF) was set up for post-evaluation monitoring.

If NGOs and other humanitarian agencies are to respond to the challenges thrown down by recent critiques of their work they need to be clear about their values and ethics and how these relate to international humanitarian law and the Human Rights and Refugee Conventions, as the evaluation of Oxfam's Great Lakes programme suggests:

In the case of humanitarian organisations the base line for determining humanitarian intervention should derive from International Humanitarian Law (IHL), Human Rights Conventions (HRC) and the Refugee Convention (RC).[5] These provide basic, but absolute, rights to protection and assistance for people affected by conflict. They constitute an internationally agreed general reference point for humanitarian intervention — an obligation on and a right of the international community ... IHL, HRC and RC provide the internationally accepted norms which justify intervention and determine accountability for those who intervene. (Zetter 1998)

This must then be complemented by becoming more vigilant, at an operational level, about setting consistent objectives and monitoring both changes in the context and in the impact of an intervention, and how these weigh up in the light of the growing body of standards that NGOs are starting to set for themselves.

Ethics and organisational practices

If impact assessment has to incorporate considerations of ethics and organisational practice, how would this work? Hugo Slim has set out a possible framework for ethical analysis (see Summary 5.1). Slim reminds us that relief agencies in conflict situations are always responding to the violence of others, and that the difficult moral choices they face are normally due to the immoral choices of others. He outlines the important characteristics of a moral dilemma (a choice between two evils) and distinguishes it from other 'tough choices' that can masquerade as moral dilemmas. In impact assessment, being clear about the types of choices and decisions that are or were available to agencies is a first step in analysing its actions and responsibilities in a given situation.

The next step is to determine what code of ethics the organisation adheres to and whether it is essentially 'duty-bound', like most of the medical profession or the ICRC, which undertake certain actions because they believe they are intrinsically right. The responsibility for the consequences of those actions is more dispersed; for instance, a doctor cannot refuse to treat a patient because of what he or she may do in the future. The alternative to being duty-bound is to be 'goal-bound' like many development NGOs, which involves a complicated and uncertain process of anticipating the wider outcomes of one's actions and holding oneself, at least partially, responsible for their long-term consequences. Once this basic point is addressed, other questions (relating to an organisation's motivations, prior knowledge, capacity, deliberation, mitigation, and organisational conscience) may be relevant. Answering these will allow a systematic review of an agency's ethical standards.

Slim's framework provides a useful if untested tool for undertaking an element of institutional and policy analysis that is usually lacking. When combined with other tools and approaches for looking at organisations and impact assessment, such as those described in Chapter 7, perhaps it will help to make the link between significant changes in individuals' lives and the organisational context in which they occur. An organisation's values and ethics (or lack of them) are an important indicator not only of how decisions are taken but also of which projects or policies will be delivered, and what value is placed upon the impacts that are achieved.

Summary 5.1: A framework for ethical analysis adapted from Slim (1997)

What code of ethics?

Is the organisation secure in the belief that its actions are always good in themselves? Or does it believe that it needs to have a sure grasp of the wider consequences of its work to be certain of the goodness of its work? Answers to this will determine how much moral responsibility an agency assumes for conditions surrounding its work.

How are different intentions and motivations balanced?

Is the agency acting out of the best motives and intentions or doing the right thing for the wrong reasons? How does it balance different organisational motives such as compassion, income, publicity, and influence; which tend to win out?

What knowledge is sought?

To what degree has the agency made every effort to gather all information relevant to its decision-making? If the agency did not have all knowledge at its disposal could it have reasonably been expected to collect it?

What capacity is available?

Did the agency have the capacity (resources, influence, power) to do anything about it? An agency can only he held responsible for not doing something it could have done, but chose not to do.

Is deliberation valued?

Did the agency make very effort to counsel, consult, debate, and weigh carefully the various aspects of the problem? A commitment to ethical deliberation should be a part of responsible programme design.

Did the agency seek to mitigate any negative impacts?

Did the agency seek to minimise any likelihood of negative impacts? In a choice between 'two evils', did it seek to limit the damage caused?

Is there an organisational conscience?

Do senior managers promote a moral ethos and ensure that staff have the ethical skills and a knowledge of past dilemmas to increase the likelihood that they will make sound decisions in difficult moments?

As far as other organisational practices are concerned, recent work by the Sphere project recognises that 'without clearly defined, systematic organisational policies and procedures the implementation of high quality programmes will not be possible' (The Sphere Project 1998). This approach complements Slim's ethical framework and the project has developed a set of organisational best practices which provide the means to achieving agreed minimum standards for humanitarian assistance. These are described in Summary 5.2.

Summary 5.2: Organisational best practices for humanitarian agencies (Sphere project 1998)

Philosophy

The agency's goals reflect universal humanitarian principles as outlined in the humanitarian charter and the Code of Conduct.

Accountability

The agency is accountable to the recipients of its services, to staff, and to donors.

Management and support of staff

The agency recognises that the effectiveness and success of humanitarian programmes depends on all the people working for them. Human resources issues are therefore central to strategic plans.

Analysis

Interventions are based on an understanding of the context and a clear analysis of need. Any response is based on the culture(s), needs, and rights of those it is intended to assist.

Co-ordination

There is commitment to a co-ordinated response, which takes into account the views of all the stakeholders and where local authorities take a lead if appropriate.

Participative programme planning

Programming decisions are consistent with the agency's philosophy and involve all stakeholders in the process. Programme characteristics are determined through application of the planning cycle which facilitates monitoring and accountability.

Gender integration

The agency considers gender aspects in all programming decisions.

The special needs of children

Programmes address the special needs unique to children affected by calamity or conflict.

Environment

The agency takes a proactive approach to environmental concerns in all programming decisions. Prevention of environmental damage should be the norm rather than the exception.

Protection

The agency demonstrates concern for the physical safety of disaster-affected persons. Although protection is the responsibility of states, agencies have a responsibility to be knowledgeable and aware of the implications of interventions.

Security

The agency demonstrates concern for the security of local and expatriate staff.

In each of these areas, Sphere gives detailed information which attempts to further define best practice. This is cross-referenced to thematic minimum standards (for example for water supply, nutrition, food aid, shelter, health-care, and site planning) so that each thematic areas has standards of analysis for assessment and monitoring and evaluation processes; minimum standards related to the thematic area in question; and some related capacity and competence standards on the part of the agencies involved. Although many of the standards and associated indicators are not impact indicators in the strict sense, they are qualitative and quantitative output measures which, if reached, could reasonably be expected to make a significant difference to people's lives in emergency situations.

These sorts of standards and guidelines for best practice can, therefore, make an important contribution to assessing performance and in the development of clearer accountability. However, NGOs are increasingly combining operational relief efforts in humanitarian situations with lobbying and advocacy work, so any assessment of overall impact has to also explore this other aspect of their work. The next chapter attempts to do this in some depth.

6

Impact assessment and advocacy[1]

This chapter looks at the particular challenge of assessing the impact of advocacy initiatives, in terms of both designing an assessment and selecting tools and methods for it. The material presented uses three main ways to examine the impact of advocacy and policy work. The first analyses activities designed to change policies and through reasoned argument seeks to predict or explain their general impacts. The second assesses to what extent various groups' abilities have been enhanced, and what they can now achieve. The third approach is to examine how policies are implemented in practice and what the actual, specific impact on people's lives is. The chapter concludes that a major challenge is to bring these different approaches together in order to make an overall assessment of impact. In addition it is suggested that the findings from impact assessment processes can themselves be used as important evidence for advocacy work in the future.

Non-government organisations have in recent years put a growing proportion of their time and resources into 'advocacy' work. Advocacy is sometimes defined simply as the pursuit of change in policy or practice for the benefit of specific individuals or groups of people. However, some would argue that NGO advocacy should be defined more specifically as 'the strategic use of information to democratise unequal power relations and to improve the condition of those living in poverty or who are otherwise discriminated against'[2]. This is because NGOs seek to improve the situation for a particular constituency, and because they should seek to do so in a way that strengthens that constituency's power to influence others on their own terms.

Advocacy may therefore involve direct lobbying, public campaigning, public education, as well as capacity-building and creating alliances in order to achieve desired changes in people's lives. Many large agencies now have dedicated policy departments which carry out research and lobbying on specific issues, and the NGO presence at major international events — such as the Conference on Environment and Development in Rio de Janeiro in 1992, the Conference on Population and Development in Cairo in 1994, the Copenhagen Social Summit in 1995, and the World Conference on Women in Beijing in 1995 — has increased dramatically. Both Northern and Southern NGOs have invested time and money in trying to influence the outcome of these events. However, like any other aspect of their work, NGOs need to be able to justify this investment to themselves and to other stakeholders and to improve their ability to achieve an impact in this way.

Yet many, within and outside the NGO sector, still have doubts about advocacy work. Are NGOs drifting away from what they are supposed to be good at — running field projects or 'grassroots' work — into areas where they have limited competence and even less leverage? Or is it high time that they tried to attack the root causes of poverty? Who determines the policy agenda, and who assesses the impact of policy change? Does the increasing level of subcontracting threaten NGOs' ability to promote change in the policy arena? Is there a trade-off between undertaking advocacy oneself and building the capacity of others to undertake their own advocacy? What proportion of resources might most effectively be allocated to advocacy compared with other work? Does advocacy ultimately make a difference to the lives of people living in poverty — or does it result, at best, in changed rhetoric and empty promises, and at worst in the development of policies and practices which actually leave marginalised groups worse off? These are the kinds of questions that are currently being debated within and between NGOs and that any impact assessment exercise must bear in mind.

Particular problems with assessing the impact of advocacy work

NGOs need to demonstrate that their advocacy work is not only effective but also cost-effective and has impact in the sense of making a positive difference to people's lives. They must show that lasting change in policy and practice actually results in improving the lives of men and women living in poverty and that this achievement is due, at least in part, to their research, capacity-building, and lobbying efforts. NGOs also need to know under what conditions they should advocate on behalf of others and when they should be strengthening others to speak for themselves. They have to demonstrate that they are going about this work in a professional and competent manner, and use the monitoring of this work to learn and to improve future performance. These are not new issues: the same criteria should be applied to grassroots projects. However, advocacy work presents some particular challenges.

A large proportion of advocacy work is long-term; it may lack dramatic moments when it is possible to say that a significant change has occurred. Policy change is often incremental and slow, and implementation lags significantly behind legislative change. Although there may be exceptions to this, particularly in single-issue campaigns, the relationship between these 'victories' and long-term policy change is complex and difficult to untangle. In addition, policy- and decision-making processes are subject to a large number of influences. The necessary change in policy or practice may happen in a place far removed from where impact is sought; policy and practice changes may need to occur at the local, national, and international level. Combining and cross-checking assessments from multiple levels can be 'like trying to force pieces from different puzzles into one frame' (Oxfam GB 1998). This complexity becomes even greater in trying to demonstrate that advocacy has prevented something from happening. For example, how can one prove that violent conflict would have occurred if not for an NGO's influencing work to persuade opposing parties to resolve their conflict by non-violent means?

A great deal of advocacy work takes place through networks and coalitions. Positive results are often achieved through a rich mix of strategies, with some agencies taking a confrontational line and others conducting an 'insider' debate; indeed, sometimes individual agencies may adopt both approaches at once. This combination may be effective, with the public campaigners forcing open doors for others, but it can make attribution and impact assessment very difficult. It may be counterproductive for a particular agency to say exactly how its own efforts contributed to the final outcome, either because this will be seen to undervalue the contributions of others, or because disclosure may compromise future initiatives.

Even when the objectives of a piece of advocacy work are clear, the means by which they are achieved are often less certain and usually have to be adapted over time, making it difficult to draw up predetermined plans and select progress indicators. In advocacy work, it is necessary to invest in a variety of activities and cultivate a large number of contacts in order to cover a range of potential opportunities for influencing. Many of these may not bear fruit in the short term, or even at all, but it is often not possible to determine this beforehand and some 'failures' or 'lost causes' may eventually lead to changing future policy and practice in a positive way.

Much advocacy work is unique. Seizing opportunities and innovation are often critical components of successful advocacy; there is relatively little repetition, which prevents the gradual accumulation of knowledge across a series of 'projects'. Lessons are more likely to be about the relative merits of various strategies in addressing specific audiences, as well as different sequences and combinations of tools and methods, than about developing a single model of change or assessment.

As Rick Davies has noted, if one adopts the dictionary definition of advocacy as 'verbal support or argument for a cause' then an advocate is often a broker or mediator between two parties: the 'client' and the 'audience'. Impact assessment therefore needs to look at the advocate's relationship with both parties. Davies recognises that there are particular problems with relating to 'clients'. In some cases the 'intended beneficiaries' may not know that they are the 'intended beneficiaries'; in many cases they do not have a choice about who will undertake the advocacy role and lack influence over their advocate. The balance of power in the relationship between audience, advocate, and client is not in favour of people living in poverty; and it may be more seductively attractive for the advocate to talk to powerful people than to the poor (Davies 1997). Moreover, if an agency is seeking to change policies which may have an impact on many thousands or even millions of people (such as debt relief) then the logistical and practical difficulties of consulting with them become enormous. In this type of advocacy work, talking to the ultimate beneficiaries and understanding their perception of impact becomes even more difficult than in grassroots projects.

Some of the above issues, as discussed in earlier chapters, also apply to long-term development work: it does not produce dramatic breakthroughs, attribution is difficult, it requires an appropriate mix of approaches, and the work is often unique. This is particularly the case as one moves away from narrow project-based assessments and towards the examination of long-term programmes and relationships with other actors.

Designing an impact assessment process for advocacy work

Defining the purpose and the types of impact to be assessed

Returning to the arguments in Chapter 3, impact assessments of advocacy work need to be clear about what the purpose of the assessment is, and who it is for. Similarly, as outlined in earlier chapters, certain assumptions about how policy change happens and what types of impact are to be examined must also be made explicit. I am using some examples from the case studies, but as few of them looked at advocacy in depth, I am also drawing on material from other sources.

The NK and GSS case study from Bangladesh sets out a clear model of change which is mainly based on the development of group cohesion and the groups' subsequent ability to advocate and push for change in policies and practice at a level beyond that of the village. The following stages in group cohesion are identified and then tracked over time.

1 Group formation
2 Group carries out activities
3 Group sets up or joins a federation beyond the village level
4 Movement is launched which takes on groups with vested interests
5 Groups of poor are involved in framing legislation and have control over resources

This approach focuses mainly on assessing the capacity of groups of people living in poverty to have a growing say in their lives and to influence the agenda of the more powerful. At the same time the study explores the necessary levels of support that are required from intermediary organisations at each level of group cohesion. This relationship is explored in more depth in Chapter 7.

The CYSD study in Orissa, India, analysed their programme in terms of first-order change (outputs), second-order change (effects), and third-order change (impact). First-order change was measured in terms of the numbers and types of groups that were formed as a result of the project, such as village development committees, self-help groups, forest protection committees, farmers clubs, and *mahila samiti* (federation of women's self-help groups). Second-order change was assessed in terms of the evolution of these groups through membership drives, formal registration, creating a community infrastructure, and in terms of changes in the growth of community activities, the roles and regularity of meetings, and the use of community centres. In assessing the impact at community level (third-order change), it was examined if and how groups shared approaches and techniques or used them more widely; how many and what kind of proposals and demands the community made; what changes occurred in community norms and behaviour (for example, in terms of gender or dependence/ self-reliance); and what degree and range of activities the groups believed they could accomplish.

The CYSD study was particularly interested in the links between the three levels of change. All results from the three villages where the detailed study was undertaken were compared with a control village. Looking at impact in this way (for example, comparing those villages which had a community centre provided by the project with the control village which did not have a centre) also allowed a comparison between the abilities of the communities to influence others. One of the ways this was done was to list the proposals and demands made by each of the communities and their effects (see Table 6.1). The control village — although it has generally made fewer proposals and demands – like two of the other villages has submitted a proposal for legal rights to encroached land. This suggests either that the project's influence has spread beyond the initial villages, or that the ability to submit proposals is not attributable to the project. The fact that its proposal has not had a result yet, whereas those from the other villages have, may or may not point to differences in an ability to not only submit proposals but to have them acted upon. Using a control group allows these kinds of questions to be asked, even if further investigation will be required if they are to be answered.

Table 6.1: Assessing community proposals and demands, CYSD, Orissa

Village	Proposals and demands	Effect and level of the action
I	Submitted proposal for forest protection rights	Forest protection right over 30 acres granted by Forest Department of the Government of Orissa
	Submitted proposal for transferring legal right to their encroached land	Eight households received legal right to encroached land
	Submitted proposal to the displacement officer for rehabilitation compensation on their displacement	All villagers received reasonable compensation
II	Submitted proposal for a water harvesting scheme	Accepted by block office, now in progress
	Submitted proposal for care feed system	Villagers are getting food items from block office
	Submitted proposal for transferring legal right to their encroached land	Eight households received legal right to encroached land
	Submitted proposal for loan for starting poultry farm	Bank has assured loan
	Proposal for protection rights over 320 acres of forest	No result as yet
III	Submitted proposal for forest protection rights	Forest protection right over 75 acres granted by Forest Department of the Government of Orissa
	Submitted request for more canal water to be released to the village	More water now allotted to the village
	Submitted proposal for road-construction scheme	Accepted by block office; road has been constructed
Control	Submitted proposal for transferring legal right to their encroached land	No result as yet

This example demonstrates that advocacy is often part and parcel of local projects and of setting local priorities for development, rather than only about international lobbying, campaigning, and summits. In the following, I present two examples of approaches to impact assessment concerned with high-level lobbying, drawing on work by Oxfam GB's Policy Department and by the New Economics Foundation.

In the past, the Oxfam Policy Department has tended to focus on the policy outcomes of its work, distinguishing between different stages of the advocacy process in the following way:

1 Heightened awareness about an issue
2 Contribution to debate
3 Changed opinions
4 Changed policy
5 Policy change is implemented
6 Positive change in people's lives

This approach postulates an implicit hierarchy of change, from getting an issue on the agenda of decision makers through to changing policies which eventually make a positive change for people living in poverty.

Both the authors of the NK and GSS case study and Oxfam are at pains to point out that they recognise that in reality, policy change is neither as linear or as predictable as these simple hierarchies suggest. However, one must recognise the usefulness in distinguishing between different stages in this way, and establishing indicators that can monitor progress. Clearly there are many cases where a change, or several changes, in practice or legislation trigger policy change, rather than vice versa — in fact, the importance of creating precedents (for instance, winning a particular victory such as the case of the Narmada dam) which may then lead to broader policy change (relating to all future dam construction) may be an central advocacy strategy. In a similar way, much advocacy, particularly local advocacy, may move directly from engaging on a general issue to changing practice and bringing about specific immediate benefits, such as successfully pushing for the sacking of a corrupt official.

In its research on the effectiveness of NGO policy work the New Economics Foundation builds on the work of Jane Covey, among others. It proposes a framework for understanding the process of policy change that brings together the effects of advocacy both on policy and on the emergence of civil society or its ability organisations to undertake advocacy work (Covey 1996). The following kinds of questions can thus be addressed:

To what extent has the alliance, through its organisation and campaign strengthened the institutional base for citizen political action? Has it nurtured informed grassroots participation for the long haul, or simply mobilised groups for acts of protest? Has it contributed positively to an inclusive political culture, and public resolution of conflict through peaceful means? (Covey, quoted in NEF 1998)

NEF's model sets out a similar, but simpler, hierarchy of policy change to the Oxfam one shown above, and distinguishes between three different but overlapping phases. During the formative phase, issues begin to take shape and moves are made to place it on the policy agenda; at the discursive stage, the aim is to achieve policy change; and with the paradigm shift, new policy is implemented and practice changed.

Fig 6.1: The policy time line, with policy and civil-society aims

adapted from New Economics Foundation 1998

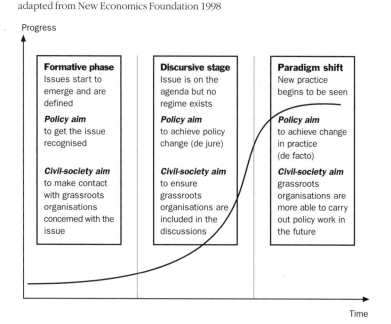

This model also elaborates the aims regarding civil-society participation in policy change, which is seen as part and parcel of the long-term advocacy agenda. Of course this process is unlikely to be as neat, ordered, and linear as this, but the time line does lay out an explicit model of change to be assessed.

An example of an assessment which uses this kind of framework is found in a study of advocacy work and the promotion of peace in East Timor and Angola by CIIR.[3] This research takes forward the two dimensions of capacity-building and policy impact, differentiating between declaratory and implementation impact (similar to NEF's distinction between the discursive stage and the paradigm shift). CIIR define capacity-building impact as the extent to which an organisation has accumulated the necessary skills and resources to carry out effective advocacy and the extent to which they have translated this into action. Declaratory policy impact means the degree to which advocacy has produced a change in the rhetoric of decision-makers and in their legislation. Implementation impact refers to the extent to which new legislation has been translated into new administrative procedures or institutional practices.

CIIR also sought to distinguish between 'Northern' and 'Southern' outcomes for each of these dimensions,

on the grounds that while it is important to assess the effect of NVO [Northern Voluntary Organisations] advocacy on Northern institutions, it is also important to ascertain what effect NVOs advocacy has had on the situation in the South. (CIIR 1997, p.6)

Figure 6.2 illustrates how this effect is rated on a scale from 'low' to 'high'. CIIR used a relatively simple graphic, with a range of symbols representing specific types of impact and annotations of these symbols to show change over time. The first graphic, for example, shows that capacity-building impact in both North and South has progressed positively over time in the case of East Timor; but implementation impact has remained low despite some change in rhetoric. In the case of Angola, progress on capacity-building has been more modest, and implementation is also low.

This model indicates how the crucial link between the 'advocate' and the 'client' can be explored, and the degree to which trade-offs between policy change and capacity-building may have occurred. In addition, it allows change over time and at different levels to be examined — for example, this approach could be used to explore differences between outcomes at the national and local level within a country. CIIR learned important lessons about the importance of generating public concern in the North; the need to focus on achievable policy goals; the requirement of establishing a clear division of labour between, and effective co-ordination of, grassroots organisations, development NGOs in the South and North, and policy institutes; and the need for campaigns of this nature to take a long-term view and be supported by adequate resources.

Figure 6.2: A model for rating the impact of advocacy work by Northern-based voluntary agencies (NVOs) (produced by CIIR)

Source: *Making Solidarity Effective* (Baranyi, Kibble, Kohen, O'Neill 1997)

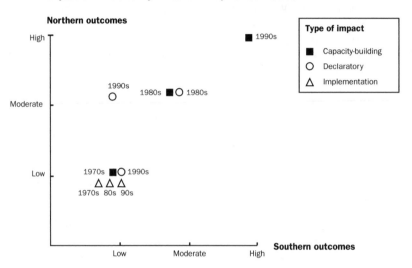

Impact of NVO activity on East Timor, 1970s–1990s

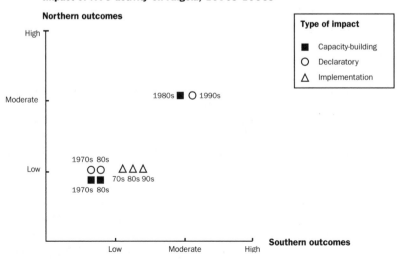

Impact of NVO activity on Angola, 1970s–1990s

These examples indicate that two broad dimensions of impact need to be explored — policy change and impact, and capacity-building and impact — within which more specific indicators can be developed, depending on the specific nature of the advocacy work undertaken. All assessments — whether examining local, micro-level advocacy work (NK/ GSS in Bangladesh and CYSD in India) or advocacy work on a wider, macro-level scale (NEF and CIIR) — suggest that it is important to look at these two dimensions together in order to explore the relationship and potential trade-offs between them. A recent study by Edna Co on advocacy for policy reform in the Philippines, commissioned by a group of Northern and Filipino NGOs, deliberately includes an assessment of the degree to which the advocacy work had equalised power relations and strengthened grassroots organisations and movements. Not only did this legitimise the advocacy work but 'a grassroots constituency gave public actions credibility and effectiveness' (Co 1999). Indeed, the sustainability of much advocacy work is dependent on local organisations ensuring that any agreed policy or practice is actually delivered.

However, these example also illustrate that although NGOs are starting to assess more than just the outcomes of advocacy work they still tend to concentrate on outcomes or effects (changes in policies or practices, or changes in capacity to advocate), rather than on ultimate impacts (significant changes in people's lives). This is understandable, because — as in the case of CYSD — the ultimate impacts have yet to be felt. Presenting a reasoned argument for the likely or plausible impact, based on what has been achieved to date, is all that can be done. In some cases, the fact that a policy has been changed or that people feel more capable of advocating in the future can in itself be deemed an impact, because it can lead to significant changes in people's self-confidence, self-belief or self-worth, even if other benefits that had been sought have not (yet) materialised. This is certainly the case in those communities in the CYSD study which specifically explored change in the degree and range of activities which communities believe they can accomplish.

It may impossible, unnecessary, or extremely cost-ineffective to demonstrate ultimate impacts, for instance in cases where one is trying to mitigate negative impacts. It is already medically established that vaccinating children against polio will have a significant effect on their lives (because it eliminates the possibility of them catching the disease); it is therefore sufficient to assess the outputs of a polio vaccination campaign, such as the proportion of children vaccinated every year, rather than demonstrate that a representative sample of children did not get polio as a result of the vaccination. Similarly, in the case of land mines it would probably not be possible, or necessary, to demonstrate — except through reasoned argument — that if fewer land mines are planted this will lead to fewer injuries or deaths. Rather, it will be necessary to ensure that policy and practice change actually leads to fewer land mines being planted (an outcome rather than an impact). On other hand, if the ban on land mines does not lead to any changes in practice, as some fear, or if funds that would otherwise have gone to mine clearance are diverted, there may be a need to assess the impact of the campaign in these terms.

Assessing impact remains critical for advocacy work, not least because those involved must ensure that what they are doing actually makes a difference to people's lives, and that they can demonstrate this. There are enough examples of how changes in policy, practice, or legislation fail to lead to significant changes in people's lives. However, there may be occasions when the actual demonstration of impact, other than in the form of reasoned argument agreed by key stakeholders, is either unnecessary or too costly to make it worthwhile.

What are the units of assessment?

As the above examples show, several dimensions of impact can be explored in advocacy work through a range of units or levels of assessment. Impact assessment in case studies has tended to focus on the level of the individual, the household, the community and local NGOs, with less emphasis on the wider institutions which may be targeted by advocacy work. As the CYSD study described above reveals, this approach can give important insights into changes in the capacity of local organisations to undertake advocacy work, as well as into the ultimate impact of changes in the political, economic, and social environment. However, a list of critical success factors for advocacy at the macro level identified by Oxfam GB (see Summary 6.1) indicates that it is not only targeted lobbying which creates changes in policy and practice, but that influencing public opinion can play a crucial role. While this may not tell us directly about impact it helps to understand how particular outcomes, which may have achieved an impact in the past or are likely to do so in the future, were brought about.

Summary 6.1: Critical success factors for advocacy suggested by Oxfam GB

When Oxfam and its partner organisations have been most successful in bringing about policy and practice change through advocacy, this has been based on a number of critical factors:

- solid research and analysis and clear achievable propositions for policy change;

- credibility built on being able to link practical experience to broader policy issues — making micro-macro links;

- the ability to build upon past investments in local contacts, partner organisations, networks, and alliances (many of which had been built up over several years);

- the readiness and ability to seize sometimes unexpected opportunities to push for change;

- the involvement of credible, skilled, and experienced lobbyists, who have good intelligence about, and contacts within, the lobbying targets;

- excellent media work founded on good contacts with journalists.

For some issues — for example, on land mines, debt relief, or structural adjustment programmes — the generation of demonstrable public concern in both the North and the South has also been critical in creating a favourable environment for policy and practice change.

Source: 'Fundamental Review of Strategic Intent' (Oxfam GB 1998)

Table 6.2, building on a similar table in Chapter 3, attempts to synthesise some of the advantages and disadvantages in exploring impact with a range of stakeholders in the advocacy process. Clearly the balance between groups will depend on the purpose of the study and the nature of the advocacy work. However, sensible judgements about advocacy work should combine a good understanding of the inputs and outputs of the process as well as an estimation of the impacts. As the consultants who assessed Oxfam's advocacy work regarding the Great Lakes region, and who were unable to examine ultimate impacts in any systematic way, stated in their report:

Some NGOs use proxies to try and measure the effectiveness of their advocacy (how many press releases and briefing papers were sent out etc.). But these are output measures, which may show that people are working hard — but they have little to do with whether they are making an impact.

In this evaluation we have focused on interviewing people who have been on the receiving end of advocacy messages, because we fell this is what might be termed 'the least worst' method of evaluating advocacy. (Development Initiatives 1997)

In many NGOs the assessment of the worth of advocacy will ultimately depend on the reasoned judgement of senior managers. The perspectives of the actors included in the table below can present important information for making that judgement as well as being a means of cross-checking analysis — as explained later in the chapter, it is often in the interests of several of the parties involved, including NGOs themselves, to exaggerate their role in promoting policy change. However, as impact cannot be proved statistically or scientifically, managers will have to make a trade-off between devoting resources to the assessment of impact and the actual advocacy work itself. This in turn will also help determine both the absolute number of individuals or organisations who might be involved in a process of impact assessment, as well as the proportion of contributions from stakeholders.

In broad terms, these stakeholders provide different perspectives on various parts of the 'impact chain': for instance, ultimate beneficiaries, local people, and local organisations are central to our understanding of ultimate impact or significant change in people's lives. Staff from local and international organisations who are specifically involved in the advocacy which is being assessed can not only provide insights into the precise role they played but can often also compare and contrast the specific roles played by various agencies. The targets of advocacy – legislators and governments as well as their staff and civil servants — can give an important insight into what it felt like to be on the receiving end. Journalist and academics can give slightly different 'outsider' perspectives, while assessing public opinion can provide a useful barometer of direct and indirect changes in attitudes.

Table 6.2: Advantages and disadvantages of different units of assessment for examining the impact of advocacy work

Unit of assessment	Advantages	Disadvantages
Ultimate beneficiaries, at the individual and household level	Permits an understanding of: • ultimate impacts and changes in people's lives; • local capacity for collective action and advocacy; • sustainability of impacts.	It may be difficult to link changes to advocacy outputs. A focus on this level may ignore other influences. It may be difficult to aggregate impacts.
Local NGO/ community-based organisation/ local activist groups	Permits an understanding of: • capacity for collective action and advocacy; • capacity to support and sustain changes at individual level; • the scope that has been created for advocacy; • impact of advocacy on community norms.	Exact membership is sometimes difficult to assess. Dynamics within and between groups is often difficult to understand. It may be difficult to compare impact using quantitative data.

Table 6.2: Advantages and disadvantages of different units of assessment for examining the impact of advocacy work (continued)

Unit of assessment	Advantages	Disadvantages
Advocacy staff	Permits an understanding of: • inputs to and outputs of the advocacy process; • perceived models and indicators of change as well as strategies for achieving it; • comparison of different agencies' roles.	Advocacy staff may tend to exaggerate their role, often to ensure their own organisational survival. Advocacy staff may be detached from others in the organisation who work with local actors.
Decision-makers	Gives insider perspective of policy process. Permits comparative analysis of different forces and influences for or against change. Can provide vital information for future strategies.	Decision-makers tend to exaggerate their role in promoting change. May be moved in the next cabinet reshuffle, election, or coup, and therefore not be a reliable guide to the future.
Civil servants and agency staff	May have longer-term perspective than politicians. Are often well placed to explain procedural and bureaucratic mechanisms and obstacles to policy change and implementation. May be able to expose inner workings and politics of organisation as well as disagreements which can be exploited in the future.	May not have access to overall understanding of policy process. May be naturally conservative in their views about future change.

Table 6.2: Advantages and disadvantages of different units of assessment for examining the impact of advocacy work (continued)

Unit of assessment	Advantages	Disadvantages
Journalists	Can give another perspective on the politics of the policy process.	May tend to sensationalise the mundane.
	Can give insights into the inputs, outputs, and impact of media work in achieving change.	Tendency to exaggerate their role in promoting change.
	May have access to insider information not available to others, as well as information on public attitudes and opinions.	May be unable to reveal sources and may need to 'trade' information for other favours.
Academics, research and policy institutes	Can give another perspective on the politics of the policy process.	May tend towards an overly academic analysis of impact biased by their particular discipline.
	Can give insights into the inputs, outputs, and impact of academic and research work in achieving policy change.	Tendency to exaggerate their role in promoting change, often for their own career purposes.
	May have access to insider information not available to others, as well as information on public attitudes and opinions.	May actually be isolated from reality of policy process and public opinion.
Public opinion	Gives an understanding of change in public attitudes, how this may have been brought about, and how they may have shaped decision-making and policy changes.	Greater problems of attribution given that causality is difficult to untangle.
		Expensive to get representative view.
	Can in itself be used for advocacy work so as to demonstrate public concern.	Difficult to aggregate while retaining an understanding of differences of opinions between groups.

What information already exists?

Once the model of change and the types of impact to be assessed are clear, the next step is finding out if the required information already exists. Apart from exploring project documents, official records and surveys, records of parliamentary debates, politicians' voting patterns in national assemblies, and public opinion polls can often provide evidence of changing opinions and attitudes as well as examples of action taken as a result. In some settings historical or anthropological material, newspapers, government and development agencies' reports, and so on may be all be relevant not only for determining what change has been brought about by a given project, but also for comparing past dissent and protest or lobbying capacity with the current situation. Although it may be very difficult to discover what caused these changes, such information can paint a backdrop to more focused impact work. In addition, it can help determine whether particular changes in opinion occurred widely in a given population or only in specific groups of people who may have been targeted by a campaign.

Who should be involved in the evaluation team?

The choice of evaluator or assessor will be subject to the same kinds of concern as raised in Chapter 3: it will depend on the level of experience available 'in-house', the degree of independence or 'objectivity' that certain stakeholders may demand, and the extent to which the exercise is viewed as a training or capacity-building process in its own right. Additionally, an impact assessment of advocacy initiatives needs to give thought to the evaluators' access to, and credibility with, advocacy targets if these are to be contacted. If evaluators are already known to the target, either personally or by reputation, this may gain them access to people who are invariably busy and may well have better things to do. Similarly an evaluator who does not respect people's time constraints, who behaves in an unprofessional way in an interview or consultation process, or who does not appear knowledgeable about the issue in question, not only risks collecting poor quality information, but can also undermine the credibility of the organisation commissioning the evaluator and thus its access and impact in the future.

The issue of baselines

Chapter 3 stated that where baseline information exists it can help track change over time, but that even if baseline data is collected it may not include information which is subsequently revealed to be important, or the information may not be organised in such a way as to make it accessible or usable for comparisons. So although it is important to collect relevant baseline data which is appropriate to the desired change (see Summary 6.2) it is often necessary to reconstruct baseline data from project documents, other organisations, key informants, other stakeholders, and so on.

Summary 6.2: Key lessons for baseline data collection for advocacy work

- Aim to collect only information that is seen to be particularly relevant to assessing the outcome and impacts of the advocacy work and that will be difficult to collect through recall or baseline reconstruction methods.

- Collect only the amount of information that the organisation actually has the capacity to analyse, organise, and store.

- Make sure that the data collected is properly recorded, filed, and stored. The organisation must know where these files are held and what they contain, and have an adequate system for retrieving this information when it is needed.

- Recognise that it is impossible to predict all the information that might be needed and that any baseline will have to be updated.

- Explore the possibility of creating 'rolling baselines' by following changes in a particular number of people, groups, or advocacy targets over the life-time of the project.

- Explore the possibility of using new individuals, campaign groups, or targets which can act as a baseline for comparing existing participants.

In advocacy work — particularly in a policy environment which is subject to rapid and unpredictable change, where seizing new opportunities is critical to success, and where attribution is usually difficult to assess — the monitoring of ongoing change in the relationship between outputs and impact is likely to be more useful than extensive 'before and after' surveys. This suggests a greater emphasis on systematically recording ongoing evidence (both anecdotal and statistical) and making a reasoned assessment of past impact on a regular basis, than on collecting data on a large number of predetermined indicators. This is not to say that the latter is unnecessary but that it should not be done at the expense of ongoing impact tracking.

Dealing with attribution

In Chapter 3 I looked at several ways of dealing with the problem of how to attribute change to a given intervention. I explored the use of control groups and non-project respondents; the possibility of searching for other explanations of change; and how secondary data and other key informants can help clarify attribution. For advocacy work the problem of attribution may be even more complicated, and the gap between action and ultimate impact even greater. An internal report written by Oxfam's Policy Department illustrates the problem.

The difficulty of attributing impact, in its ultimate sense (i.e. alleviating poverty, distress and suffering), to Policy Department work is fraught with difficulty. It would seem that we therefore need to be concentrating more on outcomes i.e. what we are willing to be held accountable to achieve and then providing a logical and reasoned account of what the consequences of us doing that are, in terms of wider impact. This means concentrating on something more than activities (workshops held, support visits made, publications produced) and something more specific than vague goals and objectives. It means focusing on what has changed or what is different as a result of an activity. This does not mean that, from time to time, we need not also to test our assumptions, for example by assessing the impact on people's health of the withdrawal of user fees in Zimbabwe. This however will only be possible where field programmes [or partner organisations] have the ability to assess impact at this level or where the impact and causal attribution is particularly clear. (Oxfam 1995)

Focusing on change rather than outputs, Oxfam's Policy Department has recently attempted to plot its major pieces of work in a graphic (Figure 6.3) along two axes: one represents a scale of impact (from profiling an issue, through changing policy to change in people's lives), the other charts an assessment of attribution.

This method is an attempt to disentangle the extent to which various agencies contributed to the success (or failure) of a particular campaign and the degree to which one can be certain about that finding. Since this will always be difficult to prove and will involve a subjective assessment it should be made explicit so that it can be challenged. It would then be interesting to compare and contrast the views of various agencies involved in the same campaigns to corroborate or contest these findings.

Figure 6.3: An attempt by Oxfam GB's Policy Department to assess impact and attribution of advocacy work

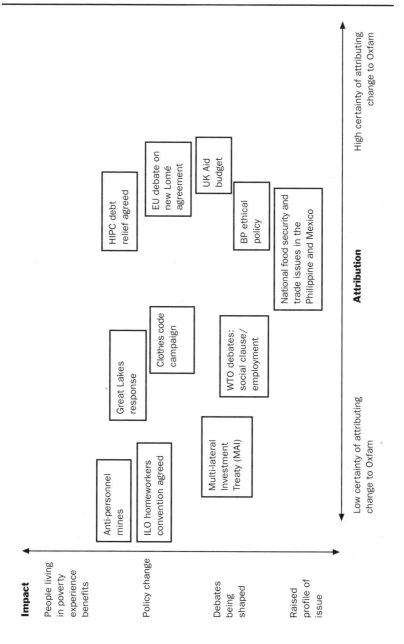

This approach has the merit of simplicity as well as a clear recognition of the importance of making judgements explicit. However, the case studies described earlier in the book suggest that this sort of approach could be usefully complemented by seeking out the views of non-project respondents and comparing them with those of people involved in the project. In the case of advocacy, this might include:

- comparing the views of decision-makers, politicians, or journalists targeted by advocacy work with those of their peers who were not targeted;

- comparing the opinions of members of the general public targeted by campaigning work with those of people who were not targeted;

- comparing the positions of individuals in countries where specific policy change has occurred with those in countries where it has not.

Although these groups are not strictly comparable (they are unlikely to have started off sharing the same views) allowances can be made for this. In addition to providing insights into what difference advocacy work has made in the past, this approach can also provide important information for the future. For example, in an assessment of the 1995 NGO campaign against aid cuts in the UK, discussions with members of parliament revealed important differences between those sympathetic to the NGO position and those less so, as well as a feeling that NGOs had failed to build a sufficiently broad coalition to defend the aid budget. As a result, in the following year institutions and organisations with an interest (such as trade unions and businesses) were more widely targeted, and the advocacy work was better tailored to the different interests and positions of the groups and individuals targeted.

Of course other variables in advocacy work combine to produce change: the national and political context; the media; changes within an organisation that NGOs are trying to influence; and continual changes within broader society. In building the case for attribution one must situate advocacy work within the context of these and other key variables. Only then can the question 'would this change have happened anyway?' be answered with a little more confidence.

The importance of cross-checking

The difficulties of attribution as well as the very nature of the advocacy process, where it may in the interests of many of those involved to exaggerate their own role in promoting change (see Table 6.3 and the section on aggregation and interviews below), make cross-checking a vital part of assessing the impact of advocacy work. The Oxfam GB Guidelines for Advocacy state that *[i]mpact assessment always runs the risk of being influenced by an organisational or individual desire to stand out or to be seen as successful or to blame others for a lack of success. But advocacy monitoring or impact assessment may be exposed to manipulation beyond that ... advocacy monitoring is particularly vulnerable, because it takes place during a campaign. Different stakeholders may each have their own reasons to either exaggerate or downplay the impact of NGO advocacy. Do not expect a member of parliament or an official to give an honest answer to the question whether he/she believes that NGOs are effectively advocating a certain issue. The answer maybe 'yes', while in reality the person is trying to keep the NGOs' in a marginal position by making them believe they are successfully lobbying. The reverse can also happen. The impact of NGO advocacy can be ridiculed, precisely because it's influence is felt and to prevent it from becoming more successful. Just as the art of advocacy itself, advocacy impact assessment requires a high-level political consciousness and, practically, multiple sources of information to be cross-checked.* (Oxfam GB 1998)

The methods of cross-checking explored in Chapter 3 — by employing a range of research methods, by comparing the findings of various researchers doing similar research, and by comparing respondents or sources of information – are all relevant to the assessment of advocacy work. Given the very different interests and levels of power of those involved as stakeholders in advocacy work, cross-checking can be an important means of exposing bias.

Summing up: The problem of aggregation

For many agencies involved in advocacy a critical question is what proportion of resources it should devote to specific types of advocacy work (research and lobbying, public campaigning, direct action, longer-term education, and so on), or indeed to advocacy work in general. Agencies would like to allocate their resources on the basis of what works, in other words what achieves greatest impact. Senior managers therefore often request information which allows them to compare the impact of different strategies, which requires an aggregation of findings from different campaigns and lobbying activities in ways that make them comparable. Given that often the allocation or re-allocation of resources is the ultimate purpose of this comparison, the tendency of those involved to exaggerate their role and impact is understandable. There may also be a resistance to aggregation across campaigns because it means simplifying reality. Campaigns are often, rightly, perceived as unique and not comparable with past or future work: strategies which may yield important results for debt relief may not work in a campaign against land mines or the small arms trade. One must not simplistically replicate strategies that have worked in the past without considering a changing context and a changed subject area.

Chapter 3 outlined ways of summarising the findings of an impact assessment of an individual project which minimise the loss of the richness and diversity of the data collected, for example by allowing different stakeholders the opportunity to provide feedback on the aggregated findings; by ensuring that any report retains certain data in a disaggregated form; and by exploring means of communicating findings other than the usual report, such as participatory video, in order to retain the original voices and analysis of people themselves which can complement other data. While these ideas also hold good for advocacy work, an examination of its impact must take into account that policy change is the result of a combination of factors such as direct action, change in public opinion, media exposure, and insider lobbying. This may occur as the result of a single agency's work or, more commonly, through the work of several actors. Therefore any aggregation of advocacy work needs to retain a holistic understanding of the influencing process and the relationship between different strategies employed.

Table 6.3 offers an analysis of the anti-roads campaign in the UK, which has seen the virtual collapse of the roads lobby, a swing in public opinion against road building, and a transformation of the culture of the Department of Transport. In this case a diverse coalition of agencies was instrumental in achieving change, including professional research and lobbying bodies such as Transport 2000, environmental NGOs such as Friends of the Earth and the Council for the Protection of Rural England, as well as local and direct action groups such as Earth First and Reclaim the Streets. This combination of actors and the division of labour between them were beneficial to all of them, giving focus and credibility to each. Although the British government would not talk to certain groups because of their perceived links with direct action, they would meet with the professional research and lobbying groups, while the media interest generated by the direct action groups clearly strengthened the hand of the lobbyists too.

This evaluation does not look at impact in the sense of change in people's lives which has resulted from the policy and practice outcomes. However, it is useful to look at the outcomes of the range of generic advocacy methods employed and the relationship between them, in order to draw conclusions about the ultimate impact and what brought it about. Case studies carried out in similar ways may demonstrate the appropriateness of different advocacy mixes for specific issues. This approach — while recognising the need for aggregation — attempts to do so in a holistic way, rather than through a narrow functional division of information.

Table 6.3: Exploring the impact of various elements of the anti-roads campaign (UK)

Generic method	Features in campaign	Comments on outcomes
Professional research and lobbying	Research from academic bodies, including government-appointed ones, invalidated the case for road-building. Transport 2000, an independent research and lobby organisation, presented a coherent analysis of the roads programme and had access to politicians.	The publication of one specific report was perhaps the most significant event in the campaign, because it refuted the road builders' main line of argument. It was essential that widespread opposition to roads was supported by credible alternative solutions.
Lobbying by consumer groups and constituents	Friends of the Earth and the Council for the Protection of Rural England led various lobbying campaigns. Lobbying through public enquiries soon proved ineffectual because of their anti-democratic nature.	Lobbying helped supplement active local opposition but was probably not significant in isolation.
Surveys and petitions	Over 13,000 people objected to widening the M25.	Not a significant feature of campaign.
Local action	A network of active local campaigning groups was linked through, and supported by, ALARM UK. 200 active groups linked to ALARM UK at its peak. Community groups generally folded once the local campaign was completed (obviously leaving residual opposition).	Local campaigning helped make the roads programme a soft target for cuts during a series of tough expenditure discussions in the British cabinet. Local action created splits in the ruling party (for example, members of the Conservative Party in areas affected by the M25 widening ended up opposing it).

Table 6.3: Exploring the impact of various elements of the anti-roads campaign (UK) (continued)

Generic method	Features in campaign	Comments on outcomes
Direct action	From Twyford Down onwards, direct action was a significant, and apparently dominant, feature of a number of anti-roads campaigns.	Media interest kept the anti-roads campaign in the public eye.
	Through continual development of innovative campaigning stunts, activists maintained media interest and the high profile of the anti-roads campaign.	Direct action increased the cost of road building (for the government, not for contractors). But no roads were stopped by direct action; it followed local action and was only relevant in tandem with it.
	Direct action probably only involved a couple of thousand activists, even at its height. Impact has almost certainly been overestimated.	Significant only because it reflected existing public sentiment.

Assessing the ultimate impact of this advocacy might include exploring to what extent air quality and the incidence of respiratory diseases have changed as a result. This will vary for different groups of people: those living on busy roads may benefit if more by-passes are built, at least in the short term, whereas those living near the new by-pass may suffer. This underlines the importance of ensuring that in aggregating results that the views and situations of both winners and losers of policy change are included and not hidden from view.

Choosing tools and methods

Surveys

Chapter 4 shows that surveys are a useful way of gaining an overview of a given situation by collecting comparable and quantifiable data from a representative sample. Many of the issues arising from the case studies regarding questionnaires are relevant to assessing the impact of advocacy work, and I summarise them in the following.

Before carrying out a survey, it should be clarified how problems that arise during the course of data collection will be dealt with. For instance, if some respondents are unavailable during the survey period the lower than expected response might bias the results. Questionnaire surveys should concentrate on key issues asking questions such as *how many? what? how often?* and *when?*, rather than *why?* and *how?*, which are often better answered by less formal or structured methods. Adequate thought must be given to ensuring that the survey will seek not only to find out what change or impact has occurred, but also to verify the degree to which given interventions might plausibly have led to those changes.

The assessment team should recognise that surveys can be used to compare situations before and after a project or a campaign, which is a critical part of impact assessment. This can be done through simple ranking or scoring of people's perceptions now and some time ago, for example of their attitudes towards specific issues, their quality of life, or their capacity to influence others.

The choice of the number and type of respondents must be considered with care, particularly in relation to how representative they are of a given population; whether there is adequate coverage of various groups according to gender, age, and so on; the degree to which they should incorporate a control group; and the capacity of the organisation to actually analyse and summarise the results that emerge.

In addition, questionnaires should be pre-tested and refined before the survey is implemented, and assessors should consider carefully the selection of enumerators and ensure that they are properly trained and briefed.

Interviews

Recent evaluations of advocacy in which Oxfam GB has been involved4 chose to interview a range of people close to the policy-making process. The first example is an assessment of the 1995 inter-agency campaign of nine British NGOs to prevent cuts in the official aid budget. This assessment was undertaken by external consultants over a six-week period and involved interviews with 23 people on an unattributable basis, half of them carried out face-to-face, half on the telephone; discussions lasted between 20 minutes and two hours. The evaluation focused on how key decision-makers and decision-formers who were targeted by NGOs (ministers, Members of Parliament, Chairs of select committees, civil servants and parliamentary advisers, journalists, opposition spokespersons, and academics) rated the actions of the various NGOs, their effectiveness in influencing the levers of power, their accuracy, and their timing.

The second case is an evaluation of Oxfam's advocacy and communications work on the Great Lakes region of Africa during the period from 1994 to 1996. This involved over 50 interviews, both within Oxfam, among its peers, and with key decision-makers and other observers. It thus looked at internal processes of policy formulation as well as the external effects of advocacy.

The third example is a request to Kenneth Clarke, former British Chancellor of the Exchequer, to give Oxfam feedback on its debt-relief campaign in which he was a key target.[5] Although again these examples do not directly evaluate ultimate impact, they do teach important lessons about the potential of interviewing advocacy targets in order to understand one part of the advocacy 'impact chain'. This approach has proved a relatively cost-effective way of talking to a small sample of the key audience for lobbying, asking them what changed as a result, and finding out what was the most effective means in achieving this. The costs of doing this in a more extensive or statistically valid way may be prohibitive and unnecessary, particularly when 'insider' lobbying is involved. By giving direct feedback from a lobbying target to those conducting an advocacy campaign this method has provided useful insights into the following areas:

- How one agency's advocacy is perceived compared with that of other agencies working on the same issue, and whether stakeholders can actually distinguish between them. For example, Oxfam discovered that civil servants often find it more difficult to distinguish between its lobbying and that of other agencies than politicians or journalists who were often able to recall what specific actions they had taken as a result of Oxfam's lobbying.

- How Oxfam's and other NGOs' advocacy, for example on debt, affected the British government's position as well as that of other actors such as the World Bank and the IMF.

- How NGO advocacy is used by its targets in their own advocacy, for example by the British government to strengthen their hand in negotiations on debt relief with other G7 countries.

- What kind of advocacy strategies politicians welcome and which strategies may be counterproductive.

- What strategies are likely to be more effective in the future (for instance, suggestions were made to use more personal lobbying rather than sending letters, briefing papers, and so on).

- When a campaign would need to start in order to fit better with existing decision-making processes.

- What other actors could add political weight to a given campaign.

As noted in previous chapters, people are sometimes economical with the truth and politicians may try to put a particular 'spin' or interpretation on events that makes them look good. For example, Kenneth Clarke describes Oxfam's lobbying as 'supportive' and 'helpful' in taking forward an initiative where 'Oxfam was pushing at an open door as far as John Major and I were concerned', whereas the Oxfam Campaigns Department's constituency contact during the multilateral campaign recalls that when the concept of debt relief was first raised with Kenneth Clarke in 1987 he dismissed the idea as 'Mickey Mouse economics'.[6] This demonstrates not only how far attitudes and policies had changed but also how key advocacy targets may be unwilling to admit this, at least in public. Indeed, as Clarke stated in his letter to Oxfam,

[i]n all lobbying it is always a good idea to acknowledge that the Government is being helpful, and a little recognition of what is being done makes the lobbying more welcome. (letter, Kenneth Clarke 1997)

This also suggests that key lobbying targets may have a tendency to downplay the impact of a particular campaign or lobby in order to demonstrate the importance of their own efforts and in order to discourage the perception that they can be easily influenced. Once again this suggests that a healthy dose of scepticism and a strategy to cross-check findings from a variety of perspectives are important components of any impact assessment process.

Analysis of interviews must happen during or soon after a particular campaign has ended or a particular breakthrough has been achieved, in order for interviewees to be able to remember the process of decision-making and what influenced it, and also in order for the agency to maximise the utility of the findings so that strategies can be adapted accordingly. However it may be the case that politicians who are no longer in power, or civil servants who are no longer in post, can offer a more objective and honest account of decision-making than those still involved.

Finally the distillation of semi-structured interviews of the type used, means that researchers impose some interpretation. Any report should make it clear where there are differences of opinion and where the judgement of evaluators differ from the views reported.

When interviews are not possible

The Seeds Action Network and Indigenous Woodland Management projects run by ENDA-Zimbabwe both sought to influence other organisation's approaches to the environment. However they found assessing their effect on these organisations one of the most difficult aspects of the case study. Initially they had wanted to visit and interview staff within those institutions, but by that stage of the impact work, they could not afford to do so. Instead a questionnaire was sent out by mail to NGOs, government departments, and other institutions which the community had identified as being active in the district, or which the researchers felt might need or find useful some of the data generated by the project. Fifty questionnaires were sent out, but only two responses were received, even after a telephone follow-up.

One of the reasons why the response to the questionnaire was so poor was that most people who were familiar with the projects had left and were difficult to trace.

In looking for institution level impacts it became clear that only those individuals who had direct contact with the project could attempt to respond to the questionnaire. When one considers that most people do not have the forum within their institutions to readily share experiences from workshops, this is not entirely unexpected. (ENDA case study)

This illustrates how short institutional memories can be and what difficulties one will encounter in following and tracing changes through key informants if one waits too long.

Eight months later, ENDA secured funding to pursue this activity again. A new methodology was developed in which the research team would visit the libraries of institutions doing similar work and look for texts published by ENDA as well as citations of the two projects being assessed. They would try to create a listing of how often the results of these studies have been used. (This involved establishing which were the key texts that ENDA had produced for the two projects in question.) It was assumed that the number of organisations making use of the project publications would be a good indicator of the extent of ENDA's influence at the institutional level.

Although it was possible to establish if these reports were present it was, unfortunately, not possible to establish if and when these reports had been used; sometimes it was difficult to actually locate them. Most of the libraries were for reference use only, so books were not loaned out, or the organisations in question were in the process of setting up their libraries, so material had not been sorted. Further, many of the libraries were not computerised and as such did not have a database of the material present. This led to a substantial amount of time being spent on manually searching for the publications. The evaluators encountered an additional problem: some project reports were not widely distributed or, as is usual in many organisations, they had found their way on to someone's desks and gone no further. More success was met in seeking where ENDA was cited in the bibliographies of relevant material: a total of ten citations were found, including two theses.

Although this approach allowed ENDA to conclude that it had had some kind of influence on other institutions and it was encouraging to note that

ENDA project documents had found their way onto library bookshelves, it was difficult to ascertain what changes had been brought about as a result, or how attributable these were to ENDA. It was clear that after its Indigenous Woodland Management Project, other NGOs and institutions had embarked on similar projects or programmes. ENDA can therefore infer that they may have had some influence on the inception of these projects — but not much more. Clearly this approach can be a useful adjunct to other types of assessment, but it will only be cost-effective where library records or citation indexes are computerised and thus allow rapid searches.

Observation

Chapter 4 shows that observation can be a useful tool in assessing the quality of relationships between individuals or groups. It can therefore also have a role in the field of advocacy, particularly in assessing the changed capacity to influence as well as changed behaviours or actions of those being influenced. Bob Hammond's observation cited above of Kenneth Clarke's changed attitude and language regarding the issue of developing countries' debt is a good example.

Observation is not just about sitting in on meetings, observing changed behaviour or ways of living in a community, or observing change over time; it is also about keeping one's eyes open on all occasions to changes that are occurring and recording them. The following comments made by two supermarket chains in the UK about Fair Trade issues are a good example of observed changes in behaviour, and at least rhetoric. In the summer of 1994, Sainsbury's reported that 'a handful of letters arrive every day asking about ethically traded goods'. One year later, Safeway stated that 'if people don't buy it then we don't sell it and it is as simple as that'. In the autumn of 1996, Safeway had changed their mind: 'It's not about a niche market any more. It's about making sure that all products in all superstores in Britain are ethically produced'. And in spring 1997 Sainsbury's said: 'We are responding to public demand' (in developing a code of conduct).

This sort of data provides useful evidence of change which can lead to further questions such as: what brought it about? Has it led to real changes in purchasing policy? What is the ultimate impact it has had on poor producers? However, this approach also means being alert to change and disciplined enough to record it. Good observation and recording are skills which can be developed, and which need adequate preparation. Preparing for advocacy work might make use of the following basic questions:

- What specific changes in behaviours and actions are hoped for and are observable?

- Who should be observed (for example, the lobbying target, those whose capacity has been built, ultimate beneficiaries, the public at large)?

221

- How should they be observed — as participant or onlooker, overtly or covertly, through public or private statements?

- When should they be observed — at particular events, times of the day, or seasons?

- How should these observations be recorded and communicated — notes, tape-recording, video, by other means?

RRA and PRA/ PLA tools

The potential for adapting participatory tools and methods for the assessment of advocacy work appears large, although neither the case studies or other examples previously cited have specifically used the tools in this way. What follows are examples of similar work that has been done which seems to lend itself to a participatory approach undertaken at different levels: with beneficiaries, advocacy staff, or with other agencies and stakeholders.

Time lines

Time lines are a useful way of situating specific projects in a longer historical time-frame (see Chapter 4). Emergency and development work often needs to reconstruct the history of a given project as well as the context in which it evolved, partly because of weak baseline data and poor record-keeping, but also because of changing circumstances and a revised understanding of what information is relevant. Constructing this history is particularly important for advocacy work which seeks to bring about policy changes over a long period. Additionally — given the difficulties of attribution mentioned above — time lines such as that in Table 6.4 can help set out the outputs and potential impacts so that the relationship between the two can be explored.

Table 6.4 covers five years of Oxfam's involvement in campaigning for debt relief and attempts to record outputs directly related to the campaign, as well as other closely related work. A separate column summarises the effects of advocacy and information on impact, including a mixture of quantitative data from commissioned polls of public opinion; qualitative data elicited from lobbying targets; qualitative and quantitative data relating to the process of policy change and the timing and scale of the changes introduced; and observed events which Oxfam considers important indicators of progress towards impact. These include, for example, the President of the World Bank's comments to the Ethiopian minister, or the fact that the UK Treasury had to print proforma responses to cope with the numbers of campaign postcards it was receiving urging it to take action.

In fact, the last column provides us with no impact data in the sense of ultimate change in people's lives. Clearly questions remain about whether the policy changes that have occurred will ultimately lead to a significant impact, and about the degree to which these changes were attributable to Oxfam, pressure from NGOs in general, or the general economic and political climate. But this systematic collection and presentation of information can at least be a starting point to answering such questions and tracking change over time. For instance, in the near future it should be possible to determine whether promised debt reduction has led to increased expenditure on health and education services in Uganda, and whether this is correlated with improved health statistics.

If other agencies involved in advocacy on debt were to construct similar time lines one could compare perceptions of the change process as well as the complementarity between different levels and types of change. This would need to include local Ugandan or Honduran agencies involved in the establishment of local debt-relief advocacy networks and relevant government officials, as well as advocacy agencies and targets in the North. This might not only be a useful way of cross-checking perceptions but also help to deepen all the agencies' understanding of the different roles they played.

Table 6.4: Time line of Oxfam's campaign on debt 1993-99

Date	Oxfam campaign outputs	Outcomes/ effects/ impact
1993	Launch of 'Africa Make or Break' report and campaign in the UK.	President of World Bank asks Ethiopian Minister: 'Have you read the Oxfam report?'
	338 MPs contacted in person or by letter.	Cross-party MP caucus to promote debt relief formed in British Parliament.
	Letters to John Major, British Prime Minister. Visits to Kenneth Clarke, UK Chancellor of the Exchequer, and meeting with Lynda Chalker, UK Minister for Overseas Development.	Clarke backs Trinidad Terms at World Bank/ IMF autumn meetings in Washington DC.
	Letters sent to Clarke prior to IMF/ WB meeting.	15,000 letters from Africa presented to WB/ IMF finance ministers.
	Letters sent to Japanese Finance Minister calling for adoption of Trinidad Terms.	G7 Economic Summit in Tokyo: debt on the agenda, but no agreement on Trinidad Terms.

Table 6.4: Time line of Oxfam's campaign on debt 1993-99 (continued)

Date	Oxfam campaign outputs	Outcomes/ effects/ impact
1993	UK media stunt drawing on image of the four horsemen of the apocalypse. Oxfam partner/ overseas staff visits: public meetings and local media coverage.	10% public awareness of 'Africa Make or Break' campaign among top socio-economic groups A & B (6% of total UK population). More than 40 features in UK press since campaign was launched. 30,000 statements of support delivered to Prime Minister's home in Downing Street, and 4,000 campaign messages from Oxfam donors sent.
1994	Campaign postcards to Clarke about Uganda debt. Visits to British MPs about Uganda debt. Lobbying visits to candidates in the European parliamentary election in 50 constituencies. Campaign 'birthday card' to the World Bank President about health user fees. Visits to Japanese Embassy in London and Edinburgh.	British MPs make follow-up visit to Clarke, and UK Treasury has proforma responses printed to reply to campaign postcards. Economic Secretary to the Treasury says in the House of Commons that debt relief for Uganda 'has been raised by many of our constituencies'. WB/ IMF Summit in Madrid: Clarke puts forward proposals to sell IMF gold stocks to reduce debt repayments of some heavily indebted countries, including Uganda. G7 Economic Summit in Naples: agreement to reduce debt-stocks and to move beyond a 50% limit on debt write-off, but no agreement on gold stocks.

Table 6.4: Time line of Oxfam's campaign on debt 1993-99 (continued)

Date	Oxfam campaign outputs	Outcomes/ effects/ impact
1995	Oxfam's Basic Rights campaign launched. Letters to Clarke expressing concern about debt.	WB/ IMF meeting: UK proposal on gold stock sales submitted. Similar motion on sale of gold stocks presented to G7 Summit. Uganda gains two-thirds reduction on bilateral debt repayments.
1996	Oxfam's Constituency Contacts visit MPs and candidates across the UK lobbying on debt, trade, and aid in the run-up to UK general election. Oxfam report published: 'Debt relief and poverty reduction: New hope for Uganda'.	At G7 meeting, Germany blocks gold stock sale; no agreement reached on bilateral debt. WB/ IMF meeting in Washington DC agrees Heavily Indebted Poor Countries (HIPC) initiative, increasing potential bilateral debt write-off from 67% to 80% and including provision for multilateral debt relief funded by IMF and WB (equals $80m per year in debt relief for Uganda).
	Letters to Clarke about improving the terms and speeding up the implementation of the debt initiative.	Letter from Clarke: 'It only remains for me to thank you for Oxfam's encouragement and support over the last two years. I am very grateful for your help in getting the initiative off the drawing board to the point of implementation.' Clarke and UK Director of IMF comment on number of letters they have received.

Table 6.4: Time line of Oxfam's campaign on debt 1993-99 (continued)

Date	Oxfam campaign outputs	Outcomes/ effects/ impact
1997 and spring and summer 1998	Intensive lobbying on Uganda with respect to delays in receiving HIPC debt relief.	After lengthy delays, WB and IMF approve debt relief of $900m for Bolivia, Burkina Faso, and Uganda.
	Oxfam Constituency Contacts make 102 visits to MPs urging them to write to Tony Blair, new British Prime Minister, asking how the UK government will check its progress towards the 2015 goals (part of which is debt relief for poverty reduction).	Letter from Kenneth Clarke to his Oxfam Constituency Contact states that the campaign gave credibility and impetus for reform, and galvanised key individuals to take action which they might not otherwise have taken.
	Oxfam GB issues briefing papers and public information materials on poor country debt relief: on debt relief for Mozambique and Tanzania (launched with Julius Nyerere); on the impact of debt and poverty on children.	British Department for International Development White Paper asserts that radical debt relief is necessary to meet 2015 poverty targets.
	Jubilee 2000 and Debt Crisis Network (of which Oxfam is a member) merge to form a broader, more effective alliance.	70,000 people form a 'human chain' at G8 Summit in Birmingham to illustrate 'break the chain of debt' campaign theme.
Autumn 1998	Campaign mailing urging UK Chancellor to take action at IMF and World Bank autumn meetings to ensure investment in human development within HIPC.	IMF and WB autumn meetings: further review of HIPC agreed in broad terms.
Winter 1998	Campaign mailing calls for debt relief for Nicaragua and Honduras following Hurricane Mitch; briefing paper on Central America links debt to reconstruction and development after natural disaster.	Substantial media coverage on Central America also clearly makes link between debt and the catastrophe of Mitch. Debt servicing suspended for Nicaragua and Honduras.

Table 6.4: Time line of Oxfam's campaign on debt 1993-99 (continued)

Date	Oxfam campaign outputs	Campaigns outputs
Spring 1999	Launch of Oxfam's Education Now campaign: first phase links debt and education. Oxfam makes formal submissions to the HIPC Review, showing how investment in human development could be ensured. Direct letter, postcard, and email actions to Gordon Brown, Chancellor of the Exchequer, urging him to 'drop the debt' at the G8 Cologne summit. 177 MPs visited by Constituency Contacts on education and debt.	Widespread media coverage in UK. The Guardian praises 'new' Oxfam angle linking debt to impact on poor people's access to education. First stage of the HIPC Review recognises failings in HIPC and highlights Oxfam's and other NGOs' alternatives. Oxfam presents its approach to Gordon Brown and Clare Short, Secretary of State for International Development. UK government proposals on HIPC for the HIPC Review strongly support debt and poverty linkages, as well as broader improvements to HIPC.
Summer 1999	Hand-over of action cards linking education and debt to Downing Street prior to G8 Summit in Cologne. Campaigners and Oxfam International supporters join Jubilee 2000 supporters at G8 summit and at 'human chain' events in the UK. About 25,000 signed action cards collected at UK pop festivals linking IMF to debt; new Oxfam supporters write to Michel Camdessus, IMF Managing Director, about debt relief delivery at IMF autumn meeting.	Downing Street call Oxfam to enquire about number of Oxfam cards handed over. At the Cologne Summit, G7 agree important changes to HIPC initiative which will speed up and increase debt relief to eligible countries Tony Blair mentions Oxfam in House of Commons, following G7 debt agreement.

Ranking

The full range of ranking methods (wealth ranking, problem ranking, performance ranking and satisfaction matrices, and impact ranking) described in Chapter 4 can all be useful in exploring the significant differences within groups or communities that need to be taken into account when exploring impact.

As discussed in the section on aggregation, organisations may face great difficulty in choosing between different advocacy strategies on the basis of impact; they therefore find it hard to allocate resources on this basis. The process of ranking and comparing the merits of different approaches, projects, or strategies offers one way of doing this. More importantly, it can make explicit the different criteria that people may have for comparing approaches — a critical step in starting a dialogue and defining clear success criteria.

Venn Diagrams or chapati diagrams: influence and power

The example of the use of Venn diagrams in Chapter 4 shows the perceived relationships of villagers in India with internal and external institutions and how these has changed over time. In this case, the relationships were symbolised by the distance of symbols representing the institutions from the central symbol, which represented the community. The respondents were asked to do this for the current situation and as it was a number of years before.

Given that advocacy is fundamentally about seeking to influence relationships of power and changing the ability of people living in poverty to influence decisions that affect their lives, tools that facilitate discussions about changes in relationships over time will be particularly useful. This use of Venn diagrams may be appropriate in the following situations:

- in assessing changes in the ability of groups or organisations to influence different institutions;

- in assessing the changes in linkages and coalitions between those carrying out advocacy work on similar or related issues;

- in mapping changing relationships between actors in the policy-making process, for example in assessing their relative influence on or proximity to decision-makers.

Such tools not only allow an assessment of past change but can also help to identify 'levers' or 'pressure points' to promote change in the future. Recent experience in using Venn diagrams to explore the perceived access of different groups to decision-making[7] indicates that they can be a powerful means of indicating exclusion and providing a visual trigger for discussion. However it was also found that, like other techniques of this kind, unequal power relations within the groups constructing the diagram determines what is and is not represented, and that the very nature of the exercise can create artificial or unhelpful boundaries between institutions or groups. If the diagrams and its subsequent discussion are to be shared between groups or made public, thought must be given to the effect that this is likely to have on other groups represented in the diagram.

Impact flow charts and trend analysis

These tools, as illustrated in Chapter 4, are useful for indicating the impact of a given intervention, policy change, or event and for documenting changes over time. The impact flow chart done by the men in Yiziiri village in northern Ghana (Figure 4.2) indicates the significant impact that a government immunisation scheme was perceived to have on not only health, but also on food security, income, and education. This tool can therefore help in identifying the potential impact of future policy change, as well as an analysis of past policy changes. This is particularly helpful in identifying future negative impacts, which may not have been anticipated, as well as identifying less obvious secondary impacts that may have occurred.

Similarly, the trend analysis from Demon village in Ghana (Table 4.18) is a good illustration of the impact of conflict in relation to other dimensions of people's lives and how these have changed over several years. From the point of view of advocacy impact assessment, trend analysis can provide a simple way of understanding relative change in people's lives over time, which can then be linked to particular policy changes. In addition, a better understanding of relative levels of change over time should help determine whether policy changes actually make a difference to existing trends. This is a critical issue for impact assessment in that it allows some analysis of the counter-factual (in other words, what would have happened anyway without any change in policy), a particularly tricky problem.

Participatory tools and methods thus hold some unexplored possibilities for impact assessment of advocacy work, both in exploring the process of policy change and its impact, but also in exploring changes in the ability of people living in poverty to advocate their own agenda and to influence others. Perhaps, as recent experiences with participatory poverty assessments suggest, they also hold the key to the difficult task of relating changes in policy to changes in people's lives. However, all the concerns about participatory methods outlined in Summary 4.5 remain relevant.

Other participatory tools

The use of theatre and video to give people a 'voice' rather than a 'message' is a means to strengthen their ability to advocate for desired changes. Augusto Boal's Theatre of the Oppressed and Legislative Theatre, which focuses on participatory means of devising and changing laws, are two examples.[8] The use of theatre and video for evaluating the impact of advocacy work is still in its infancy, but experiences with using these tools for evaluative purposes[9] show their potential in providing feedback on how policy is actually implemented in practice which would otherwise have been difficult for the communities to air in a more formal way. This feedback can have an effect on changing matters at the same time. For example, Malian villagers staged plays depicting how members of the forestry service behave towards them. The Forestry Chief heard about these plays and took steps to reduce the repressive measures that his forestry officers were using. In this case, the plays acted as a means to assess policy implementation and to change aspects of it simultaneously.

Case studies, combined methods, and sequencing

Chapter 4 set out that case studies are an approach to gathering comprehensive, systematic, and in-depth information about one or more cases of interest. Since they are particularly valuable where broad, complex questions have to be addressed and where the number of variables is usually be greater than can be controlled for, they are especially relevant to advocacy work.

Creating case studies will usually mean breaking down the component parts of advocacy work into various, overlapping elements such as specific projects or programmes or campaigns; specific policies; specific institutions or targets; specific countries or regions; specific clients of beneficiaries.

This will allow cases to be selected, depending on the purpose of the impact assessment and the kinds of case study being undertaken (see Table 4.19). Much advocacy work is unique, so a case-study approach to assessing impact offers a number of advantages. However, it would be a mistake to assume that this uniqueness prevents learning about impact from a number of cases. Over time synthesis studies or cross-case analysis, which attempt to draw wider, more generic lessons will be useful. Their quality will be improved if case studies ask key common questions (focusing on change over time and what has caused it), or if a variety of cross-cutting case studies using a range of perspectives is chosen (for example, one looking at a particular campaign, one looking at specific targets, on looking at a particular group of clients).

The examples in this chapter use three ways to look at the impact of advocacy and policy work. The first analyses projects and campaigns which are designed to alter policies by investigating their inputs and outputs, and by predicting or explaining, through logic and reasoned argument, the general effects or impacts that these changes have had or will have on people's lives. The second approach concentrates more on assessing the degree to which the abilities of others, and of people living in poverty in particular, have been enhanced and what this allows them to do and to achieve. The third approach examines how policies are implemented in practice and what the actual, specific impact on different people's lives is; this can usually only be done in a limited way or through a case study, by sampling the population in question.

It is a major challenge to bring these different approaches together in order to make an overall assessment of impact. Earlier examples from NEF and CIIR indicate ways forward on combining the first two, but to date, relatively little seems to have been done in ensuring that the third element is properly integrated. However, there is a growing number of attempts which combine participatory research methods that explore the impact of policy with an assessment of the policy-making process itself that at the same time seeks to strengthen the voices of those involved.[10] These offer an intriguing glimpse of possible ways forward.

Conclusion, lessons learned, and ideas for the future

Several agencies' work in this field points to similar general lessons regarding the assessment of advocacy work.

Be clear about advocacy objectives. Even if it is difficult to assess impact, it should at least be possible to explain lucidly what one is trying to achieve. Without this, even 'management by deviation' (in other words, focusing on *why* plans were changed and introducing accountability after the event), as opposed to management by objectives (which can lead to sticking over-zealously to predetermined plans), is very difficult. Much advocacy work is non-routine, so the gradual accumulation of knowledge by repetition does not happen. Learning by examining the deviation between planned and actual activities may provide an attractive substitute. This might mean placing as much emphasis on developing more internal learning and monitoring systems as on external evaluation; and it also means investigating the unexpected or unpredictable outcomes and spin-offs that are an inevitable part of any project.

Do the simple monitoring well. NGOs should record the concrete inputs and outputs of the work so that they can at least be held accountable for these, if not entirely for the final impact. This monitoring needs to include tracking relevant changes in the external environment.

Take every opportunity to record and log concrete evidence of outcomes and impact. In the all too frequent absence of 'hard' quantitative data, it is crucial to be systematic about collecting, and active in reporting, 'anecdotal' evidence of impact as well as any available evidence that can help deal with the attribution question.

Assessments need to provide useful and timely information. Those involved need fast, appropriate information so that strategies can be shifted and activities adapted in an effective way. In a fast-moving policy environment this is essential. Although post-hoc evaluations may be appropriate from time to time, monitoring and learning by doing is vital.

Impact assessment of advocacy will always be more of an art than a science. Subjective judgements about the value of advocacy work will continue to be important. Cross-checking those judgements by asking the 'audience' and the 'client' some key questions will be a critical means of ensuring veracity and credibility. Summary 6.3 builds on questions that Rick Davies has drawn up in order to assess impact and attribution.

Summary 6.3: Key questions for assessing advocacy work with clients and audiences

Audience	Client
Who was supposed to hear the message?	If clients are not already working with the NGO, how are they contacted in order to ensure that the NGO is acting appropriately on their behalf?
Who has heard the message?	
How did they interpret the message?	To what extent have NGOs shared their advocacy activities with the people they are working with?
How was it different from other messages?	Has there been any attempt to get beneficiaries to rank advocacy work against other activities which they might see as more relevant?
What did they do in response?	What effort has there been made to provide feedback to intended beneficiaries about the results of advocacy work?
Have they heard of the sender/ advocate?	To what extent do beneficiaries feel more confident about their capacity to advocate on their own behalf?
How do they differentiate the sender/ advocate from others who might be communicating similar messages?	What effort has been made to seek people's assessment of results and get their confirmation of assumed impact?

Adapted from Rick Davies (1997)

Finally, there is some potential for impact assessment to become an important tool for advocacy itself. Several of the results of the case studies — in Wajir, Ikafe, Matson, and Ghana — are being used to promote change of policy and practice, or at least discussions are taking place about how the results can be so used. The very nature of impact assessment, its focus on change and what is ultimately important in people's lives, generates information not just about the impact of a single intervention but about people's overall quality of life and its determinants. Government and donor policies were often cited as particularly important in promoting significant positive changes, for example in health and education. In some cases they were also identified as having negative effects through the withdrawal of services, poor co-ordination, and lack of transparency. The more impact assessment can be seen, and used, in this way, the more likely it is that its full potential for development will be realised and its cost-effectiveness improved.

7

Impact assessment and organisations[1]

This chapter looks at some of the theory and the practice of organisational assessment; in particular, I present examples of organisational self-assessment and ways of assessing collective action, leadership, and sustainability. The second half of the chapter considers the challenges facing organisations in designing impact assessment systems, as well as the best practice emerging in this area. The chapter concludes by analysing the effect of these impact studies on the organisations involved and suggests that, overall, there is a need for greater mutual assessment between agencies in order to assess how together they can achieve more.

The preceding chapters in this book have all alluded to the role that organisations play in the process of achieving, or failing to achieve, impact. These organisations include informal groups or community organisations, intermediary NGOs, local and national governments, international NGOs, international donors, and many other public and private sector agencies, and they are important for several reasons. In development, humanitarian and advocacy work does not take place in a vacuum; projects and programmes are designed, implemented, and evaluated by men and women who are part of different organisations, each of which has its own systems, values, and culture. Systems, values, and culture are products of the society in which the organisation exists, and the organisation reproduces them in turn.

The battle for changes in policy and practice — which can potentially have greater impact on people's lives than discrete projects — is often played out between organisations and is determined by the relationships between them. This suggests that organisations are more than simply a means of delivering projects; they are also one of the key vehicles for setting the context in which projects and policies evolve and for determining which projects or policies will or will not be supported or delivered. Organisations set the value that is placed upon the impacts that are achieved and determine, at least in part, whether their impacts are, or are not, sustained.

Impact assessment therefore needs to go beyond analysing programmes and projects, and explore the influence and roles of the various organisations involved. In fact, one can argue that the analysis of projects cannot be separated from analysis of the organisations which run or fund them (Fowler 1995). Impact assessment also requires a broader understanding of various institutions such as the family, market, state, and community in order to assess whether change is also occurring at these levels. This means looking at the effect of interventions or projects on those organisations that embody relations of authority, power, and control. Institutions (including NGOs) are not neutral actors, they are made up of individuals with differing interests. As such, they may well conceptualise and measure impact in ways that will perpetuate those interests. In looking at impact assessment, we cannot ignore this.

This chapter therefore explores the relationship between impact and organisations, examining in particular how the influence of projects and programmes on organisations can be assessed (especially if this was an ultimate aim either through capacity-building or advocacy programmes) and how organisations approach and manage impact assessment.

Assessing change in organisations

This study defines impact as significant change in the lives of people brought about by a given intervention. In this sense, the changes that might be brought about at the level of organisations is not an impact but rather a means to achieve impact. However as many programmes and projects seek to achieve those impacts through changes in organisational policies and practices, it is important to assess whether such change has occurred. This is done in two broad ways: through allying with, and strengthening the capacity of, formal or informal groups (sometimes called partners or counterparts) to bring about change; or through bringing pressure to bear on other organisations through influencing or advocacy work. In either case, for the purposes of impact assessment, this requires a judgement to be made as to what organisational change has occurred, what has brought about that change, and what the broader effects or impacts of that change have been. In this section I summarise a small selection of the growing literature on organisational assessment elements before looking at what some of the case studies actually discovered.

Organisational assessment theory

There are many suggestions, at least for NGOs, of what organisational assessments should or might include (see Uphoff 1987, Drucker 1990, Fowler 1995, Zadek 1996). The list below is a synthesis of some of the common elements these authors propose.

- Identity and values;
- Purpose, vision, and strategy;
- Human and financial resources;
- Systems and procedures;
- Organisational culture;
- Structure and organisation;
- Control and accountability;
- Programmes and services;
- Performance and results;
- Learning and change;
- Leadership, management, and decision-making;
- External linkages and relations.

These elements are often related to each other in various models which distinguish between internal processes, external relations, and performance (see Fowler 1995). Deborah Eade in her book on capacity-building suggests five different approaches to organisational assessment: stakeholder analysis, social audit, social relations analysis, appreciative inquiry, and historical analysis (see Eade 1998). In much of the literature it is suggested that an external facilitator can help in providing a 'critical mirror' in these processes (in other words, reflecting back a group's perceptions to them while at the same time introducing questions).

Assessing gender and organisations

Other authors place more stress on the importance of looking at specific interests within organisations such as interests based on gender, class, or ethnicity. Anne Marie Goetz argues that this can be done by starting with the outcomes or products of an organisation and exploring how these affect men and women differently (Goetz 1996). It is then possible to find out the reasons why a particular organisation produced a specific outcome. If, for example, an agricultural extension agency only provides advice to male farmers, this might be because it does not employ many female staff. This finding would lead one to explore why it does not recruit women extension agents, or why it does not undertake research into crops grown by women. This might expose the assumptions this organisation makes about agriculture, and who in the organisation is making those assumptions. This helps to understand how organisations are gendered — in other words, how they function in ways that reflect gender relations and inequalities in society as a whole — and the concept of gendering (organisations will tend to reproduce those inequalities that exist in society). Goetz suggests that 'the key to understanding how such outcomes are produced is to trace the way institutional structures, practices and agents embody and promote gendered interests'. The diagram in Figure 7.1 illustrates how these interact.

Figure 7.1: The links between organisational structures, practices, and agents

Source: adapted from Goetz 1996, p.4

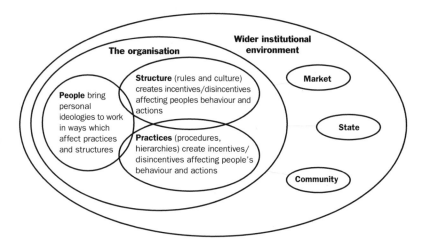

Goetz further argues that although structures and practices in organisations create incentives and disincentives for staff to behave and act in particular ways, those individuals create and recreate the structure and practice. Understanding this link can give important insights not only into how change might be affected in an organisation, but also into how policy directives can be blocked or subverted. This is particularly significant for advocacy strategies, which may need to be adapted to take this into account, or to confront such issues directly. Table 7.1 summarises some of the questions which Goetz suggests for uncovering the 'gendered archaeology' of organisations.

This way of exploring gender in organisations provides an interesting framework for understanding how one set of interests (in this case male interests) is institutionalised and reproduced. Similar analyses could be done for other relevant sets of interests such as class, caste, race, religion, or ethnicity.

This section has indicated that organisational change can be assessed in a variety of ways, and that it is important in the process of impact assessment to understand the role that different organisations might have played. The next section examines how this might be done in practice.

Table 7.1: Towards a gendered archaeology of organisations (after Goetz 1995)

Aspect of the organisation	Line of enquiry
Institutional history	Who was involved in establishing the organisation? Who was not?
	How was this done?
Ideology	What are the academic disciplines that animate the organisation?
	What are the underlying assumptions these disciplines make about gender roles?
Participants	Who makes up the organisation?
	What is the gender division of labour?
	What is the gender profile of the different levels of the organisation?
Space and time	Are working hours convenient for women employees?
	Are meetings or social activities held at times which might make women's participation difficult?
	Is provision made for career breaks, child-care, and so on?
	Does the organisation demand travel away from home as part of the job?
Authority structures	Can women command authority for their approaches and views in the organisation?
	Do women have to take on 'male' attributes to be heard?
	What is valued in terms of achievements in the organisation?
Incentives and accountability	Do performance objectives focus more on quantitative rather than qualitative targets?
	Do the lines of accountability go upwards, downwards, or are they horizontal?

Organisational self-assessment: the practice

Despite what the literature may say, the tendency in the case studies examined in this book, at least when assessing village-level and community-based organisations, was not to draw up a list of skills or capacities and then assess them, but rather to explore with the groups or organisations in question which elements of organisational development *they* considered important, and how these had changed over time. This was usually done through a process of self-assessment which was facilitated by an external person acting as the 'critical mirror'. Other methods of assessment that were used are outlined in the following.

Gathering information from a range of stakeholder perspectives. This was done especially to explore an organisation's evolution and to explore changes in the nature and scale of collective action and leadership (further discussed in this chapter). It was also a method used to monitor wider changes in the community, for example in community norms and behaviour in terms of gender and self-reliance. Chapter 6 describes how this was done in the CYSD case study.

Attending organisations' meetings. Evaluators can look on as an observer to identify the level and the quality of participation and decision-making, the conduct of leaders, and also the kinds of issues and problems being discussed. This method was used primarily in the Matson Neighbourhood Project, described in the section on direct observation in Chapter 4.

Holding discussions and informal conversations. Talking to committee members and project staff helps to explore, among other things, their ideas for innovation, future plans, and strategies for organisational sustainability. Again, the Matson study in particular used this approach.

The first step in some of the case studies was to identify with the organisation being assessed the key capacities or criteria to be explored. This was usually done simply by asking staff to identify, for example, the ten things that would indicate that an organisation was 'healthy' and the ten things that would signify that an organisation was 'sick', or to identify the key capacities that every organisation needs for it to function properly. Participants then analysed changes in these capacities in a number of ways. The examples below from Wajir and Ghana illustrate how this was done in practice.

In Wajir (see Table 7.2), key capacity-development indicators, as identified by the Wajir volunteer group, were ranked before and after Oxfam had provided training, funding, and assistance. In the reranking, zero signifies low capacity, and ten represents high capacity.

Table 7.2: Changes in key indicators of capacity development at Wajir volunteer group

Indicator	Score (before)	Score (after)	% change
Equipment	0	8	100%
Accounting/book-keeping	1	8	88%
Networking with donors	1	7	86%
Management skills	1	7	86%
Fund-raising	1	5	80%
Monitoring and evaluation	2	9	78%
Follow up/assessments	2	9	78%
Proposal development	2	7	71%
Policy advocacy	2	6	67%
Networking with business	2	5	60%
Legitimacy	3	7	57%
Networking with NGOs	5	8	38%
Group participation	5	8	38%
Networking with communities	7	8	13%
Networking with government	7	8	13%
Voluntarism	9	6	-50%

Combining this analysis with other findings, the assessment could infer that Oxfam's assistance had contributed to significant changes in the capacities of local organisations to implement development programmes in pastoral settings. But these changes have not been without costs, as indicated in relation to the declining voluntarism within this group.

In Ghana, a similar exercise was undertaken with a number of organisations. In this case, once the key capacities had been identified, a five-point scale[2] was agreed against which these capacities could be rate for the past (five years ago) and present. In order to visualise the results and to compare changes across the range of capacities identified, participants were asked to draw a simple bar chart (for an example of one organisation's findings see Figure 7.2).

Figure 7.2: Organisational self-assessment exercise, northern Ghana

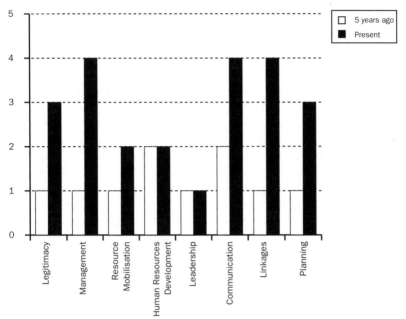

Note

1 = minimum or little capacity, just starting

2 = unsatisfactory, a great deal of improvement required

3 = adequate to poor, much improvement required

4 = satisfactory, but still some room for improvement

5 = very satisfactory, little or no room for improvement

This exercise not only allowed individual organisations to analyse and reflect on their situation, it also allowed members of the Northern Ghana Network for Development (NGND) to compare themselves with others. This revealed some common patterns across the network: resource mobilisation was considered the least developed capacity among all organisations; decision-making, management, and planning had improved dramatically over the past five years as a result of training; and leadership and linkages with other organisations had changed least. This insight into past performance in capacity-building gave an indication of where future efforts might be directed.

Change over time can also be displayed graphically in the form of a spider diagram. In the Ghana study this visualisation technique was used to compare changes in capacity for priority areas identified by the organisation, as well as to set out future targets. Figure 7.3 is an example of a spider diagram drawn by

241

members of the Galayri Suntaa Women's Group, illustrating their perceived progress in leadership, resource mobilisation, monitoring and evaluation, and training. It also shows what progress they seek to make on these issues in the future.

Agreeing a scale for scoring as described above in the case of Ghana, rather than simply asking people to score from one to ten, as in Wajir, adds a degree of consistency and comparability to the assessment. For example, in some of the Ghana cases, the ranking of key capacities was done individually by different members of the organisation. When large differences in scores occurred this indicated important disagreement between staff about what had been achieved and what room for improvement existed. Because the criteria for the scoring had been agreed beforehand such disagreements could be more fully debated. If this had not been done, comparison would have been more difficult as different scores might simply have indicated different opinions of what a 'low' or 'high' score meant to people. For the purposes of organisational assessment, which usually seeks to explore the past while increasing an organisation's capacity for the future, resolving such differences of opinion is important.

Figure 7.3: Spider diagram of Galayri Suntaa Women's Group, northern Ghana

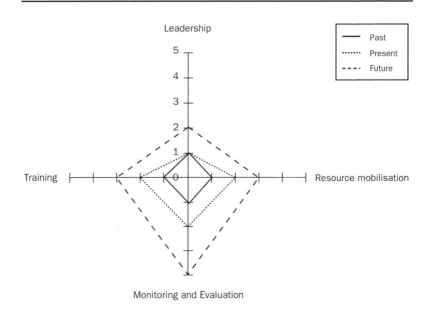

This sort of participatory diagnosis is important because it leaves the categorisation and classification of organisational elements in the control of members or staff, rather than imposing a prescribed model or a number of general indicators developed elsewhere. The result is therefore more likely to reflect *their* priorities and concerns. And although it may miss out some of the elements that others feel should be included, what is missed out is, in itself, an indication of the stage of self-analysis an organisation has reached. Tracking the dimensions that a self-appraisal process focuses on is therefore an important means of assessing organisational development and change.

Assessing collective action

An analysis of collective action figured strongly in several of the studies (see Chapter 6). Some saw this as a crucial method of assessing the performance of local organisations, as well as of the NGOs which support them. In the Ghana study, a historical analysis of collective action proved a useful means of understanding whether community capacity had changed over time. In addition, it produced more generic indicators for successful and less successful villages and CBOs in promoting collective action (Table 7.3).

Participants were asked to list all kinds of collective action in the community's recent history on cards; sort the cards by source of initiative (local or external); sort them chronologically; analyse a few examples of collective action from each period in depth; compare the time periods and analyse whether community capacity has changed and how, and determine the trends and forces contributing to this; and to draw conclusions.

Again this process is designed to assess past change as well to understand the source of that change. This in turn can help participants to differentiate between blockages to future collective action which they can address, and those for which they may need help and support. When participants went on to look at the reasons for differences in the capacity of different groups to undertake collective action it became clear that many of these related to the nature of the social relations within that community. This underlines that different impacts are likely to occur as a result of the same project because of the unique nature of the communities and organisations involved. It is therefore crucial to understand how the context and the activities of a given project combine to produce change in varying ways, depending on the initial conditions into which a specific action is inserted.

Table 7.3: Indicators of strong, middle, and weak community capacity for collective action (northern Ghana)

Aspects of community	Capacity for collective action		
	Strong	**Middle**	**Weak**
Communal spirit	High communal spirit A sense of common purpose	Factionalism Chieftancy dispute	Low communal spirit Divided community Monopoly of resources held by one group
Leadership	Trust of leaders Able leadership Strong leadership	Weakened leadership due to out-migration Good but declining leadership	Few individuals decide for the majority Poor leadership Chief's greedy attitude has killed community spirit Selfish leaders Dormant leadership
Ability to undertake collective action	Undertake activities themselves	Difficult to mobilise people	Apathy Inability to undertake collective projects
External links	Good external linkages		Low linkages
Ability to mobilise resources	Good resource mobilisation Effective fund-raising		Inability to mobilise resources
Organisation	Effective record-keeping Regular payment of dues	Inadequate record-keeping	No regular meetings Poor payment of dues Poor record-keeping Poor communication

Assessing leadership

As the Ghana case demonstrates, the issue of leadership — whether in a community or an organisation — emerges as a critical element in achieving change. Other case studies, notably the CYSD and the NK/ GSS studies in Bangladesh, also explore this issue and remark on its importance.

The NK and GSS study goes furthest in developing a framework for assessing leadership. It asks: 'Common sense suggests that leadership is a critical factor in group dynamics and the development and sustainability of village organisations, but what shape does leadership take?' (Rao and Hashemi, p.10). Rao and Hashemi have developed five leadership types which they believe cover the spectrum for village organisations in Bangladesh. *Entrenched patrons* describes those leaders who generally have higher status and wealth than group members and who use the group to further their own personal economic or political ends. *Emerging patrons* are those leaders who generally have higher status and wealth than group members. Although they may gain more from group activities than other members, they will normally seek to share at least some of the economic and status gains with them. *Representational leadership* refers to the style of leaders who, although they may have higher status or wealth than the group members, do not seek personal economic gains from their involvement; rather, they are committed to organising group members so that everyone gains collective benefits. *Egalitarian leadership* refers to groups where there is little difference between leaders and members in terms of status and wealth. In these cases, the interests of the leadership and group members are basically the same. *Satellite leadership* refers to leaders who depend on another group for deciding their main course of action: for example, women's groups are highly dependent on a male group in the same village.

For each of these types Rao and Hashemi explore clashes of interests between leadership and community, the leaders' autonomy or dependency, the nature of decision-making, and how gains are shared. Table 7.4 outlines these relationships.

These findings suggest a number of key challenges, particularly to intermediary or NGO-support organisations who seek to work with and through community-based organisations. Egalitarian groups in which gains are equitably shared are likely to be, and remain, heavily dependent on external support. Across all groups, economic gains build cohesion, but for groups which engage in riskier activities that challenge entrenched interests, failure can be much more damaging and lead to a backlash that causes a group to disintegrate. In patron-led groups, autonomy is relatively high, although participation is low, because without economic success this model could not sustain itself since patrons need to be able to distribute 'favours'.

Table 7.4: Leadership typologies of village organisations, NK and GSS, Bangladesh

Dimension of leadership	Leadership type				
	Entrenched patrons	Emerging patrons	Represent- ational leadership	Egalitarian leadership	Satellite leadership
Homogeneity of interests	Great variance in wealth between leaders and members; leaders use village organisation for personal ends.	Significant variance in wealth or status between leaders and members develops over time.	Great variance in wealth, education, or status between leaders and members.	Low variance between leaders and members; all interested in employment and income.	Where variance is significant, leaders shape how the organisation functions.
Autonomy from NGO	High autonomy from NGO in day-to-day affairs; high dependency on NGO on issues that go beyond the village.		Low dependency on the NGO in day-to-day affairs; in some cases, also in planning and implementing collective actions.	High dependency on NGO for economic projects, group management, and wider issues.	Dependency is on another group rather than the NGO.
Decision- making	Leaders make all decisions and are perceived as exploitative.	Leaders make decisions but are perceived as fair.	Leaders persuade members to follow the leaders' decision.	Leaders and members actively participate in decision- making.	Leaders make day-to-day decisions but follow the stronger group on wider issues.
Partcipation gains	Leaders take all economic resources and gains in political status.	Leaders gain more but share economic resources and gains in status with members.	Gains are shared but leaders control resources.	Gains are equally shared but economic gains are few.	Status gains accrue to leaders; in cases of high homogeneity, economic resources are shared with members.

246

Lastly, NGO leverage in promoting more 'democratic' or 'egalitarian' behaviour is lowest in those groups which need it most, although it may be greater when it comes to supporting cross-village issues that require intermediation with state actors or foreign donors.

From the point of view of impact assessment it is clear that leadership can make a difference not only to the levels of change that may occur, but also to how the gains (or losses) from given interventions are distributed, and how long they can be maintained. In addition, leaders can determine the nature of the relationship between a community or grassroots organisation and intermediary and international NGOs. This in turn will influence the sustainability of interventions, in particular the transfer of responsibility from NGO to CBO, both of which are critical in achieving impact.

Assessing handover, sustainability, and the relationship between organisations

Transfer of responsibilities and handover

At its simplest level, handover often means simply the transfer of responsibilities for running a project from one organisation to another. In the case studies, an intermediary or international NGO usually handed over responsibility to a community-based organisation. This generally meant identifying the critical functions involved in running a given project, and exploring who undertook these in the past and who is undertaking them now. Below is an example from the Ghana study of an assessment of changes in responsibility between an intermediary NGO and a CBO it supports (see Table 7.5). It includes an assessment of who within the CBO has assumed that responsibility: all the members, or the 'animator' or group facilitator. This assessment was done during an organisational self-assessment exercise by asking participants to identify key responsibilities, and then to score them in terms of who performs more of each task, taking ten as complete responsibility, and zero as none.

Table 7.5 reveals that although there has been a transfer of responsibility from the intermediary NGO to the CBO in certain areas (such as reporting and training), there are other areas such as running meetings, credit disbursement, and monitoring and evaluation where the NGO is doing more than it did in the past. It seems that within the CBO, although the responsibilities of the animator are increasing, this is at the expense of the members whose responsibility is generally declining.

Table 7.5: Transfer of responsibilities chart for two organisations, Ghana

| Responsibilities | Intermediary NGO | | CBO | | | |
| | Management | | Animator | | Members | |
	Past	Present	Past	Present	Past	Present
Reporting	8	6	2	3	0	1
Project planning	2	4	1	1	7	5
Running meetings	0	2	1	3	9	5
Credit disbursement	2	5	1	2	7	3
Loan recovery	1	1	1	6	8	3
Training	9	7	1	2	0	1
Monitoring and evaluation	4	6	2	2	4	2
Resource mobilisation	4	3	1	1	5	6
Average	3.75	4.25	1.25	2.5	5	3.25

This sort of exercise can provide important insights into the relationship between organisations over time. It can provoke debate, in this case about the rather alarming decline in responsibility that seems to have occurred at the level of the CBO membership, and the overall growth in responsibility by the management of the intermediary NGO. This in turn can stimulate discussion about strategies for future handover and associated training needs. In addition, it can allow some assessment of the performance of staff, animators, or community workers who may be specifically engaged in building local capacity and promoting a transfer of responsibility. In the CYSD study, specific assessments by communities of these local 'cadres' was seen as an integral component of the impact assessment study. This helped reveal that although

the project is in its phase out stage [it] has not yet adopted any follow up strategy for sustaining these village level cadres. These cadres were functioning well as long as they were provided with incentives. But a strategy for raising these incentives in the future is not yet articulated. In such a condition the sustainability of these cadres ... is questionable. (CYSD case study)

The common response to this problem is to ensure that handover and the transfer of responsibilities is built into the project from the start and continually monitored. One of the ways to do this is to determine a scale of levels for group or organisational development, and a similar scale for the levels of involvement of the support organisation. The NK and GSS study by Rao and Hashemi in Bangladesh did this, although retrospectively. Table 7.6 outlines the criteria used to define levels for both the local group and the support NGO in order to create a composite index.

Table 7.6: Indices of NGO involvement and group cohesion

Rating	Level of NGO involvement	Level of group cohesion
0	No NGO involvement.	No group, or total disintegration of an existing group.
0–1	Intermittent attendance at group meetings, no provision of advice or direction to the group, or no interest in group development.	Group formation: inactive group (meets infrequently, no activities; high level of conflict within group).
1–3	Regular attendance at group meetings, keeping of accounts, conduct of relief distribution.	Normal group activities ongoing; regular meetings; resistance to harassment of individuals; low to medium conflict within group.
4–6	Motivation of potential group members, conscientisation at group meetings; lead role in group discussions; conduct of training for group members; provision of logistical support for group activities.	Group carries out activities at the village level (for instance, arbitration); benefits accrue to few rather than the collective; organised resistance against attacks on the group.
5–8	Development of strategies for social actions; planning economic activities; conflict management and mediation (within and between groups).	Different groups combine together beyond village level for a collective end and collective benefits.
8–9	Decision on and leadership in group social actions; providing legal assistance; political brokering with state mechanisms; providing a national forum for local issues.	Movement launched by local organisations which has a national impact and takes on highest echelons of political power and business interests.
10	No group involvement in decision-making; NGO is completely in control of all decision-making.	Groups of the poor take over political control at the sub-national level (for example, they are involved in framing legislation, and have complete control over resources).

This then enabled the researchers, through discussions with group members, the NGOs, and others to plot graphically the relationship over time between grassroots groups and the support NGOs. The example below is typical of their findings which gave rise to the title of their report 'Institutional Take Off or Snakes and Ladders?', after the children's board game in which players try to progress to the end by climbing 'ladders' but often slip back down the 'snakes' towards the starting point (see Figure 7.4). Their findings showed that group development did not progress smoothly as the intermediary NGO's involvement declined, but that group cohesion and NGO involvement were closely linked and characterised by significant fluctuation between progress and decline.

Figure 7.4: Analysis of relationship between NGO involvement and village cohesion for men's group in Madhyapabantair, Bangladesh

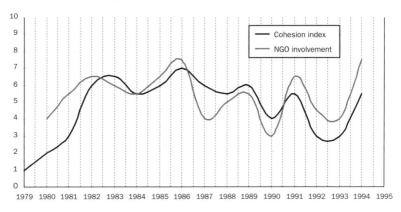

Apart from the study's innovative methodology for exploring the relationships between the organisations, its findings shatter many of the common assumptions about organisational sustainability and the linear nature of group development. They found that group development is punctuated by short-term, issue-specific actions which, if successful, lead to greater cohesion; if unsuccessful, they result in increased inactivity, at least temporarily. The momentum on issues that crossed village boundaries and were more 'political', was maintained not only by the groups but also by the leaders of support NGOs — often because of the backlash and retaliation against groups which confronted more powerful economic or political actors.

Rao and Hashemi argue that the common assumption about group sustainability and handover, in the case of Bangladesh at least, are often highly unlikely and stem from a view of poverty that sees a lack of resources as its primary cause, rather than inequality and injustice which are built into unequal power relations. The empirical work they did indicates that when local organisations started to tackle the strategic aspects of poverty — addressing power relations beyond the village level — they needed as much support as before, if not more, albeit of a different nature. This suggests that although a project may achieve handover for activities at a community level, if the objective is to change the underlying order that created and perpetuated poverty in the first place, then such an approach to sustainability is at best naïve, and at worst an acceptance of the status quo.

Financial sustainability of organisations

Chapter 4 described ways in which the economic impact and the sustainability of individual projects can be assessed through various kinds of cost-benefit analysis. However, at another level the financial sustainability of organisations themselves may be an issue. Clearly, the nature and purpose of an organisation will determine the degree to which it can or should strive for financial sustainability. Johnson and Rogaly distinguish between three different levels: subsidy-dependent, operational efficiency, and fully self-sufficient (see Johnson and Rogaly 1996).

Level 1: subsidy-dependent. Most if not all of the organisation's costs are funded by donor grants and subsidies and are likely to remain so. The main focus here will probably be assessing the current and future ability of the organisation to raise its own funds efficiently and effectively without compromising its overall objectives and purpose. In some cases it may be appropriate for some aspects of the organisation to start moving towards operational efficiency .

Level 2: operational efficiency. Some or all of the recurrent or running costs of the operation (such as salaries, administrative costs, and so on) are covered by programme revenues such as payment for services, income generation, or interest on loans. Here assessment will mainly examine the degree to which the organisation is covering its costs, how efficiently it is doing this, and whether it can and should do more to move towards the full self-sufficiency or profitability .

Level 3: fully self-sufficient or profitable. The organisation is generating, or plans to generate, a positive return on its assets, even when inflation is taken into account — this includes sufficient revenue to cover recurrent costs and financial costs; in other words, capital is raised though loans not grants and income is sufficient to cover the costs of these loans as well. Here assessment issues are likely to centre on the organisation's longer-term profitability, on whether it can sustain a comparative advantage over its competitors and keep its best future legal status as a not-for-profit organisation, a co-operative, or limited company.

Undertaking these sorts of assessments entails complex analysis of the trade-off between impact, sustainability, and the purpose and values of an organisation. However, some basic financial ratios can be useful in doing this. The first is the ratio between recurrent costs and total costs, which gives an idea of an organisation's financial structure, its potential financial sustainability, and, sometimes, of its efficiency. Recurrent costs are generally defined as those costs that involve maintaining the basic functioning of the organisation (for example, salaries, vehicle running costs, and office costs). For example, the proportion of recurrent costs to total costs of the Oxfam operation in Wajir was 36 per cent, whereas for the local Wajir volunteer group supported and strengthened by Oxfam, the figure was 7.5 per cent. This suggests that although the Oxfam operation may have been valid in terms of start-up costs, particularly in terms of the needs for institution-building, the financial benefits in transferring responsibility to a local organisation over time are high. It may be very difficult for NGOs to determine and agree upon what precisely recurrent costs are, not least because these costs are, rightly or wrongly, often associated with unnecessary bureaucracy or administrative 'overheads'. Organisations which seek to continue to raise money from donors and to cover some of their recurrent or core costs will usually have to give a justification and breakdown of costs.

Another financial ratio is the payment or repayment rate and, related to this, the arrears and default rates. In effect, these are measures of the performance of the income a NGO has earned from payments for its services or, in the case of credit and savings organisations, from the repayment of loans. In essence these rates compare the proportion of repayments actually made with those that are due, judge how late these repayments might be, and estimate what proportion of repayments are never likely to be made. They give a good indication of future sustainability for these kinds of institutions, particularly in terms of the ability to cover recurrent costs (level 2 in the above list). They also give a relatively rapid indication of problems that may affect future sustainability if they are not resolved quickly. For example, if an organisation has a very high arrears or default rate which is greater than the provision it has made for losses of this type, then it cannot continue to sustain loans if it wants to survive.

Lastly there are two ratios which provide an overall organisational picture and can allow comparison between organisations. One of these is the sustainability index (Havers 1996), which looks at the percentage of total costs covered by revenue during a given period.

$$\textbf{Sustainability index} = \frac{\text{total income during the period}}{\text{total costs incurred during the period}} \times 100$$

For credit schemes, the break-even interest rate defines the interest rate that the scheme would have to charge its borrowers if it was to be self-sufficient.

This can then be compared to other schemes and official rates in order to assess the degree of subsidy required and the scheme's future viability. For both of these ratios, estimates of future liabilities, interest, and inflation rates are needed for costs to be calculated properly. Organisations which aspire to self-sufficiency will find this rate essential, given that future revenue may need to be discounted in line with inflation and future costs increased in line with inflation and interest rates. This information is necessary in order to get an accurate and realistic picture of future financial sustainability.[3]

Assessing funding relationships

An organisation's funding relationships will usually be critical in determining, at least in part, not just how it reports but also how it plans, implements, and evaluates its work; they will affect who is recruited and retained; how it relates to others — including its own staff and ultimate beneficiaries — and ultimately, how it grows and survives. The behaviour of donors may therefore be a significant determinant of the impact that the organisation in receipt of their funding achieves.

Recent studies on this issue (Moore and Stewart 1998, INTRAC 1998) underline the fact that being a 'good' donor requires a lot more than doling out cheques: it includes having good local knowledge, the capacity to assess organisations as well as projects, and sensitivity to the impact one's funds and corresponding demands can have on local organisations. Moore and Stewart, in a study of Nepal and Zimbabwe, distinguish between three models of funding.

Arm's length. This is funding at a distance, often from outside the country, for large projects well established organisations.

Handshake. This kind of funding — often from Northern NGOs with Southern-country offices — works through more frequent contact and exchange, including the provision of small grants and accompaniment; it may also include organisational funding, rather than project funding.

Hand-in-hand. The donor and the local organisation work jointly on a particular project or in a specific region, with regular contact.

Moreover, these relationships are characterised by varying demands for reporting or specific formats for funding submissions, which will also be determined by the attitude of donors. Rick Davies has developed a continuum of attitudes, characterised below, and suggests that more thought and effort needs to go into how donors solicit information. For example, they might specifically try to obtain beneficiary-centred information, which in turn may lead to the funded NGOs having 'to enter into contracts or understandings with their own beneficiaries … [t]his itself may be empowering for those beneficiaries' (Davies 1997).

Laissez-faire attitude towards receiving information. Funded NGOs should be trusted to do as they say, and not harassed by donors.

Minimalist (defensive) attitude. Donor information demands can distract and undermine the effectiveness of NGOs in their work and should therefore be minimised.

Minimalist (self-interested) attitude. Donors are overwhelmed with the practical tasks associated with funding (identification, appraisal, approval, disbursement, and documentation) and do not have sufficient time to read and make use of information about project activities and impact. As a result, they do not bother asking for much more than what they already receive.

Apologetic/ realist attitude. Donors have obligations to their own donors and thus must ask for information from the NGOs they fund, although they feel or know that this can be a burden on the funded NGO.

Facilitator attitude. Information is needed from funded NGOs so that other NGOs can learn from their experiences. A related rationale is the need to support development education in the donor's own country.

Interventionist attitude. The process of requesting information can have a positive impact on NGOs' institutional development (defined, as above, in terms of increased responsiveness).

Hard-line attitude. Funded NGOs have signed a contract and therefore have an obligation to supply information.

Although the case studies did not systematically examine the nature of relationships between the organisations involved and their donors, some cases made it clear that donor pressures, for example to spend money on agricultural technology by a certain date in the CYSD study, led to less impact being achieved. Indeed, in some cases the continued financial relationship between Oxfam GB or Novib and those undertaking the case studies influenced the case studies themselves, in terms of which programmes were chosen for assessment (ENDA), as well as in terms of management tensions during the process (Ghana).

For the purpose of impact assessment it is important to recognise that the relationship between donors and NGOs can have an important effect on many aspects of organisational development, not least the psychological health[4] and feelings of dependence local staff. Knock-on effects in terms of effectiveness, efficiency, and impact must be assessed. This demands a more mutual assessment of this relationship, rather than treating the local organisation as if it was isolated from the demands placed upon it. Donors have to understand that this relationship is more than simply an input to be charted in a log-frame.

One of the future challenges for impact assessment work will be to help determine the role of NGOs in broader processes of transformation — in relation to the strengthening of civil society, the creation and maintenance of social capital, and the role of civil-society organisations in promoting good governance. Although there are some attempts to do this, such as Kees Biekart's work on *European Private Aid Agencies and Democratic Transition in Central America* (see especially pp.125-131), much remains to be done to link this kind of analysis to assessments of change in the lives of ordinary women, men, and children. This is vital if NGO strategies are to be tested against whether they really make a difference.

How organisations approach and manage impact assessment

Choices are made at different levels in organisations — choices about where to work, who to work with, how to allocate scarce resources, and what focus to choose for individual programmes. Implicitly or explicitly, criteria are used to make these choices. Impact is perhaps the most elusive one, especially when broad choices are being made, and yet it is one of the most important.

Although perhaps the emphasis on impact assessment is relatively new, most development organisations have invested in some kind of monitoring and evaluation processes. Summary 7.1 outlines some of the classic problems associated with these.

Summary 7.1: Classic problems and failures of monitoring and evaluation (M&E) systems

Information produced for M&E systems is irrelevant, late, or in a form that is not usable, and M&E systems are not integrated into project management.

Evaluation/ impact systems are seen as a threat to jobs rather than as a learning experience.

The over-ambitious design of M&E systems leads to too much data with poor understanding of the consequences of managing and analysing it; there is little emphasis on minimum or light systems.

Evaluation is often at the expense of monitoring because focus on local staff or beneficiaries is often secondary to donor or organisational needs.

Poor marginal groups, particularly women, are often ignored in M&E processes, and results are not cross-checked with them or fed back to them.

Poor quality of data because of various methodological problems:

- the approach used lacks or is based on weak baseline data, objectives, and indicators;

- the approach used fails to recognise that proving statistical significance of data often requires an inordinate amount of time and cost – this investment requires a conviction that it is better to be 'long and legitimate' than 'short and dirty';

- the approach used over-emphasises large surveys which require the measurement of complex input-output indicators, rather than using proxies and 'subjective' indicators which may be considered soft or biased;

- the approach used attempts to prove cause-effect relationships which are at best uncertain, based on linear notions of development.

Systems designed for learning tend to be slow to learn and adapt themselves.

Organisations and individuals are very clever at fending off the conclusions they do not like with a variety of tactics.

After Coleman (1992) and Pettigrew (1974)

Several of the case studies encountered some of the same difficulties and are attempting to redesign their planning and monitoring and evaluation systems as a result. Some of the common elements and challenges that emerge from this are described under the following headings. These include questions about which approach to adopt, who to ask for information, how to synthesise and communicate information, and how to encourage learning and create incentives for changing policy and practices as a result of that learning?

Methodological pluralism
Any organisational system has to recognise that no one method or approach will be adequate in undertaking impact assessment, and that any system must be adapted to the particular needs of the organisation in question, and must also be flexible enough to accommodate the organisation's variety of programmes and projects.

[T]here is no 'optimal' approach but … better practice is about 'achieving fit' in meeting specific objectives of the impact assessment at an acceptable level of rigour, that is compatible with the program's context, that is feasible in terms of costs, timing and human resource availability. (Hulme, quoted in Johnson 1998)

Multiple sources

The incentives offered by an organisation's various stakeholders contribute to determining its performance and impact. Analysing to whom the organisation is accountable, and how multiple accountability is managed, is equally important. Any organisational system therefore has to consciously seek out the views of a wide variety of stakeholders and cross-check their opinions. It needs to be clear about whose views count in case of differences of opinion.

Two tools developed by the New Economics Foundation in collaboration with three NGOs seem particularly appropriate as a framework for analysing and pulling together data on this issue: they are the organisation-ranking grid and the social audit. The first lays out various stakeholders' assessments of an organisation in order to establish the degree of coherence between them. This approach suggests that effectiveness, of NGOs at least, rises with the level of coherence. Social auditing takes this a step further. It seeks to make public, in the same way as company accounts, the assessments of a range of groups regarding the social and ethical behaviour of the organisation (Zadek 1996). As the case studies in this book demonstrate, the voices of some stakeholders rarely get heard, and the impact of programmes and policies upon some groups is often ignored. These are usually the groups who had no say in programme design in the first place and whose views, values, and needs are not taken into account in the monitoring of policy and project implementation.[5]

Aggregation and information-sharing

Some of the organisations in the case studies mention that their previous M&E systems were 'too slow' or took 'too long', with all staff getting the same information whether they needed it or not. Some also note that field and middle-level staff did not feel a sense of ownership of the process, or of the outputs, of monitoring systems which were mainly designed for the needs of others. However, several of the studies highlight the importance of impact tracking or monitoring. If even part of the data collected by monitoring systems is not relevant and useful to those collecting it, then the quality of that data is likely to suffer in quality. When this happens, aggregated data can give a very false sense of confidence that what is reported as occurring is actually happening.

But just as not all information is needed by everyone in an organisation, not all analysis has to be undertaken at the same level. Indeed, the idea of 'meta-evaluations' which pull together learning across several evaluations or case studies is becoming increasingly used by many agencies in order to draw out generic lessons across a range of contexts and activities.

[I]t is extremely difficult to compare the results of participatory poverty assessments across locations, particularly at the regional and national level…

BRAC works all over Bangladesh. Although its beneficiaries are almost homogeneous in terms of their economic status, their needs are heterogeneous and therefore so are their perceptions of poverty as they live in different socio-cultural rural settings. (BRAC case study)

In order to overcome this obstacle, some agencies are seeking to adopt a ranking system for comparing the performance of different programmes as assessed by local managers. While this has the value of simplicity it contains a number of risks: in the absence of agreed quality criteria, or cross-checking in other ways, the ranking may simply represent an individual's views. The quantification of performance that this will allow may lead to simplistic comparisons which are invalid if taken in isolation; if linked to resource allocation this will result in greater manipulation of results in order to secure future resources.

In the end, different stakeholders will have different information needs. A large organisation should consider how individual project appraisal or monitoring, which is vital for beneficiaries and project staff, can still be sampled by other stakeholders. Managers or trustees may need proportionately more cross-programme or thematic analysis which is related to broader strategic aims. However, no matter how carefully designed reporting and information-management systems are, they can never replace face-to-face encounters and dialogue. These are essential for overcoming hierarchy in organisations and complementing other forms of reporting and reviewing progress.

Learning, culture, and attitude

The ultimate purpose of impact assessment is to learn about what works and what does not, and how to apply these lessons in the future. There are a number of well-known bottlenecks to promoting organisational learning, some of which were apparent in the case studies. These include high staff-turnover, poor systems for recording storing and retrieving information, and poor linkages between learning and training. This is compounded by lack of rewards or incentives to learn and share learning; as a result, little time is devoted to it. When learning is hived off to specialist units, staff may see it as the specialists' responsibility, rather than everyone's. Lastly, NGOs are not seen as particularly adept at dealing with the kinds of discordant information that learning processes are liable to reveal (Roche 1995 and 1996, Edwards 1996).

Summary 7.2 suggests some of the questions that can be explored in order to assess the degree to which the organisational context within which impact assessment occurs will be conducive to absorbing its lessons.

Summary 7.2: Questions related to organisational learning[6]

Who learns in the organisation and how?

What kind of learning is rewarded?

To what degree are errors admitted and analysed?

What forms of knowledge are defined as legitimate, and how?

What constraints are there to learning?

How does information flow in the organisation?

How is institutional memory constructed; how accessible is it, and for whom?

What changes occur through self-learning, rather than other ways of learning?

How does the organisation react to learning which challenges its assumptions?

Is the organisation better placed than it was, in the light of what it has learned, to anticipate change in its environment and adapt accordingly?

What changes are being made to the organisation's learning systems?

From the case studies some clear messages emerge about the elements of organisational culture that are likely to underpin a learning organisation. The Pakistan study recommends to 'start a recording habit, be curious and cross-check, be honest'. The CYSD study notes how critical individual attitudes and behaviour are; they emphasis that one should not approach people with prejudice or pre-conceived ideas, but rather be open and curious, as the researcher in this example.

[T]he researcher walked directly with a friendly smile into the field and acted as an outsider who is interested to know about his cultivation. This pleased the farmer and he was glad to delineate his experience since the intervention of the project. (CYSD case study)

The same study reminds us that perseverance counts: 'the reward of good work can only be delayed, but can never go to waste'. Finally, becoming and remaining externally focused is vital. What happens at the interface of an organisation in its relationships with the outside world and its primary stakeholders, and how these shift over time, gives an interesting insight not only into how open an organisation is to its stakeholders but also into how well it adapts in the light of that learning.

Towards some solutions and good practice

Creating demand, incentives, and accountability

Good recording and reporting, curiosity, cross-checking, honesty, openness, perserverance, and an external focus are behaviours which will not be practised unless they are rewarded. Learning, reflection, and sharing of knowledge will not happen if they are not valued. In several of the case studies, comments were made about the time and effort that the impact assessment work required, and how the absence of co-researchers, lack of time, and staff turnover or transfer made the work especially difficult and sometimes stressful. If impact assessment work and subsequent improvements in quality are to take place then resources must be made available and such work must be seen as an integral part of everyone's work, not an 'add-on' or a luxury.

This also means creating demands and incentives for impact assessment to become a central element of development work, and articulating these demands through the organisation's structure and policies. The following example on the lack of gender-disaggregated data reported by project staff concludes that

[o]verall the problem is not so much the lack of gender awareness by field staff and researchers, but the lack of sufficient perceived demand by higher levels within agencies like Action Aid for gender differentiated results. If this demand had been in place it could have acted as a counter influence to the pressures felt by staff to aggregate and summarise research results from multiple meetings in multiple villages. (Goyder et al., p.49)

This study suggests some criteria for assessing the degree of participation in impact assessments (which in turn could be used to encourage particular ways of going about it) such as the extent of differentiation between different groups — particularly, but not only, between men and women; the frequency at which views are obtained from various groups; the degree to which new indicators, rather than predetermined ones, are allowed to emerge; and the extent to which information provided actually produces change in practices or policies.

In addition to creating incentives for those 'below' from 'above', a key issue is how to establish the accountability of those in positions of institutional power to those whom their organisations exist to serve. Impact assessment is one of the ways of doing this, along with processes such as stakeholder reviews or social audits where the results are actually made public. In assessing the accountability of senior staff or managers some key questions might include the following.

- What proportion of time do senior managers spend with programme staff or those who have contact with other organisations?

- What proportion of time and money is devoted to meetings and skill upgrading of programme staff?

- To what extent are senior managers open to continuous quality control by the organisation's counterparts and other stakeholders?

- How much insistence is there on the development of flexible, bottom-up quality-control measures?

- To what degree are the findings of such bottom-up processes made available both within and outside the organisation?

- To what extent do senior management support innovation through encouraging the analysis of past failures?

- To what degree is the organisation (its board, trustees, general assembly, staff and so on) representative of, or able to represent, those whom it seeks to serve?

Good practice in impact assessment systems

So what might good practice for impact assessment be? As is the case for monitoring and evaluation systems in general, there is a danger in supposing that impact assessment is going to solve more than it can reasonably be expected to. Moreover, impact assessment is linked to other important elements of organisational development such as learning, accountability, and reward systems. However, there seems to be a growing consensus about at least some of the elements that are needed for organisational impact assessment systems to function well. These emerge not only from the case studies presented in this book but also from other recent studies (Goyder et al. 1998, Oakley et al. 1998) and I outline their general conclusions in the following.

Keep impact assessment simple and user-friendly. Build on what people know and are able to do, and make sure that they understand, use, and benefit from the system. Keep the system simple, flexible, and focused on a few key topics, but allow a variety of means of assessing them. Make the findings visible and accessible: it shouldn't require reading pages and pages of text or figures to see what is happening. The system should allow one to discover quickly whether progress towards overall goals has been made or at least whether there has been deviation.

Embed impact assessment in all phases of the project-cycle. Do the basics well by ensuring that impact assessment is embedded in all phases of the project cycle. It is hard to carry out impact assessment without relevant baseline data, objectives, and indicators, although retrospective techniques can overcome some of the problems associated with a lack of this information. Make sure that there are clear mechanisms for ensuring that feedback is incorporated into new phases of programming or organisational development.

Focus on the key questions. Has there been change over time? How significant was it, and for whom? Was it good or bad, intended or not? How does this change compare with other periods, with other groups, and with the costs involved? What caused the change, in terms of the project and its context?

Recognise diversity and cross-check. The information that is collected should always be dissagregated so that different groups views and conditions are taken into account, especially those of men and women. Records and reports need to recognise that different people in an organisation have different needs and, if possible, tailor reports to those needs. There should be more than one channel for monitoring information in order to ensure that the system contains checks and balances to double-check information.

Ensure that the system evolves, too. It should be the responsibility of one person or group to make sure that the monitoring system itself evolves and adapts over time, selecting and learning from useful variations of existing tools and methods. It is often better to see how efficient existing sources of information can be used better, rather than to adopt completely new systems, which are likely to be costly, time-consuming, and often not comparable with old ones.

Ensure organisational coherence. Organisational incentives, rewards accountability, and other systems must be compatible with the impact assessment system at the very least; ideally, they should promote and encourage its functioning. This requires a commitment from senior mangers to ensure coherence with other systems; to keep the organisation's work focused on its programme and the external environment; and to provide an accountability framework in which 'bottom-up' quality-control measures are properly represented along with those of other stakeholder interests.

The impact of impact assessment

Although all of the impact studies demanded a lot of time and effort, the agencies involved generally seem to think that this was justifiable, because in many cases it allowed the ultimate beneficiaries of the programme to have their say, and also improved the beneficiaries' overall perception and understanding of the intervening agencies. In this sense the impact studies increased mutual accountability to some degree.

The studies also provided critical information about certain policy implications, notably the tendency of several programmes to benefit the relatively 'less poor' and, inadvertently, to exclude the poorest. They pointed out the importance of dynamics within households and communities — particularly relating to gender, class, kinship or ethnicity, and the nature of leadership — in determining whether inputs and outputs were translated into wider, sustained impacts and who benefited and who lost. Impact assessment shed light on the significance of community self-confidence and pride in creating a positive 'feedback loop', starting with what the community has achieved which in turn motivates people to continue; however, the negative 'feedback loop' was also apparent.

The studies highlighted the vital role played by intermediaries or 'outsiders' in supporting communities or membership organisations when they seek to influence institutions and wider power relations; and the role played by both community-level organisations and intermediaries in integrating and harmonising the actions of several actors and sometimes facilitating the dialogue and co-ordination between them.

Apart from leading to a growing recognition of the importance of impact assessment, the studies underlined some of the current weaknesses and challenges which agencies face: the absence of adequate baseline or monitoring data that allow change over time to be properly estimated; the difficulty of quantifying, aggregating, and reporting on much of the impact they achieve; the absence of a coherent or adequate overall planning, appraisal, monitoring and evaluation framework within which impact assessment would be integrated; the difficulties of proving attribution and the need to assess how various actors combine to produce positive impact; and the question of finding a reasonable balance between undertaking systematic assessment of impact — which is adequately resourced — and continued programme work

In the end, 'the proof of the pudding is in the eating' and to this extent the results are encouraging. BRAC, in response to the results of its study which indicated a recent bias in member selection towards the relatively 'less poor', has

initiated steps to enter the hard-core poor. Over 200,000 women have been already identified. A survey is being conducted to assess their problems and need to evolve a suitable programme of intervention for this bypassed group.

CORDES will attempt to institutionalise the assessment method it piloted during this case study and use it is a critical adjunct to their planning process in order to adapt their strategic direction in the light of its findings.

As a result of the organisational learning generated from their impact assessment, Proshika have initiated an organisation-wide strategy for developing a more coherent approach to all its work — not just impact assessment—based on much more participatory methods and ways of working.

The Northern Ghana Development Network now wants to develop a research and advocacy strategy, focusing on issues the study identified as criticial, such as health financing and food security. They recognise that their members will need to gain a better understanding of both local and national policy issues.

Conclusion

Understanding the influence, roles, and relationships of the range of organisations and institutions involved in a given programme or region is a critical part of assessing impact; it is also important in developing stronger mutual accountability in partnership arrangements. This means overcoming a number of methodological and institutional challenges in terms of synthesising and sharing multiple perspectives and stimulating learning. In the first instance this requires a desire on the part of each agency, including donors, to undertake systematic self-assessment of its performance and relationships. This makes mutual assessments more feasible — but if they are to be truly mutual, communities must be encouraged to assess the intermediary organisations which support them, and intermediary organisations encouraged to look critically at their funders. This is not always going to be straightforward, given the unequal power relationship between them. However, it needs all actors in the process to collaborate in seeking to understand how, together, they are maximising their impact.

8

Conclusion

In the introduction to this book, I described a vicious circle in which many NGOs are trapped. Before returning to look at what the findings of this book suggest about these wider issues, and the creation of a more virtous circle, I explore some of the more specific issues that the case studies set out to address, notably:

- the key elements of impact assessment;

- how impact assessment can deal with issues relating to the unequal power and participation of the range of stakeholders involved;

- what has been learned about various approaches to undertaking impact assessment;

- what the implications of the findings are in relation to the organisational context in which impact assessment takes place.

The essence of impact assessment

As we have seen, it is the constant and fluctuating interaction between a given set of actions (in this case, a project or programme) and the context in which these are situated, that produces change. If impact assessment is essentially about looking at change, it may be useful to review the various ways in which the studies did this. In practice, they focused on a number of very simple questions: Has there been change in people's lives — yes or no? In what areas has there been change: in health, income, happiness? Has the change been positive or negative? How much change has there been, in a relative sense (for example, income has doubled compared to last year) or in an absolute sense (for example, income has shrunk by $5 a month)? What brought about that change?

However, *comparing* these changes with other factors was critical in the studies for the purposes of impact assessment. The research findings were compared to the following elements:

- other groups (for instance, men and women, 'rich' and 'poor', control groups, non-project respondents, and so on);

- other changes (for example, improvements in health compared with improvements in education);

- baseline information (ranging from the simple, such as last year's data, to longer time-series or longitudinal data);

- the costs invested;

- changes in the context (for example, even if people became worse off because of general trends, did the intervention contribute to those it supported being less worse off than they would otherwise have been?).

Quantification of change

In those instances where this kind of comparison was not, or could not, be made, researchers may have felt that they needed data on absolute change rather than relative change, when in fact information on relative change would have been sufficient. For example, in the Wajir study the differences in the relative perceptions of respondents within and outside the project area regarding changes over time in quality of life, water reliability, and security allowed important conclusions to be drawn. However, if the study had felt it necessary to gather absolute figures regarding, for example, water reliability or income this would have probably required resources beyond the budget and time-scale of the study. A focus on absolute figures can also lead to excluding the views and perceptions of those who may not be able to put numbers to changes in their lives, but who can quite clearly prioritise and rank different changes and their importance.

There were also cases where a greater quantification of change was necessary and possible, but was seemingly avoided. In more than one study, participatory exercises at the community level showed clearly that there had been a positive change in people's lives, but they gave no indication whether this referred to two people or 2,000, to men or women, to 'rich' or 'poor'. Again relatively simple questions and exercises, such as ranking or scoring, could have helped in understanding not just what had changed, but its scale and significance. This is important, because as we have seen the difference between impact assessment and other types of assessment or evaluation is precisely that it explores significant or long-lasting change brought about by a given project or programme.

In the end deciding how significant or long-lasting a change is, and how attributable it is to a given action, is a matter of judgement. The decision depends particularly on the context and, of course, who decides what is significant, and means recognising that change is the outcome of multiple and complex processes as well as of the struggles, ideas, and actions of various and unequal interest groups. This is different from seeing development as a managed process undertaken by development agencies and NGOs through projects and programmes. Simple models of cause and effect, linking project inputs to outputs and impact, will usually be inadequate for assessing the impact of what NGOs do; we need models which embrace the wider context of influences and change processes that surrounds projects and programmes, and the wide variety of the resulting impact.

The contingent and uncertain nature of change as well as the possibility of discontinuous or catastrophic change puts a premium on impact monitoring, learning, and adaptation. What is certain is that the unexpected will happen, and that we cannot plan for every eventuality; any action we take might produce dramatic and significant change that was not predicted. This puts the onus on those who intervene in processes of change to monitor the impact of what they do, on a regular basis, and adapt their actions as a result. Is it simply not good enough to say that impact cannot be measured until after a project has finished, when significant — and negative — change can occur very early on in the lifetime of a project or programme. Impact assessment must be able to cope with turbulent, non-linear change as well as gradual and linear change (Roche 1994).

The issue of power and participation

If impact is defined as significant or long-lasting change, the key questions concern not only what has changed, whether it is significant, and to what degree it can be attributed to a given set of actions, but equally who makes the judgement.

Despite the efforts made in the case studies, in many situations certain groups, notably women and children, are consistently excluded from 'participatory' exercises. In some emergency situations there may also be logistical and political limits to participation. The case studies also reveal that even among the group of participating NGOs there are several interpretations of the term 'participation', as well as different criteria for assessing its quality or depth. Given the growing importance that is being attached to participation, not just by NGOs but also by bilateral and multilateral agencies, the absence of clearer agreements and standards for assessing the quality of participation is particularly problematic.

While the scientific tradition sets out clear criteria for judging the quality of research, based on notions of internal and external validity, reliability, and objectivity, there is no such broad agreement as yet on criteria for assessing the quality of participatory research. Some attempts to develop a model have been made, for example by Jules Pretty and others, building on the work of Guba and Lincoln. Pretty has adapted the criteria used to assess the quality of conventional research in order to find equivalent ones for participatory processes of inquiry. These are based on based on the criteria of credibility, transferability, dependability, and confirmability (Pretty 1994, Guba and Lincoln 1989). Table 8.1 summarises these criteria as well as those commonly used in scientific research.

Table 8.1: Criteria for judging the trustworthiness of information

Conventional scientific criteria	Participatory criteria
Internal validity: the proof of causal relationships (A leads to B).	**Length and depth of engagement of actors:** discovering what has changed and why, based on sufficient trust and rapport to gain quality information.
External validity: the degree to which findings can be applied to other contexts or groups.	
	Persistent and parallel observation: identifying and focusing on key issues; using a number of observers at one time.
Reliability: the degree to which the findings could be repeated if the enquiry was replicated in the same or a similar situation.	**Cross-checking:** combining various sources, methods, and investigators, as well as participant checking.
Objectivity: the extent to which multiple observers can agree on a phenomenon, ensuring that the results are not due to the researcher's biases.	**Expression of difference and negative case analysis:** searching out different views and explanations from a range of stakeholders, particularly on the basis of gender and class; analysing change for the worse.
	Research diary and peer review: making transparent the means by which the information was collected as well its sources (so that an audit of the inquiry would be possible).
	Impact on stakeholders' capacities to know and act: the process of inquiry should be empowering in and of itself and generate new insights for all concerned.

The important difference between the two approaches is the degree to which the researcher or observer is considered capable of remaining independent of what is observed or measured. In the scientific method this is deemed essential, and therefore a lot of effort goes into designing measurement tools, experiments, and methods of analysis which attempt to ensure this. Participatory and qualitative research accepts that researchers or observers are necessarily part of what they observe, and that their own attitudes, beliefs, and behaviours will determine, at least in part, the information gathered. It therefore emphasises the quality and depth of engagement, as well as cross-checking findings from several perspectives.

These differences are often couched in terms of an opposition of objectivity and subjectivity, when in fact the issue may be more usefully debated in terms of how one can avoid bias in any given method of assessment. If we pose the question in this way we can ask whether the prolonged process of participant observation adopted in the Matson study may have been biased towards the views of particular groups within the community. We can ask whether the household survey undertaken in the BRAC study reduced bias by ensuring that a representative sample of village organisations was selected for study. In other words, the context of the study and the kind of activity being assessed will determine the approach adopted and the mix of methods and tools employed. The tools and methods within that mix will be subject to different criteria or standards: a questionnaire survey which seeks quantitative information from a representative sample of a given population would have different quality criteria than a series of focus-group discussions exploring how changing attitudes to gender relations have been brought about. However, the findings of the study as a whole and the individual methods adopted should be judged according to the degree to which the views and perceptions of staff, external assessors, as well as different groups of local people and other stakeholders, were, or were not, taken into account and cross-checked with each other.

The different approaches to impact assessment

The project in question, its context, and issues of power and participation determined what was assessed in the case studies, as well as how. Three main approaches were adopted. The first was mainly focused on an individual project and involved clarifying and specifying project objectives and indicators and then assessing the degree to which they had been met. In some cases, this involved a careful analysis of the links between outputs, outcomes, and impacts with a limited number of indicators being verified at a each level of the impact chain. In some studies, control group or individuals outside the project areas were compared with those in project areas.

The second approach focused on the projects being assessed, but looked more broadly at the potential changes that might have occurred as a result. A range of stakeholders were asked to identify the most important changes brought about by a given project, and how they happened. In some cases, this involved using a broad checklist of potential areas or dimensions of change.

The case studies in the third catgeory were interested first and foremost in the overall changes in people's lives and sought to explore with them the significance of these changes and their causes, including the project in question. This approach seeks to situate changes brought about by a particular project within the context of other changes.

Change, objectives, and indicators

Most case studies examined change at an individual or household level, although some, particularly those which included advocacy, explored wider changes at the level of the community, the organisation, and in policy. However, certain areas or dimensions of change are seen as significant in all the case studies:

- income, expenditure, and assets, including access to land and credit;

- health, education, literacy, and other skills and knowledge;

- infrastructure, including access to water and sanitation facilities in particular;

- food security and production;

- social relations, social capital, unity, and changed community norms;

- women's ownership and control of assets, mobility, access to income-generation activities, child-care, freedom to express their views, power in household decision-making, ability to control violence; and the household division of labour;

- peace and security, law and order, declining levels of sexual violence, human-rights abuses, and destruction of lives and property;

- ability to cope with crises;

- self-confidence, self-esteem, independence, potential and capacity to make claims and demands;

- overall quality of life.

Although the indicators people choose for identifying significant change in their lives may be different, the above list perhaps represents a common core of dimensions that are important to people which is not location-specific. But the priorities and order that various groups — men and women, old and young, rich and poor — assign to those changes will vary both within and between regions or locations, and over time. In addition, as the Pakistan study suggests, the aesthetic, cultural, religious, or spiritual dimensions of people's lives are affected both positively and negatively by projects and programmes, yet tend to be ignored. This may mean that, for impact assessment purposes, the search for common or generic indicators is perhaps much less vital than understanding which areas of change certain groups of people prioritise, and how these relate to each other in different contexts. In this sense, indicators become more a means of exemplifying why and how change within a particular area has occurred, rather than simply a means to verify a project's progress against predetermined objectives.

Tools and methods

A wide variety of tool and methods were used in the studies; these were explored in some detail in Chapter 4. Perhaps the most important conclusion is that the selection of a judicious mix, and sequence, of tools and methods is heavily dependent on being clear about the purpose and focus of the assessment, and designing it in a way that is appropriate to the context, the project in question, and the organisations involved. The ability to develop appropriate method combinations and sequences, and the ability to adapt and innovate as the study progresses, seem to be as important as the knowledge and skill required for individual methods.

A number of key findings relate to the families of methods explored. First, it is evident that full use must be made of existing data — whether it has been collected as part of the project or is available from other sources. The production of synoptic documents that pulled together many years' worth of project reports and files proved especially useful in some cases. In addition, local government sources, education and health records, data from agricultural research stations, also proved an important source of information where the context was explored, despite many limitations.

Even where existing information was of high quality, and a great effort had been put into compiling baseline data, nearly all the case studies had to reconstruct at least part of the history of not only the projects, but also of the wider changes in the lives of individuals and communities. This applies particularly to situations where project plans and documents are weak or non-existent, as in emergency situations where rapid changes in the context may have led to changing priorities which may not always have been documented. Chapter 4 detailed many ways in which researchers managed to reconstruct information.

271

Although large-scale household surveys suffer many limitations, and have received quite a bad press in recent years, the case studies indicate that they can serve a useful function if they are focused, pre-tested and adapted, if enumerators receive adequate training and preparation, if findings are properly cross-checked and sequenced with other more qualitative data, and if there is adequate capacity to analyse the results. Mini-surveys and the kind of questionnaire used in the Wajir study which combined participatory tools and standard questions offer useful alternatives to fully-fledged surveys.

The wide range of interview, workshop, and focus-group methods adopted in the case studies threw up some critical questions regarding the advantages and disadvantages of individual versus group processes — issues that are rarely addressed in many of the manuals on participatory research or study design. Yet the case studies showed examples of individuals answering the same questions differently in group or individual settings; individuals disagreeing in private with conclusions reached in in a group setting; particular groups (for instance, women, young people, and members of the least well-off households) being consistently excluded from, or ignored, during group exercises. On the other hand, there were also examples of group exercises generating new insights for participants, sometimes as a result of sharing sensitive information (for example, on domestic violence); strengthening a feeling of solidarity and common purpose; and bringing together previously marginal voices in a way that allowed them to be heard.

Direct and participant observation also often does not receive much attention as a method in monitoring and evaluation texts. Yet in a number of the studies the advantage of 'resident researchers' and people simply 'hanging around' and keeping their eyes open is quite evident. In particular, observation of this kind helped to build trust and rapport with local people and project staff and allowed them to gain new insights that were unlikely to be obtained from asking questions or facilitating discussions. Observation permitted a deeper understanding of relationships not only within communities but also between the community and other actors, and allowed a high degree of cross-checking of information collected in other ways. This technique is highly dependent on the skills of the observer and is resource-intensive; on the other hand, these skills can be nurtured and developed, and this sort of approach can be less demanding of local people's time. Given the concerns raised below regarding the time-consuming nature of some of the participatory approaches adopted, this is worth bearing in mind.

Although a comprehensive range of participatory techniques was used in the case studies, there are perhaps a limited number which seem to be particularly relevant and useful for impact assessment purposes. These would include time lines, well-being and preference ranking, impact flow diagrams, and trend analysis. This kind of participatory work has to give greater recognition to existing power and social relations within communities; it must pay greater attention to people's time constraints and the opportunity cost to them of getting involved in an assessment. Again, these tools should be combined with other methods and sources of information in order to address the need for clearer standards of assessing the quality of processes of participatory inquiry. The findings from the case studies suggest that (in addition to the criteria mentioned in Table 8.1) in situations where impact assessment is primarily initiated by external agencies, the following criteria should be considered:

- a process or time-schedule agreeable both to the men *and women* in the communities and the researchers;

- efficient use of existing sources of information so as not to waste people's time collecting data that is already available;

- the development and continual adaptation of methods, based on a mutual analysis of their strengths and weaknesses;

- the extent to which the information that is gathered actually has an impact, in other words, actually produces change in practices or policies of the project or organisation being assessed.

The use of case studies (of individuals, communities, projects, and organisations) was prevalent in nearly all the countries involved. Case studies are particularly useful in complex situations where many variables interrelate and where outcomes and impact are likely to vary across different populations. What kind of study is chosen needs to be to be consciously thought through. Well chosen case studies and cross-case study analysis can add a lot of value to an assessment, particularly if they relate to wider policy matters which are of major interest.

Finally, the issues of attribution, cross-checking, and the importance of feedback remain, issues which are discussed throughout this book. None of the tools and methods used *on their own* can solve the problem of determining attribution, and even in combination they cannot prove it. However, if properly cross-checked, they provide a body of evidence that can be agreed, disputed, or amended, which can in turn contribute to a reasoned and plausible judgement. As Roger Riddell has stated:

In short, it is unnecessary to concentrate time, effort and resources on project or programme evaluation if firm conclusions can be drawn without using sophisticated techniques. Similarly if judgements made about qualitative aspects of projects are not substantially challenged by the relevant 'actors' or groups ... then purist worries about objectively assessing these factors become largely irrelevant. (Riddell 1990)

The organisational context

The previous chapter goes into some detail about how the case studies assessed the impact of projects and programmes on organisations, as well as how organisations in general approach and manage impact assessment. At the workshop that brought together many of those involved in the case study work, the issue of how organisations can help or hinder various forms of impact assessment was a recurring theme. This is linked to the growing interest, particularly among gender analysts, in the role that organisations and institutions play in producing and reproducing various forms of inequality, and in how their cultures, systems, and values determine what impact they achieve. In this sense, impact assessment also requires looking at the deep-rooted impact on those structures that embody relations of authority, power, and control and that determine the degree to which individuals and groups can exercise choice.

Development agencies, including large NGOs, are not immune from the problems confronting other bureaucracies in terms of complacency, hierarchy, inertia, and poor information flow, which can lead to loops of self-deception as feedback from activities is distorted, or manipulated as individuals seek to protect themselves. Senior managers who subscribe to the view that 'if it ain't broke, don't fix it' will tend to go along with positive news and carry on without any checks until something 'breaks'. As Robert Chambers has suggested, this kind of institutional blindness has led to the most remarkable feature of development efforts over the last few decades: that 'we' were so wrong when 'we' thought we were so right (Chambers 1994).

Much of the good practice that emerges from the case studies and from recent work on impact assessment in other agencies (summarised in Chapter 7) focuses on ensuring that impact assessment processes are kept simple, relevant, and useful. Experience also underlines that an organisation needs to align its incentives, rewards, and systems so that they are compatible with a real desire to learn, and adapt its work and ways of working in the light of that learning. This requires a commitment from senior mangers to ensure a coherence with other systems, to maintain the external and programme focus of the organisations' work, and to provide an accountability framework in which 'bottom-up' quality-control measures are properly represented and balanced with those of other stakeholder interests.

This means that any process of assessing impact not only has to be appropriate in terms of the complexity and the cost involved, but also has to be flexible and produce relevant, timely, accurate, and useable information that can satisfy different interests or stakeholders. The challenge for most organisations will be to develop appropriate processes and methods of impact assessment, which recognise the limited time and financial resources available, and which are in harmony with the skills and experience of those at the 'sharp end' — especially those whom our efforts seek to benefit and those working on programmes 'in the field'. The approaches, tools, and methods presented in this book provide some answers to this challenge.

Much of the literature suggests that the past emphasis on 'independent' external, one-off evaluations as mechanisms of quality control often brought little of value to project managers, who saw the process as a justification, control, or policing function. This does not mean that external impact evaluations may not have their place, but rather that NGOs need to refocus on the 'front-line' and instil in staff a major preoccupation with learning systems at the programme level as a vital internal project activity. This is not only because unused or unusable information will not lead to any changes in practice; the problem is more fundamental. If information systems and evaluations are, or should be, largely based on the ongoing recording of project processes and on regular interaction with beneficiaries, then the quality and honesty of that recording becomes the critical issue. If this information is of poor quality, or simply a distortion of reality, then entire organisations can find themselves locked into a false picture of what they achieve as they synthesise, aggregate, and analyse primary data which is fundamentally flawed.

Providing the right incentives for this basic level of information collection properly is vital, and there is no better incentive than self-interest. In this case, self-interest relates to how useful the information will be in future to the person or organisation that collects it. A recent Action Aid study on impact assessment concluded that for

most local NGOs reporting, whether for their own Head Offices or for their donors, is a chore and for many, evaluation and impact assessment is assumed to be of greater interest to donors and Head Offices rather than the staff themselves. (Goyder et al. 1997, p. 47)

Seeking more reliable guidance of how things are going from the people and local staff involved in a project, and understanding how they are already monitoring impact in their own way, thus increases in significance. Our case studies provide some clues about the difficulties in meeting the diverse needs of local stakeholders and of more distant organisations, as well as indicating which tools and methods are particularly helpful in this process. However, many of these problems demonstrate not only the need to develop alternative assessment methods, but also the need to develop new organisational cultures and relationships.

Policy implications

This final section of this book explores some of the key policy implications which emerge from the case studies. These are grouped under the following headings: poverty and gender issues, resource allocation, and the future of NGOs.

Poverty and gender issues

Although the case studies' primary purpose was to explore and learn about approaches to and methods of impact assessment, the findings of these studies merit some attention. Several of the studies note that the very poorest groups, whether identified through wealth-ranking or by poverty-line measures, have either been excluded from projects or benefited less than less poor groups. This happens either because of the nature of the organisation running the projects in question (it may be a community-based or a membership organisation that the poorest do not or cannot join) or because of the nature of the intervention (for example, an agricultural project may demand labour inputs which the poorest cannot make, or a credit programme may demand repayments that the poorest do not feel able to make). However, there is also some evidence that the poorest can benefit proportionately more than richer households if they are strategically targeted, and that in some cases the incidence and severity of poverty decreased with the duration of NGO project involvement.

There is also some limited, if tantalising, evidence which suggests that poorer households when asked to compare the significance of collective services (health, education, water) which are often provided by the state, rank these higher than NGO projects, particularly those providing individualised services such as credit or agricultural extension. Better-off households rank NGO projects higher. This finding, if confirmed more widely, would clearly have important implications for the complementarity of NGO/ state roles, and indeed for the importance of NGOs not only in helping to stimulate demand by strengthening community organisations, but also in facilitating supply by advocating for adequate funding of state-service provision.

As far as women's status is concerned, most case studies report improvements in their material well-being, household relations, and self-image. However, some note that this has been accompanied by further increases in workload, little change to control over assets within the home and no change in deep-seated gender norms, for instance regarding dowry payments. As a recent OECD/ DAC study on NGOs also notes, 'what is clearly proving most difficult is to introduce processes which have a more positive and systemic impact on the status of women' (OECD/ DAC 1998).

There is also some evidence to suggest that where poorer groups and women have started to push for, and in some cases achieve, a level of systemic change, this often requires more support from intermediaries and external agencies, albeit of a nature that is different from a traditional project relationship. This has important implications for the notions of hand-over, independence, and autonomy which pervade the literature on NGO organisational development. The development of 'vertical' relationships and support networks (for example, regional, national, or international) as well as horizontal ones can provide a more appropriate framework for collaboration and advocay than single project relationships. This can allow change to be promoted at several levels simultaneously and the debate can be shifted to those organisations, regions, and capitals where the best chance of achieving change exists.

Resource allocation

The current weight given to assessing impact, rather than inputs and outputs, is welcome because it stresses the importance of understanding how a positive and significant difference can be made to people's lives. However, although past performance is a guide to future performance, it is not the only one. The relationship between projects, the organisations that run and support them, and the context in which they are situated, is a complex one which produces a wide range of possible impacts. The same inputs at different times or in different places will produce different results. These results will in turn affect various groups of people differently. This suggests first that an understanding of context, local power relations, poverty, and social dynamics is a necessary precondition to achieving impact.

Second, the ability of NGOs to listen to and learn from local people and organisations and adapt their support in the light of this learning is critical in ensuring that past impact can be sustained in the future. This, as discussed above, is dependent on organisations having a congruence between its incentives, systems, and culture that permits learning and adaptation as well as an ability to balance the interests of a range of stakeholders. Third, the ability to plan, manage, and account for funds received clearly remain important to organisational health, although the capacities and competencies needed will vary depending on the size of the organisation. Fourth, the ability to innovate and take risks will be necessary, particularly if the poorest are to be included in development efforts. Investing in projects with 'safe returns' and guaranteed future impact is likely to mean adhering to the status quo.

Finally, the ability to work with others and to use and communicate the findings of impact assessment exercises or other learning is going to be increasingly important in order to promote broader systemic change. If impact is going to be increased then this too will become a more central aspect than it has been in the past.

In short, the results of impact assessment exercises are insufficient *on their own* to make sensible decisions about resource allocation to projects or organisations. There are other criteria, notably understanding of context; the ability to listen, learn, adapt, and innovate; management capacity; and the ability to work with others and to communicate learning.

The future of NGOs: Towards a virtuous circle?

This book has tried to illustrate how a number of NGOs from around the world are struggling with the very complex set of issues which relate to assessing the impact of their work. We hope that in developing and sharing these experiences and our learning we can, in a small way, contribute to countering one aspect of the vicious circle described in Chapter 1 and thus help to develop a 'virtuous circle'.

Figure 8.1: Towards a virtuous circle?

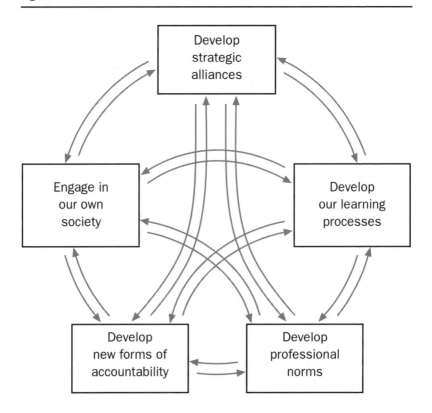

This circle, like the vicious circle, has five mutually reinforcing elements: increased recognition of the need to develop institutional learning and impact assessment processes; the development of strategic alliances with other NGOs and other sectors, including state structures; a deepening engagement with social and political processes in the NGOs' own countries of origin; the development of new forms of accountability; and the further development of professional norms and standards within and across agencies.

In order for the circle to achieve enough momentum, a number of things must happen simultaneously. The lessons from the case studies indicate that this will involve not only the development and sharing of new tools and methods of impact assessment, but also the enhancement of broader strategies for institutional learning. However, this will only make a difference if the current competition for resources, personnel, and ideas between NGOs and other actors — notably the state — is reworked into creative, strategic alliances. This, from an impact assessment perspective, means less emphasis on selfishly seeking to attribute change to an individual project or organisation, and more emphasis on how agencies *combine* to produce significant change for people living poverty. On many occasions, this in turn will mean sacrificing individual agency profile for the greater good. Impact assessment is about becoming more open and transparent about what is, and what is not, achievable in the future. Change is not likely to take place if assessment simply becomes a means of blowing the organisational trumpet even louder.

Some of the organisations in the case studies are beginning to transform themselves by putting down stronger and deeper roots in their own societies. For some, this has always been part of their identity; for others, including Oxfam GB and Novib, this means engaging even more in the UK and the Netherlands. It means making the connections between poverty and exclusion 'at home' and abroad, and demonstrating that the stories of change from Africa, Asia, Latin America, and Eastern Europe are not simply about a need for further compassion and money, but are also about inspiring, insightful, and creative work. As these roots grow deeper, accountability patterns will shift too. This is important if we wish to see a future based on notions of interdependence and mutuality, rather than dependence and hand-outs.

Change in these elements of the circle could combine to bring about a situation wich gives a more realistic portrayal of what NGOs can achieve on their own; it will have a greater degree of modesty and humility as well as a recognise the importance of working with others. This in turn will help to decrease the gap between rhetoric and reality and encourage greater realisation that the potential to solve problems 'at home' and 'out there' is enhanced by multiple perspectives based on a more effective and honest sharing of experience and ideas. It is interesting to note in this context that recent research shows that the degree of a donor country's commitment to social justice at home is positively correlated to their commitment to social justice not only in their aid programme but in all aspects of their international relations (Olsen 1996).

Change in these elements of the circle would also lead to increased trust, built on shared values *and* a respect for difference. Faed by ideologies of globalisation, the global NGO community must find ways of overcoming the danger of fragmentation and irrelevance: alliances must lead to more than mere tolerant co-existence where we agree to disagree. Our ultimate aim must be to create groupings in which organisations that do share realities based on common understanding and analysis as well as common involvement in struggles for justice and equity, can move forward together.

Moreover, new notions of 'partnership' and change could be created which are based on clear and agreed standards of performance. The reaction against the approach to development which proposes the universal blueprint of modernisation, particularly by NGOs, is to argue for the importance of context, diversity, looking at processes, and understanding difference. While this reaction is understandable, some authors argue that it has undermined the notions of universal standards and rights. If everything is different and relative, then it is difficult to imagine universally applicable standards which suggest some absolute hierarchy of values (Duffield 1995).

Fifty years after the Universal Declaration of Human Rights was ratified — and at a time when there is a resurgence of rights-based approaches to international relations — the challenge for NGOs in general, and for impact assessment processes in particular, remains to tell the stories of how individual men, women, and children, and their communities, struggle to defend their universal rights in the face of overwhelming odds, and how they can be better supported in doing so.

Notes

Chapter 2
Our overall approach to impact assessment

1 This chapter draws heavily on the literature review and preparatory reports written by Raul Hopkins and Elsa Dawson and an interim progress report by Floris Blankenberg, Margaret Newens and Chris Roche, published in Oakley et al. (1998).

2 I am grateful to Fred Wessels of Oxfam GB for this rewording of Paul Willot's work on auto-evaluation (Willot 1985).

3 See Martha Alter Chen and Elizabeth Dunn (1997).

4 I am grateful to Bridget Walker of Oxfam GB for this observation.

Chapter 3 Designing an impact assessment process

1 Goyder, H, Davies, R, Wilkinson, W (1998) *Participatory Impact Assessment*

2 Personal communication from Bridget Walker of Oxfam GB.

3 David Hulme notes that one reason why multiple regression has been rarely used, even in the area of microfinance impact assessment which one might think is more easily quantifiable, is the 'enormous demands for data on other possible causal factors', and the huge expense and technical expertise that this requires (Hulme 1997).

Chapter 4 Choosing tools and methods

1 A One Stop Shop in Britain generally provides a range of services and goods. This may include advice on employment, social services, benefits, or legal advice, as well as sales of second-hand clothes and other items. Advice workers are normally specialists in particular fields such as law or welfare benefits and offer support to anyone who seeks it.

2 The Phoenix Club is a member-led drop-in centre for residents suffering from mental health problems which is based at the offices of the Matson Neighbourhood Project.

3 For more information on how to organise a training session for semi-structured interviewing, including specific exercises, see *Participatory Learning in Action: A Trainer's Guide* published by the International Institute or Environment and Development (IIED), pp. 73–79.

4 The topics discussed are based on Chen and Mahmud's conceptual framework to assess changes in women's lives (Chen and Mahmud 1995), which identifies three pathways to empowerment (material, perceptual, and relational).

5 Goyder, H, Davies, R, and Williamson, W (1998) Participatory Impact Assessment Study, Action Aid.

6 Social mapping is another PRA method, in which participants are asked to draw a map of the dwellings in the community and to name the household or individual who live there, or to indicate details about the status of each household.

7 Bridget Walker, personal communication.

8 Kamal Kar et al. (1997) 'Participatory Impact Assessment: Calcutta Slum Improvement Project – Main Findings Report', Calcutta Metropolitan Development Authority.

9 The study has also calculated the direct and indirect economic impacts of projects.

10 See Dinwiddy and Teal (1995) for more information on how these are calculated as well as for general material on cost-benefit analysis.

11 I am very grateful to Sabina Alkire for this section, which heavily 'borrows' from her PhD thesis (Alkire 1999).

12 The IRR in this case has no distributional weights as all the projects target the same socio-economic group.

Chapter 5 Impact assessment and emergencies

1 These include a report on a workshop, 'Managing Emergency Humanitarian Aid evaluation: Lessons from Experience', held with AusAID support (Apthorpe and Nevile 1998), and a report entitled 'Good Practice in Evaluating Humanitarian Aid', submitted by DANIDA to the DAC Working Party on Aid Evaluation (Hallam and Borton 1998).

2 The SPHERE project is an effort by a large number of international agencies to draft a humanitarian charter and to identify a set of standards and best practice in delivery of services to disaster victims.

3 Hallam, A and Borton, J (1998) 'Good Practice in Evaluating Humanitarian Aid', Document No.3 submitted to the DAC Working Party on Aid Evaluation, 30th Meeting, 27–28 May 1998, DANIDA.

4 Bridget Walker, personal communication.

5 See also David Bryer and Ed Cairns (1997).

Chapter 6 Impact assessment and advocacy

1 Much of this chapter is based on an article entitled 'Assessing the impact of advocacy work' by Alex Bush and Chris Roche, published in *Appropriate Technology* Vol. 24, 1997 and preceding discussions at a Development Studies Association NGO study group meeting in July 1997. It also draws on work by Jim Coe of Oxfam's Campaigns department and detailed comments on an earlier draft by Peter van Tuijl of Novib.

2 I am grateful to Peter van Tuijl for the ideas upon which this definition is based.

3 Baranyi et al. (1997) 'Making Solidarity Effective: Northern Voluntary Organisations and the Promotion of Peace in Angola and East Timor', CIIR, London.

4 Evaluation conducted by Development Initiatives.

5 Letter from Kenneth Clarke, Chancellor of the Exchequer during Oxfam's debt campaign, to Bob Hammond, Oxfam Constituency Contact, in September 1997.

6 Letter from Bob Hammond, Oxfam Constituency Contact, October 1997.

7 See Farnworth (1998).

8 See Adrian Jackson (1997) for a description on the use of legislative theatre in the UK.

9 See Mavrocordatos (1997) on the uses of theatre for participatory monitoring.

10 See case studies in Holland, J. and Blackburn, J. (1998) *Whose Voice? Participatory research and policy change.*

Chapter 7   Impact assessment and organisations

1   This chapter in addition to the case-study material also draws upon papers and reports produced during the course of the research, notably Newens and Roche (1997) and Blankenberg, Newens and Roche (1998).

2   This scale builds on the ideas of Norman Uphoff (1987) in his field methodology for participatory self-evaluation.

3   For more on these ratios for credit programmes see Chapter 4 and Annex 2 of Johnson and Rogaly (1997).

4   Those who have any doubt about this, see Perera's analysis of the relationship between Sarvadoya and its donors (1997).

5   For an assessment of the relevance of social auditing to Oxfam see Dawson (1998).

6   See Edwards 1996, Howes and Roche 1996.

Appendix 1: Bibliography

Publications

African Rights (1994) *Humanitarianism Unbound? Current Dilemmas Facing Multi-Mandate Relief Operations in Political Emergencies*, Discussion Paper No. 5, African Rights, London.

Anderson, M and Woodrow, P (1989) *Rising from the Ashes: Development Strategies in Times of Disaster*, Westview, Boulder.

Anderson, M (1996) *Do No Harm: Building Local Capacities for Peace*, Cambridge USA.

Baranyi, S, Kibble, S, Kohen, A, O'Neill, K (1997) 'Making Solidarity Effective: Northern Voluntary Organisations and the promotion of peace in Angola and East Timor', CIIR, London.

Barrow, C (1997) *Environmental and Social Impact Assessment*, Arnold.

Blankenberg, F, Newens, M, Roche, C (1998) 'Impact asssessment: cutting through the complexity', in Oakley et al. (1998) Pratt et al. (1998) *Outcome and Impact: Evaluating Change in Social Development*, Intrac.

Biekart, K (1999) *European Private Aid Agencies and Democratic Transition in Central America*, Transnational Institute, Amsterdam.

Borton et al. (1995) 'Joint evaluation of emergency assistance to Rwanda', ODI.

Borton, J and Macrae, J (1997) 'Evaluation Synthesis of Emergency Aid', Evaluation Report EV:613, DfID.

Braden, S (1998) *Video for Development: A casebook from Vietnam*, Oxfam GB, Oxford.

Bryer, D and Cairns, E (1997) 'For Better? For Worse? Humanitarian Aid and Conflict' in *Development in Practice*, Vol. 7:4, pps 363–374.

Bush, A and Roche, C (1997) 'Assessing the impact of advocacy work' in *Appropriate Technology* Vol. 24:2, IT Publications, London.

285

Cassen, R and Associates (1986) *Does Aid Work?*, Oxford University Press, Oxford.

Chambers, R (1997) *Whose Reality Counts?: Putting the First Last*, IT Publications, London.

Chen, M and Dunn, E (1997) 'Household economic portfolios', paper prepared for an USAID-funded research project, Management Systems International, Washington DC.

Christoplos, I (1998) 'Humanitarianism, Pluralism and Ombudsmen: Do the pieces fit?', in *Disasters*, Vol. 23:2, available from www.oneworld.org/ombudsman/Ombud7.html.

Covey, J (1996) 'Accountability and effectiveness in NGO policy alliances', in Edwards, M and Hulme, D (eds.) (1996) *Non-Governmental Organisations: Performance and accountability*, Earthscan publications, London.

Dabelstein, N (1996) 'Evaluating the International Humanitarian System' in *Disasters* Vol. 20: 4.

Dinwiddy, C and Teal, F (1995) *Principles of Cost-Benefit Analysis for Developing Countries*, Cambridge University Press.

Drucker, P (1990) *Managing the Non-Profit Organisation*, Harper Collins, New York.

Duffield, M (1996) 'The Symphony of the Damned' in *Disasters*, Vol 20: 3.

Eade, D (1997) *Capacity-Building: An Approach to People-Centered Development*, Oxfam GB, Oxford.

Edwards, M and Hulme, D (1995) *NGOs – Performance and Accountability: Beyond the Magic Bullet*, Earthscan, London.

El Bushra, J and Piza Lopez, E (1993) *Development in Conflict: the Gender Dimension*, ACORD and Oxfam GB, Oxford.

Fowler (1995) 'Assessing NGO performance: Difficulties, dilemmas and a way ahead', in Edwards and Hulme (1995).

Fowler, A, Goold, L and James, R (1995) *Participatory Self-Assessment of NGO capacity*, Occasional Papers Series No. 10, Intrac, Oxford.

Goyder, H, Davies, R, Wilkinson, W (1998) *Participatory Impact Assessment*, Action Aid, London.

Guba and Lincoln (1989) *Fourth Generation Evaluation*, Sage, London.

Holland, J and Blackburn, J (1998) *Whose Voice? Participatory research and policy change*, IT Publications, London.

Howes, Mick (1992) 'Linking paradigms and practice: key issues in the appraisal, monitoring and evaluation of British NGO projects' in *Journal of International Development*, Vol.4:4.

INTRAC (1998) *Direct Funding from a Southern Perspective: Strengthening Civil Society?*, INTRAC NGO Management and Policy Series No.8 , Oxford.

Johnson, J. (1998) 'Programme Impact Assessment in Microfinance: the need for analysis of real markets' in IDS Bulletin, October 1998.

Macrae, J et al. (1997) 'Conflict, the Continuum and Chronic Emergencies' in *Disasters*, Vol.21:3.

Marsden, D and Oalkley, P (eds.) (1991) *Evaluating Social Development Projects*, Oxfam GB, Oxford.

Mavrocordatos, A (1997) 'Theatre for development, participatory monitoring and cultural feedback' in *PLA Notes* , No.29, June 1997, IIED.

Mosse, D (1994) 'Authority, gender and knowledge: Theoretical reflections on the practice of PRA' in *Development and Change*, No.25, pp.497–526.

New Economics Foundation (1998) *Towards Understanding NGO Work on Policy*, NEF, London.

Norton, A and Stephens, T (1995) 'Participation in Poverty Assessments', Environment Department Papers Participation Series 20, The World Bank, Washington DC.

Oakley, P, Pratt, B and Clayton, A (1998) *Outcomes and Impact: Evaluating Change in Social Development*, INTRAC, Oxford.

O'Laughlin, B (1996) 'Interpreting institutional discourses' in Thomas et al. (1996) *Finding out Fast*, Open University and Sage, London.

Perera, J (1997) 'In unequal dialogue with donors: The experience of the Sarvodaya Shramadana movement' in Edwards and Hulme (1997) *NGOs States and Donors: Too Close for Comfort?*, Macmillan, London.

Pretty, J (1994) 'Alternative systems of inquiry for a sustainable agriculture', IDS Bulletin Vol.25:2.

Riddell, R (1987) *Foreign Aid Reconsidered*, Johns Hopkins Press, Baltimore.

Roche, C (1998) 'Organisational Assessment and Institutional Footprints' in Tomas, A, Chataway, J, and Wuyts, M (eds.) (1998) *Finding Out Fast: Investigative Skills for Development Policy and Development*, Open University Press.

Roche, C (1994) 'Operationality in Turbulence' in *Development in Practice* Vol.4:3.

Rubin, F (1995) *A basic guide to Evaluation for Development Workers*, Oxfam GB, Oxford.

Singer, H (1989) *Lessons of Post War Development Experience 1945–88*, IDS discussion paper 260, Brighton: IDS.

Slim H (1997) 'Doing the Right Thing: Relief Agencies, Moral Dilemma and Moral Responsibility in Political Emergencies and War', Studies on Emergencies and Disaster Relief, Report No.6, Nordiska Afrikainstitutet, Sweden.

Smillie, I (1995) *The Alms Bazaar*, IT Publications, London.

Sogge, D (ed.) (1996) *Compassion and Calculation: the business of private foreign aid*, Pluto Press, London.

Stockton, N (1995) 'The Collapse of the State and the International Humanitarian Industry – The New World Order in Emergencies', Oxford University Press.

Tendler, J and Freedheim, S (1994) 'Trust in a rent-seeking world: Health and government transformed in north east Brazil' in *World Development* Vol. 22:12, pp1771–1791.

Uphoff, N (1992), *Learning from Gal Oya: Possibilities for Participatory Development and Post-Newtonian Social Science*, Cornell University Press.

de Waal, A (1996) 'Bad Aid' in *Prospect*, October 1996.

Zadek, S (1996) 'Organising NGOs for value based effectiveness' in *Development Insights*, ODI.

Unpublished papers

Adnan, S et al. (1992) 'People's participation, NGOs and the Flood Action Plan: An independent review', OXFAM Bangladesh, Dhaka.

Apthorpe and Nevile 1998 'Managing Emergency Humanitarian Aid evaluation: Lessons from Experience', a report of on the main findings of a workshop held with AusAID support at the National Centre for Development Studies, Australian National University, 13–16 March 1998.

Co, E (1999) 'Advocacy for Policy Reform in the Philippines', report commissioned by the Advocacy Working Group, Oxfam GB.

Coe, J (1998) Case studies of UK Campaigns, mimeo, Oxfam GB.

Davies, R (1997) 'Placing A Value on Advocacy Work', notes prepared for the July 1997 DSA NGO Study Group meeting in Oxford, available at http://www.swan.ac.uk/cds/rd/advocacy.htm.

Davies, R (1998) 'Donor Information Demands and NGO Institutional Development', paper originally prepared for the ODA-BOND-CDS workshop 'Institutional Strengthening of Southern NGOs: What role for Northern NGOs?' held at the University of Wales, Swansea, in July 1996. Update version available from http://www.swan.ac.uk/cds/rd1.html.

Davies, R (1998) 'An evolutionary approach to facilitating organisational learning: An experiment by the Christian Commission for Development in Bangladesh', from http://www.swan.ac.uk/cds/rd/ccdb.htm.

David, R (1998) 'Monitoring and Evaluating Advocacy Work', draft manual for Action Aid.

Dawson, E (1995a) 'Visit to Burkina Faso Oxfam UK/I programme for impact assessment research, phase III: West Africa', Oxfam GB.

Dawson, E (1995b) 'Women, gender and impact assessment: A discussion paper', Oxfam GB.

Dawson, E (1995c) Novib and Oxfam GB impact assessment research programme, Phase III – West Africa, Oxfam GB.

Dawson, E (1998a) The relevance of social audit for Oxfam GB, Journal of Business Ethics 17: 1457–1469

Dawson, E (1998b) 'Assessing the impact of emergency aid: A discussion paper', Oxfam GB.

Development Initiatives (1996) '1995 NGO aid cuts campaign: Evaluation of impact', report to Inter Agency Coalition.

Development Initiatives (1997) 'An evaluation of Oxfam's advocacy and communications work on the Great Lakes region of Africa', report to Oxfam GB.

Duffield, M (1997) 'Post-Modern Conflict, Aid Policy and Humanitarian Conditionality', ESCOR Research Paper.

Edwards, M (1996) 'Becoming a Learning Organisation, or, the search for the Holy Grail?', paper presented at the Aga Khan Foundation Canada Round Table on Systematic Learning: Promoting Public Support for Canadian Development Cooperation.

Estrella, M and Gaventa, J (1997) 'Who counts reality? Participatory Monitoring and Evaluation: A literature review', paper prepared for international workshop, The Philippines, available from IDS, Sussex; e-mail ids@sussex.ac.uk.

Farnworth (1998) 'Musings on the use of chapati diagrams', PLA Notes, February 1998, IIED.

Fowler, A (1988) 'Guidelines and Field Checklist for Assessment of Community Organisations', Ford Foundation, Nairobi.

Gell, F (1997) 'Emergency Project to Support Returning Displaced Women in Ayacucho and Apurimac, Peru: Report on Support Visit', April 1997, Oxfam GB.

Gesellschaft für Technische Zusammenarbeit (GTZ) (1988a) 'Zopp in Brief', paper, GTZ, Eschborn.

GTZ (1988b) 'Zopp: an introduction to the method', paper, GTZ, Eschborn.

Goetz, AM (1996) 'Understanding gendered institutional structures and practices', presentation for Oxfam meeting on Gender and Organisational Change.

Hallam, A (1997) 'Good Practice Review: Evaluating Humanitarian Assistance Programmes', Humanitarian Policy Programme, London.

Hallam, A and Borton, J (1998) 'Good practice in evaluating humanitarian aid', document No.3 submitted to the DAC Working Party on Aid Evaluation, 30ᵗʰ Meeting, 27–28 May 1998, DANIDA.

Hopkins, R (1995a) 'Impact assessment: Overview and methods of application', Oxfam GB and Novib.

Hopkins (1995b) 'Impact assessment: The experience of Latin American NGOs', Oxfam GB and Novib.

Howes, M and Roche, C (1994) 'A Participatory Appraisal of ACORD' in PLA Notes, No. 22, IIED.

Hulme, D (1997) 'Impact Assessment Methodologies for Microfinance: A Review (CGAP I)', AIMS Paper, Management Systems International, Washington DC.

Jackson, A (1997) 'From acting to taking action: Forum and legislative theatre' in PLA Notes No.29, IIED.

Large, J (1996) 'Breaking cycles of violence: Towards complimentarity in gender analysis and policy', unpublished paper presented to CODEP gender and conflict sub-group.

Moore, M and Stewart, S (1998) 'The impact of external funding on the capacity of local NGOs', final report no. R5968, IDS, Sussex

Moore, M, Stewart, S and Huddock, A (1994) 'Institution Building as a Development Assistance Method; A Review of the literature and Ideas', report to Swedish International Development Authority (SIDA), IDS, Sussex.

Maxwell-Stuart, L (1997) 'Domestic violence: old problems, new approaches', Links, Oxfam GB.

Newens, M and Roche, C (1996) 'Evaluating social development: Initiatives and experience in Oxfam', paper prepared for the 3rd International workshop on the Evaluation of Social Development, Netherlands, available by e-mailing croche@oxfam.org.uk.

Oxfam GB (1998) 'Oxfam GB Guide to Advocacy', Oxfam GB.

Riddell, R (1997) 'Linking costs and benefits in NGO development projects: A study by the Overseas Development Institute commissioned by the Overseas Development Administration', ODI, London.

Riddell, R et al. (1997) 'Searching for impact and methods: NGO evaluation synthesis study', paper prepared on behalf of the Expert Group on Evaluation of the Organisation for Economic Cooperation and Development, OECD, available at www.valt.helsinki.fi/ids/ngo.

Roche, C (1996) Oxfam's Cross Programme Learning Fund: An update report, mimeo, Oxfam GB.

Roche C (1995a) 'Institutional Learning in Oxfam: Some thoughts', mimeo, Oxfam GB.

Roche C (1995b) 'Impact Assessment and the Policy Department', discussion paper, Oxfam GB.

Slim, H (1998) 'International Humanitarianism's Engagement with Civil War in the 1990s: A glance at Evolving Practice and Theory', a briefing paper for Action Aid, UK. Available at http://www-jha.sps.cam.ac.uk/a/a565.htm.

The Sphere Project (1998) Humanitarian Charter and Minimum Standards in Disaster Response, Geneva.

Thin, N (1992) 'NGO reporting and evaluation: The JFS experience so far', discussion paper for JFS Edinburgh Evaluation Workshop, Edinburgh, 8-10 July 1992.

Willot, P (1985) 'S'Evaluer', mimeo, Belgium.

Wessels, F (1995) 'A Summary of the Method of Animation in Auto-evaluation of Village Groups as developed by Paul Willot', mimeo, Oxfam GB.

Zetter, R (1998) 'Evaluation of Oxfam GB's programme in the Great Lakes Region of Central Africa 1994–97: Synthesis report', Oxfam GB.

Uphoff, N. (1987) 'Participatory evaluation of participatory development: A scheme of measuring and monitoring local capacity being introduced in Sri Lanka', People's Participation Project Workshop (Ghana) on participatory monitoring and evaluation, FAO, Rome.

Appendix 2: Contact addresses and material available from the case-study participants

Bangladesh Rural Advancement Committee

Address	Materials:
BRAC Centre 75 Mohakhali C/A Dhaka 1212 Bangladesh	Husain, A M M, Mallick, D and Chowdhury, A M R (1998) An Impact Assessment Study of BRAC's Rural Development Programme: Lessons from Methodological Issues, paper prepared for the Impact Assessment Workshop in Stanton, UK 23–26 November 1998, BRAC, Dhaka. Husain, A M M (ed.) (1998), Poverty Alleviation and Empowerment: The Second Impact Assessment Study of BRAC's Rural Development Programme, BRAC, Dhaka. Mustafa, S et al. (1996), Beacon of Hope: An Impact Assessment Study of BRAC's Rural Development Programme, BRAC, Dhaka.

Centre for Youth and Social Development, India

Address:	Materials:
CYSD E-1, Institutional Area PO: RRL Bhubaneswar 751-013 Orissa India	Dash, A K, Kanungo, S, Jolly, M C, Dash, P G (1998) 'Impact Assessment: the CYSD case study', paper prepared for the Impact Assessment Workshop in Stanton, UK, 23–26 November 1998, CYSD, Bubeneshwar.

Environment and Development Activities Zimbabwe

Address:	**Materials:**
ENDA	King, B, Mawoneke, S (1998) Impact Assessment Case
P.O.Box 3492	Study undertaken by Environment and Development
Harare	Activities (ENDA) – Zimbabwe, paper prepared for
Zimbabwe	the Impact Assessment Workshop in Stanton, UK
	23–26 November 1998

Fondación para la cooperación y el Desarrollo Comunal de El Salvador (CORDES)

Address:	**Materials:**
CORDES	Lopez, M and Reyes, E (1998) 'Case Study in El
Apartado postal 5841	Salvador – Fundación CORDES', paper prepared for
27 Avenida Norte 1221	the Impact Assessment Workshop in Stanton, UK
Colonia Buenos Aires	23–26 November 1998.
No 1	
San Salvador	Lopez, M and Reyes, E (1998) 'Guia metodologica
El Salvador	para la evaluacion participativa del impacto', CORDES
	& Novib.

Lopez, M and Reyes, E (1998) 'Sistematización de la evaluacion del impacto de la Fundación CORDES en las communidades: case especifico: El Papaturro, El Sito y El Pepeto del Departamento de Cuscatlan', CORDES & Novib

Gonoshahajjo Sangstha, Bangladesh

Address:	**Materials:**
Gonoshahajjo Sangstha	Rao, A and Hashemi, S M (1995) 'Institutional Take-
(GSS)	Off or Snakes and Ladders? Dyamics and
41 Sir Syed Ahmed Road	Sustainability of Local Level Organisations in Rural
Block-A	Bangladesh', a report commissioned by Oxfam
Mohammadpur	Bangladesh, Dhaka.
Dhaka 1207	
Bangladesh	
or	
GPO Box No. 3535	
Dhaka, Bangladesh	

Matson Neighbourhood Project, UK

Address:	Materials:
Matson Neighbourhood Project	Thekaekara, S (1998) 'Does Matson Matter? A case study on Impact Assessment of the Matson
Matson Lane	Neigbourhood Project, Gloucester, UK', paper
Gloucester GL4 9DX	prepared for the Impact Assessment Workshop in
UK	Stanton, UK, 23–26 November 1998, ACCORD , India

Ross, K (1996) 'Matson Neighbourhood Project: A process evaluation for Gloucester Area Social Services Office', Cheltenham and Gloucester College of Higher Education.

Nijera Kori, Bangladesh

Address:
P.O. Box 5015
New Market, Dhaka-5
Road No. 4a
House No. 40a
Dhanmandi
Dhaka
Bangladesh

NOVIB, The Netherlands

Address:
PO Box 30919
2500 GX Den Haag
The Netherlands

Oxfam GB

Address:
Oxfam GB
274 Banbury Road
Oxford OX2 7DZ
UK

Oxfam GB in Ghana

Address:	Materials:
Oxfam Ghana PO Box 432 Tamale, N/R Ghana	Siapha Kamara, S and Roche, C (1996) 'A Participatory Impact Assessment and Advocacy Project for Poverty Alleviation in Northern Ghana', paper prepared for the 3rd International workshop on the Evaluation of Social Development November 1996, ISODEC and Oxfam.
	Nafi Quarshie, N, Pugansoa, B and Roche, C (1998) 'Ghana Impact Assessment Case Study: A Paper on Participatory Impact Assessment Research Project and Advocacy for Poverty Alleviation in Northern Ghana', prepared for the Impact Assessment Workshop in Stanton, UK 23–26 November 1998, Oxfam Ghana.
	Wolmer, W (1996) 'Local Institutions and Poverty in Northern Ghana: an Annotated Bibliography', IDS, Sussex.

Oxfam GB in Ikafe, Uganda

Address:	Materials:
c/o Oxfam GB PO Box 6228 Kampala Uganda	Neefjes, K and David, R (1996) 'A participatory review of the Ikafe refugee programme', a report for Oxfam UK&I.
	Payne, L (1998) *Rebuilding Communities in a Refugee Settlement: A Casebook from Uganda*, Oxfam GB.

Oxfam GB in Pakistan

Address:	Materials:
Oxfam GB F-191 CITIZEN COLONY Hyderabad Sindh Pakistan	Alkire, S and Narajo, H (1998) 'Oxfam vs Poverty: Assessing Impact in Pakista', paper prepared for the Impact Assessment Workshop in Stanton, UK, 23–26 November 1998.
	Alkire, S (1999) 'Operationalising Amartya Sen's capability approach to human development: A framework for identifying "valuable" capabilities', DPhil thesis, Magdalen College, Oxford.
	Alkire, S (1997) 'Impact Assessment: Oxfam vs Poverty, A field manual for Oxfam staff in Pakistan', Oxfam.

Proshiaka, Bangladesh

Address:	**Materials:**
Proshika	Naser, A (1998) 'Approach adopted for Impact
PO Box 3149	Assessment of Proshika's Develeopment
Ramna	Interventions', paper prepared for the Impact
Dhaka 1000	Assessment Workshop in Stanton, UK 23–26
Bangladesh	November 1998, IMEC, Dhaka.

Wajir Pastoralist Development Programme, Kenya

Address:	**Materials:**
Mohammed Elmi	Holden, S and Ackello-Ogutu, C (1998) 'Oxfam Wajir
Oxfam Kenya	Pastoral Development Project Economic Impact
2nd Floor	Assessment', Resource Management and Policy
Pamstech House	Analysis Institute (REMPAI), Kenya.
Woodvale Grove	
Westlands	Odhiambo, O and Elmi, M (1998) 'Participatory
Nairobi	Economic Impact Assessment of Pastoral
Kenya	Development Work: a Case Study of the OXFAM Wajir
or	Pastoral Development Project – Kenya', paper
Ojijo Odhiambo	prepared for the impact assessment workshop in
Resource Management	Stanton, UK 23–26 November 1998, REMPAI and
and Policy Analysis	Oxfam, Kenya.
Institute (REMPAI)	
P.O. Box 64559	Kinoti, W and Ackello-Ogutu, C (Eds) (1998) 'Impact
Nairobi	Assessment of Pastoral Development Work',
Kenya	proceedings of a workshop on economic impact
	assessment of the Wajir Pastoral Development Project
	hosted by REMPAI, Nairobi, 5 February 1998.

Appendix 3: Participants of the impact assessment workshop November 1998

Name	Organisation
Sabina Alkire	Consultant
Julie Allcock	Oxfam GB
Floris Blankenberg	SNV, The Netherlands
Dr Anup Kumar Dash	UTKAL UNIVERSITY, Orissa, India
Mr Pran Gopal Das	CYSD, Orissa, India
Elsa Dawson	Oxfam GB
Mohammed Elmi	Oxfam GB in Kenya
Yvonne Es	Novib
Yolette Etienne	Oxfam GB in Haiti
Mark Gale	The Gloucester Neighbourhood Project Network, UK
Ken Garland	Matson Neighbourhood Project, Gloucester, UK
Yanci Urbina Gonzalez	Oxfam GB in El Salvador
Walter Gonzalez	CORDES, El Salvador
Anamul Haque	Oxfam GB in Bangladesh
Prof. A.M. Muazzam Hussain	BRAC, Bangladesh
Andy Jarret	Matson Neighbourhood Project, Gloucester, UK
Mr Jolly M.C	CYSD, Orissa, India
Kamal Kar	Development Consultant, Calcutta, India

Name	Organisation
Conchita Lloret	Oxfam GB
Sthembile Mawoneke	ENDA, Zimbabwe
Kate Morrow	Oxfam GB
Paresh Motla	Oxfam GB
Abu Nasar	PROSHIKA, Bangladesh
Hidayat Narajo	Oxfam GB in Pakistan
Koos Neefjes	Oxfam GB
Ojijo Odhiambo	Resource Management and Policy Analysis Institute (REMPAI), Nairobi, Kenya.
Adrie Papma	NOVIB, The Netherlands
Ben Pugansoa	Oxfam GB in Ghana
Nafisatu Quarshie	Oxfam GB in Ghana
Enrique Reyes	CORDES, El Salvador
Chris Roche	Oxfam GB

Appendix 4: List of acronyms

AAIN	Action Africa in Need
BRAC	Bangladesh Rural Advancement Committee, Bangladesh
CBA	Cost-benefit analysis
CBO	Community-based organisation
CORDES	The Foundation for Co-operation and Community Development in El Salvador
CYSD	Centre for Youth and Social Development, Orissa, India
DAC	Development Assistance Committee
DFID	Department For International Development, UK
EIA	Environmental impact assessment
ENDA	Environment and Development Activities, Zimbabwe
GSS	Gonoshahajjo Sangstha, Bangladesh
INGO	International non-government organisation
ISODEC	Integrated Social Development Centre, Ghana
ITDG	Intermediate Technology Development Group
JRS	Jesuit Refugee Service
LFA	Logical Framework Analysis
LNGO	Local non-government organisation
MNP	Matson Neighbourhood Project, UK
NGND	Northern Ghana Development Network
NGO	Non-government organisation
NK	Nijera Kori, Bangladesh
OECD	Organisation for Economic Co-operation and Development
PAR	Participatory action research
PLA	Participatory learning and action
PPA	Participatory poverty assessment
PRA	Participatory rural appraisal
REMPAI	Resource Management and Policy Analysis Institute
RRA	Rapid rural appraisal
SCBA	Social cost-benefit analysis
SIA	Social impact assessment

Index

Action Aid 51, 90, 135, 149, 275
advocacy work
    aggregation 213–16
    attribution 210–12
    baselines 208–9
    case study approach 230–1
    cross-checking 212–13
    direct observation 221–2
    flow charts 229
    impact assessment process
      195–233
    interviews 217–19
    and NGOs 192–3
    participatory tools 222–31
    problems with 193–4
    ranking 228
    surveys 216–17
    time lines 222–7
    tools 216–31
    trend analysis 229
    units of assessment 203–7
    Venn diagrams 228–9
aggregation
    advocacy work 213–16
    organisations 34, 257–8
Andhra Pradesh (India), preferences
    for change 90–1
Angola, advocacy work 200, 201
anti-roads campaign (UK) 214–16

attribution
    advocacy work 210–12
    of change 79–86
    organisations 32–3

Bangladesh
    flooding 167
    see also BRAC; NK & GSS; Proshika
baselines 74–9
    for advocacy work 208–9
before and after exercises 145
beneficiaries, participation of 59, 60
bias, avoidance of 34–5, 113–14, 269
BRAC (Bangladesh)
    analysis of data 105
    baseline data 75
    case studies 151
    control group 79–81
    defining change 39
    focus groups 119
    impact of assessment 264
    indicators of change 41–2, 46
    introductory workshop 39
    overview 12
    questionnaire 99–100, 101
    research method 87
    sampling 69, 102–3
    subjectivity 34, 35
    units of assessment 52, 53